SAGE was founded in 1965 by Sara Miller McCune to support the dissemination of usable knowledge by publishing innovative and high-quality research and teaching content. Today, we publish over 900 journals, including those of more than 400 learned societies, more than 800 new books per year, and a growing range of library products including archives, data, case studies, reports, and video. SAGE remains majority-owned by our founder, and after Sara's lifetime will become owned by a charitable trust that secures our continued independence.

Los Angeles | London | New Delhi | Singapore | Washington DC | Melbourne

GLOBAL
COMMONS

Thank you for choosing a SAGE product!
If you have any comment, observation or feedback,
I would like to personally hear from you.

Please write to me at **contactceo@sagepub.in**

Vivek Mehra, Managing Director and CEO, SAGE India.

Bulk Sales

SAGE India offers special discounts
for purchase of books in bulk.
We also make available special imprints
and excerpts from our books on demand.

For orders and enquiries, write to us at

Marketing Department
SAGE Publications India Pvt Ltd
B1/I-1, Mohan Cooperative Industrial Area
Mathura Road, Post Bag 7
New Delhi 110044, India

E-mail us at **marketing@sagepub.in**

Subscribe to our mailing list
Write to **marketing@sagepub.in**

This book is also available as an e-book.

GLOBAL COMMONS

ISSUES, CONCERNS AND STRATEGIES

EDITED BY
MOHANAN BHASKARAN PILLAI
GEETHA GANAPATHY-DORÉ

Los Angeles | London | New Delhi
Singapore | Washington DC | Melbourne

Copyright © Mohanan Bhaskaran Pillai and Geetha Ganapathy-Doré, 2020

All rights reserved. No part of this book may be reproduced or utilized in any form or by any means, electronic or mechanical, including photocopying, recording or by any information storage or retrieval system, without permission in writing from the publisher.

First published in 2020 by

SAGE Publications India Pvt Ltd
B1/I-1 Mohan Cooperative Industrial Area
Mathura Road, New Delhi 110 044, India
www.sagepub.in

SAGE Publications Inc
2455 Teller Road
Thousand Oaks, California 91320, USA

SAGE Publications Ltd
1 Oliver's Yard, 55 City Road
London EC1Y 1SP, United Kingdom

SAGE Publications Asia-Pacific Pte Ltd
18 Cross Street #10-10/11/12
China Square Central
Singapore 048423

Published by Vivek Mehra for SAGE Publications India Pvt Ltd. Typeset in 10.5/13 pt Bembo by Zaza Eunice, Hosur, Tamil Nadu, India.

Library of Congress Cataloging-in-Publication Data Available

ISBN: 978-93-5388-360-7 (HB)

SAGE Team: Abhijit Baroi, Abhilash Dixit, Ankit Verma and Rajinder Kaur

Contents

List of Abbreviations   vii
Introduction   xi

Part I. Theoretical Considerations

Chapter 1	From the Tragedy of the Commons to Sustainable Commons: A Survey of the Theoretical Developments on CPR by *Bindu Balagopal and P. Chacko Jose*	3
Chapter 2	What International Law Can Teach Us about the Commons by *Julien Cazala*	12
Chapter 3	The Precautionary Principle: An Instrument at the Service of Sustainable Development by *Didier Guével*	23

Part II. Climate Change and Governance

Chapter 4	The Global Commons and the Climate Governance Regime: Effectiveness and Challenges by *Anju Lis Kurian and C. Vinodan*	61
Chapter 5	Polycentric Approach in Climate Change Mitigation and Adaptation Programme: Effectiveness and Challenges by *Sisira K. G., Govind N. and Mohanan Bhaskaran Pillai*	69
Chapter 6	International Legal Challenges of Climate Refugees by *S. Chemmalar*	84

Chapter 7	Maritime Spatial Planning: A Means of Organizing Maritime Activities Measured in Terms of Sustainable Development Goals by *Catherine Colard-Fabregoule*	95
Chapter 8	Views on Environmental Democracy in France by *Jean-Jacques Menuret*	108
Chapter 9	The Cyberspace as a Distinct Domain of the Global Commons: An Analysis of Cyberspace Governance by *Binu Joseph and Mohanan Bhaskaran Pillai*	123

Part III. Environmental Hazards

Chapter 10	The Massive Problem of Microplastics in the Global Commons: An Overview by *Kaushik Dowarah and Suja P. Devipriya*	141
Chapter 11	The Indian Ocean Garbage: Rethinking the Narrative on South Asian Waters by *Anusha Sooriyan, Namita Sharma and Mohanan Bhaskaran Pillai*	172
Chapter 12	Expanding Indian Nuclear Industry and Environmental Hazards: A Special Reference to the Establishment and Development of Nuclear Reactors in the Post-2005 Era by *K. R. Sreelekha*	191

Part IV. Poverty, Alienation and Social Exclusion

Chapter 13	Civil Society: Positing the Role of NGOs in Depoliticizing Political Action by *Arsha V. Sathyan*	209
Chapter 14	Sustainable Management Practices of the Traditional Society in Contested Landscapes by *Devjit Nandi and Debashis Sarkar*	221
Chapter 15	The Causes for the Despair of Farmers in France and India: A Literature-based Study by *Geetha Ganapathy-Doré*	243
Conclusion: Imagining Multiple Worlds in Fifty Years by *S. Ashok*		259

| About the Editors and Contributors | 269 |
| Index | 281 |

List of Abbreviations

AERB	Atomic Energy Regulatory Board
CBD	Convention on Biological Diversity
CBMs	Confidence Building Mechanisms
CCP	Cities for Climate Protection
CCX	Chicago Climate Exchange
CDM	Carbon Development Mechanisms
CERT	Counter Emergency Response Team
CFC	Chlrofluorocarbon
CFMC	Community forest management committee
COP21	2015 Paris Climate Conference
CPRs	Common pool resources
CR	Community Rights
CRR	Community Resource Rights
CSI	Cement Sustainability Initiative
DAE	Department of Atomic Energy
DDT	Dichlorodiphenyltrichloroethane
DoD	Department of Defence
EPA	Environment Protection Act
ESL	Environmental Survey Laboratories
EU	European Union
EU-ETS	European Union-Emission Trading Scheme
FRC	Forest Rights Committees
GDP	Gross domestic product
GGE	Group of Government Experts
GHG	Greenhouse gas
IMO	International Maritime Organization
IORA	Indian Ocean Rim Association
IPCC	Intergovernmental Panel on Climate Change
ITU	International Telecommunication Union

LD-PE	Low density polyethylene
MGNREGA	Mahatma Gandhi National Rural Employment Guarantee Act
MKSS	Mazdoor Kisan Shakti Sangathan
NATO	North Atlantic Treaty Organization
NCPRI	National Campaign for People's Right to Information
NGO	Non-governmental organization
NPCIL	Nuclear Power Corporation of India Limited
NSG	Nuclear Suppliers Group
NTFPs	Non-timber forest products
OECD	Organisation for Economic Co-operation and Development
OTFDs	Other forest dwellers
PCB	Polychlorinated biphenyl
Ppm	Parts per million
PTGs	Primitive tribal groups
PVTGs	Particularly vulnerable tribal groups
REDD	Reducing Emissions from Deforestation in Developing countries
RGGI	Regional Greenhouse Gas Initiative
RTI	Right to Information
SAARC	South Asian Association for Regional Cooperation
SACEP	South Asia Co-operative Environment Programme
SASEP	South Asian Seas Environment Programme
SASP	South Asian Seas Action Plan
SDGs	Sustainable Development Goals
SPS	Sanitary and Phytosanitary
TFEU	Treaty on the Functioning of the European Union
TKDL	Traditional Knowledge Digital Library
UCIL	Uranium Corporation of India Ltd
ULBs	Urban local bodies
UNCLOS	United Nations Convention on the Law of the Sea
UNEP	United Nations Environment Programme

UNFCCC	United Nations Framework Convention on Climate Change
UNHCR	UN High Commission for Refugees
UNWTO	UN World Tourism Organization
UPA	United Progressive Alliance
VPNs	Virtual private networks
WBCSD	World Business Council for Sustainable Development
WLPA	Wildlife Protection Act
WTO	World Trade Organization

Introduction

What are the 'boundaries' of human–nature interactions? Where are the 'limits' that define, describe and delimit what we are and what we can be as societies living in states of mutual interdependencies with our environments? These are traditional questions that disciplines of social sciences had asked for millennia, arguably, right from the times and spaces when these disciplines emerged with distinct but thin borderlines. The questions, and their answers, across these various life-worlds have remained relevant. This volume seeks to carry forward these discussions about such boundaries and the limits, and their reconfigurations.

The world is said to have entered a particular phase of reconfiguration of this space. Human beings, probably for the first time in history, have very clearly become the dominant force in shaping the boundaries of redistribution of nature and her forces. The vocabulary of 21st-century modern science has already called this era the Anthropocene. The term 'Anthropocene' was coined in 2000 by the Nobel Prize-winning scientist Paul Crutzen, who believed that the name change for the geological time scale was overdue (Carrington 2016). The Anthropocene marks a new period, in which, according to Professor Chris Rapley, a climate scientist at the University College, London, 'our collective activities dominate the planetary machinery' (Micu 2016). *The Guardian* quoting Professor Paul Crutzen pointed out that 'this name change stresses the enormity of humanity's responsibility as stewards of the Earth' (Carrington 2016). Human activity has pushed the extinction rate of animals and plants far above the long-term average. Thus, this is the time for us to discuss and debate, seriously, the histories of this phase of human existence and the futures that we would prefer to chart out.

The principle of a 'common heritage of humankind' determines the health of the global commons—a domain that lies outside the political reach of any one nation-state. The good health of our commons—be it lands, forests, oceans or the climate systems—has become essential in our quest for a sustainable and prosperous future world. Disciplines of advanced natural sciences have warned us repeatedly about the 'tipping points' that our environments have been facing since the advent of modern civilization. Scientists have repeatedly pronounced the points of no-return, but the significant structures of power and their mediating institutions have effected policy decisions that have often completely overlooked these warnings over the years. Modern institutions of governance have repeatedly fallen behind in the actual recognition of these events of seismic proportions. Efforts to resolve the criticalities of our 'common heritage' have been impeded time and again by the major powers themselves. The distribution and redistribution patterns of natural resources have often got aligned to favour the priorities of a few, at the expense of the many.

For instance, we live in a world where climate change theories and their multiple experiences are continuously refuted with pride by the powers that be—powers that have often been responsible for the state of our global affairs today. Climate change is predicted to have and is already having catastrophic impacts on the everyday lives of people today. The globally marginalized who have contributed insignificantly to the problems at hand are, unfortunately, often, the majority shareholders of the sufferings of our standard conditions. The quickly shifting boundaries within and between the climate system, the stratospheric ozone layer, the oceans, the biodiversity, land systems, the global hydrological cycles, the nutrient cycles that power the entire biosphere, along with manufactured chemicals, and aerosol loadings in the atmosphere are compounding the problems for and threatening the very existence of vulnerable geographies and its people.

In these circumstances, how can global commons be understood concerning our conditions of existence? As academicians and citizens, can we problematize them to understand the criticality of our existence? Can a better future be imagined—one that is more humane, sustainable and progressive—that helps guide the theory and practice of sustaining our 'commons'? These are some of the questions that haunted us when we thought of a joint book project between Pondicherry University and Paris 13 University. This venture is necessarily interdisciplinary.

Our conviction is to overcome the structural problems of global commons' excellent international coordination at the global level, a fundamental requirement. The global commons are the very foundations of our global economy and have been facing the tragedy of overexploitation and rapid degradation. With increasing pressure from people, the need for responsibility towards the preservation and management of global commons is also increasing. Conservation and the shift to more sustainable practices have proven successful at the small scale, but we are still losing ground at the planetary level. So we must bring about transformations in our critical economic systems, political leadership, knowledge and informational systems, and coalitions for change and innovation.

Thus, we have organized the volume under four distinct categories that engage with different parts of the problem, in addition to this introductory note and the imaginative narrative as the volume's conclusion. The first part problematizes the concept of the commons, attempts to define it, and identifies and describes its theoretical fundamentals. This section also attempts to recognize and acknowledge the critical gaps in these theoretical formulations and seeks to address them.

The second part of the volume deals with issues in commons and governance. The chapters in this section attempt to understand the role of global institutions of mediation like the nation-state or other institutions of the international political economy in continually redefining the boundaries of these commons while reconstructing, displacing and dispossessing the 'global outsiders'. We have arranged the third part with chapters that discuss environmental hazards.

The chapters included in the fourth part attempt at historicizing the problems related to poverty, alienation and social exclusion with the specific objective of understanding the privileges and historical responsibilities of the principal agents of this phase of humanity's long history. This part attempts to identify and map out the 'global outsiders' whose livelihoods are critically dependent on our commons and who powerlessly occupy the margins of its boundaries.

We have envisaged the concluding section as forward-looking and imaginative. Here we have discussed climate change and its relationships with the commons, articulated ideas on the newer frontiers of global commons and engaged in a creative exercise of imagining the future human–environment relationships.

In brief, this volume explores the social, economic, political, legal and cultural underpinnings and implications of global commons and their sustainable development. It also reviews how the concept of the commons had evolved in theory and practice and how the different principles derived from it got implemented in different parts of the world. Through a critical examination of the concepts and its methods, this volume attempts to imagine a way forward for our shared futures and suggests concrete proposals which could be useful in addressing the issues at hand. Through the critical interventions and insights provided in the volume, we hope to address some of the gaps in the burgeoning literature on global commons while adding constructively to the debate around an issue which truly affects all of humankind.

REFERENCES

Carrington, D. 2016, 29 August. 'The Anthropocene Epoch: Scientists Declare Dawn of Human-influenced Age'. Available at: https://www.theguardian.com/environment/2016/aug/29/declare-anthropocene-epoch-experts-urge-geological-congress-human-impact-earth (accessed on 18 March 2020).

Micu, A. 2016, 4 August. 'A private company plans to land on the Moon, but what will this precedent mean for space exploration?'. Available at: https://www.zmescience.com/science/moon-private-mining-58884/ (accessed on 18 March 2020).

PART I

Theoretical Considerations

Chapter 1

From the Tragedy of the Commons to Sustainable Commons
A Survey of the Theoretical Developments on CPR

Bindu Balagopal and P. Chacko Jose

INTRODUCTION

The term 'common pool resources' (CPRs) connotes resources common and open to all on the planet earth and from which exclusion of individuals is not possible. Fisheries, backwoods, groundwater bowls, pastures, lakes, seas and earth's climate are general instances of CPRs. At the point when numerous people make use of CPRs, the net outcome is environmental degeneration of unimaginable magnitude. The expression 'tragedy of the commons' has encapsulated environmental degradation due to overuse of CPRs. Ecological issues, for example, a planet-wide temperature boost, water shortage, environmental degradation, contamination, land debasement and biodiversity misfortune are, to some degree, the consequences of overuse of CPRs.

Mainstream economics treats the environment as resource, and problems that emanate from overuse of CPRs are considered as market failures partly, if not entirely. Markets can function adequately by establishing property rights and minimizing transaction costs. Environmental goods showcase failure when business sectors and administrations do not exist, and when business sectors do exist, the market costs do not pay much attention to their scarcity values. Through recognizable proof and estimation of these market failures, one can think of offering solutions to market failures. State intervention is a solution to reduce environmental degradations when the market fails.

Ecological debasement can regularly be the consequence of market failures. Proficient appropriation of assets is a condition to address market failures. Markets fail to work effectively in the arrangement of public good, within sight of externalities, and when property rights are not well characterized. For allocative productivity just as for productive working of the market, the cost of the item ought to be equivalent to the peripheral expense of creation. In any case, the externalities of the production process are not borne by sellers and buyers. There could be a positive externality, just as there could be a negative externality to any exchange relationship. In the issues of environmental pollution, we can notice the nearness of a negative externality. A negative externality emerges when the pollution brought about while producing a commodity is not borne by the producer alone but by the transacting parties, that is, the seller and the buyer as also the general public. Many negative externalities surface as the environmental consequences of production and use (Balagopal and Jose P. 2015–2016).

At the point when it is excessive to even think about excluding individuals from access to a natural asset for which there is competition, market allocation is likely to be wasteful. Hardin's (1968) concept of the 'tragedy of the commons' highlighted the difficulties associated with practising non-exclusion in the access to CPRs. Later, Ronald Coase recommended some approaches to overcome the issue of negative externality emerging from the absence of property rights. He contended that in order to achieve allocative efficiency, one had to deal with the parties concerned, if exchange costs were negligible. Be that as it may; here once more, the issues connected with the allocation of resources are addressed, instead of addressing the fundamental issue of environmental degradation (Felice and Vatiero 2012). Before the publication of Ostrom's studies, the solution to the tragedy of commons revolved around the idea of privatizing resources or establishing property rights. Instead, Ostrom demonstrated that a community-based bottom-up approach with appropriate government involvement could lead to a sustainable and shared management of resources, which could, at the same time, be productive from the financial point of view.

In the light of the above discussion, this chapter makes an overview of three seminal works, namely, Garret Hardin's (1968) work on 'The Tragedy of the Commons', Ronald Coase's (1960) *The Problem of Social Cost*, which examines the question of property rights, and Elinor Ostrom's (1990) work on 'Governing the Commons'.

THE TRAGEDY OF THE COMMONS

In 1833, William Forster Lloyd published a short pamphlet explaining the ideas that served as the bricks and mortar of the conceptualization known as 'the tragedy of the commons'. The pamphlet and its content remained under obscurity until 1968, when Garrett Hardin wrote an article in the journal *Science*. Thus, Hardin brought Lloyd's ideas into the limelight. For the purposes of this chapter, we use the term 'commons' to refer to any common assets that do not fall within the ambit of individual or corporate interests.

Indeed, these sources are available for use by the public. These might include public pasture land, lumber, oil, the seas, the air, natural life and fish and numerous other shared resources, such as land for eating, angling zones, backwoods for timber, water for the farmland and increasingly impalpable assets, like information, for which 'client' utilization is hard to control and delimit. The issue with these sorts of assets, as identified in the publication of Garrett Hardin (1968), is overexploitation. The sustainability of these resources is not a concern of the users. Individuals behave opportunistically (like free-riders), pocket the benefit and collectivize the costs.

The tragedy of the commons depicts how individuals regularly exploit assets that are freely accessible to them. They do not consider that if everyone overuses a comparable asset, it will provoke adverse effects for everyone, including themselves. In this exceptional situation, sharing requires that no individual has a case to any piece of the asset, but instead every individual can utilize a bit of it for his/her ideal position. The debacle is that, without a rule, each individual will, in general, misuse the assets promoting his/her latent capacity advantage, usually unbounded. In this circumstance, the assets get depleted and, in the end, demolished. The fundamental reasoning is that, if the commons, at last, will be spent, whoever impacts the most raised use stands to benefit the most. Under this condition, we are of the view that the favourable position/cost extent is cosmic. While the advantages accrue solely to the customer, the costs get spread among all others sharing the commons (Ponce 2010).

The well-known example given by Hardin (1968) includes pastureland that people use to graze their cattle. Hardin argued that when multiple users had access to the same valuable resource, the result would be a 'tragedy of the commons' to which no technological solution could be found. With the illustration of grazing land, Hardin argued,

> Each herder would keep adding cattle to his stock as long as it remained privately profitable, neglecting the costs of this activity on others sharing the commons. The consequences would be depletion and eventual destruction of the pasture. Only through the division of the land into private lots, or regulation by the state could the tragedy be averted. (Cardenas and Sethi 2016, 7)

Further, the herdsmen who indulged in excessive use of grazing land or added more and more cattle to their herd motivated other herdsmen or anybody for that matter, in the long run, to copy what they were doing. The more the herdsmen were self-centred and profit-oriented, the more the pastureland was ruined, and as a result, the herds subjected to an immeasurable amount of suffering. As Hardin rightly pointed out, 'Freedom in a commons brings ruin to all' (Hardin 1968, 1244).

Hardin authored the adage 'tragedy of the commons' to depict this complicated situation and gave social sciences one of the most compelling moral stories after Adam Smith's 'invisible hand'. Both these analogies are convincing because they depict two different social conditions.

Precisely, when social interchanges get guided by an undetectable hand, they lead to a particular choice and socially desirable results. In the terribleness of an asset, regardless of what may be healthy, individuals looking after their individual goals cause tragic implications for themselves as well as for others (Felice and Vatiero 2012).

THE COASE THEOREM

The Coase theorem, developed by the economist Ronald Coase, puts forward the idea that when clashing property rights occur, haggling between the gatherings involved will prompt a valid result, with little attention paid to which party gets ultimately granted the property rights provided that the transaction costs related to the bargaining process are negligible. In particular, the Coase theorem posits, 'If trade in an externality is possible and there are no transaction costs, bargaining will lead to an efficient outcome regardless of the initial allocation of property rights' (Haiduk 2015, 250). The Coase theorem further points out that in the matter of resource allocation, the property rights did not matter much in such situations where it was clearly defined, and the costs of making transactions were negligible. 'The Coase theorem is a method of tackling the inefficiency caused by an externality, by awarding property rights to the externality to one party and allowing the parties concerned to bargain their way to an efficient solution' (Beggs 2019, 4).

However, there are at least two reasons why society cannot always depend upon the Coase theorem to solve the problem of abuse of CPRs. First, the cost of bargaining among millions of people who are affected may turn out to be stupendous, as in the case of air pollution. It is hard to envision a massive number of individuals getting together for arrangements at sufficient ease. Second, the hypothesis takes it for granted that benefit owners can recognize the source of harm to their property and legitimately prevent harms from occurring by making the right move. For instance, on account of air pollution, regardless of whether or not property rights to air contamination got established, it is not clear how property owners would be able to identify the polluters responsible for dirtying their environment and the proportion of harm for which each one was liable. Thought in these lines, the Coarse theorem is the most relevant one for cases in which there are more than two parties involved, and the places of origin of the externalities appropriately defined.

SUSTAINABLE COMMONS

The approach of Ostrom to similar situations was very much different from that of Coase. She was of the view that the external imposition of usage rights was not feasible and desirable in many environments. As noted by Cardenas, however, 'Individuals with access to shared resources could reach tolerably efficient allocations through social norms backed by the implicit threat of decentralised sanctions. They could develop formal rules or rely on informal ones, thus engaging in what she called self-governance' (Cardenas and Sethi 2016).

Elinor Ostrom founded her study on the notion of CPR and brought out a clear differentiation between open access and common property resources. An initial phase in building her explanatory system was to make a clear-cut differentiation between assets held as common property and those subject to open access. Common property includes a well-characterized network of clients and a related arrangement of rules and norms that allow them to control each other's conduct. Those in the network demonstrate commitment—either independently or in concert—to keep outsiders from misusing the resource, regardless of whether the customary laws of the more significant political elements inside, which they get inserted explicitly, restrict such prohibitions. Models incorporate numerous inshore fisheries, touching terrains and woodland zones. Open access, paradoxically, alludes to assets from which avoidance is troublesome or inconceivable without formal state activity. Sea fisheries and the worldwide air as a carbon sink are clear examples. She concurred with Hardin that open access to resources belonging to no one is vulnerable (Ostrom 1990) yet differed when it came to scarce resources. Ostrom and others gave various instances of regular use, some of which had existed for a considerable length of time and had sustained the resources in question. The highlight is that both Hardin and Ostrom differentiated and bundled of property rights and their holders, namely,

(1) authorized entrants (2) authorized users whose rights are limited to access and withdrawal of resources; (3) claimants who hold the collective right of management; (4) proprietors, who can exclude others and (5) owners, who have the right of alienation, i.e. to sell the resource. The stability of the existence of the shared pool resources, they postulated, depended on the strength of the bundle of rights. (Schlager and Ostrom 1992, 249–262)

Based on her extensive research work, Ostrom offered following standard principles to govern commons reasonably and fairly in a community:

1. Define clear group boundaries.

2. Match rules governing the use of common goods to local needs and conditions.

3. Ensure that those affected by the rules can participate in modifying the rules.

4. Make sure outside authorities respect the rule-making rights of community members.

5. Develop a system carried out by community members for monitoring members' behaviour.

6. Use graduated sanctions for rule violators.

7. Provide accessible, low-cost means for dispute resolution.

8. Build responsibility for governing the common resource in nested tiers from the lowest level up to the entire interconnected system. (Walljasper 2011, 5)

In each one of the above principles, institutional subtleties are fundamental. Beginning from the hypothetical commitments of Ronald Coase, Douglass North and Oliver Williamson, Ostrom isolated the primary attributes of local self-government. The first condition for the institutional premise of the achievement of these instruments is the clarity of the law. Whether or not they are transparent, the standards practised must get shared by the community. That is the reason why another essential component of self-government is the foundation of the techniques for aggregate and vote-based leadership, equipped for including all clients of the asset.

Furthermore, the instruments of conflict resolution must be local, public and open in order to be available to all members of the community. Other than systems of graduated sanctions, joint control of the resources among the clients themselves must be implemented. Such control has a twofold legitimacy. To start with, those fascinated by the proper management of the resources would have a motivation to monitor the administration, and second, as clients, they have access to information on how the resources can be utilized inappropriately by the others. Finally, the rules and regulations of governance, irrespective of whether they are clear, mutual and made fruitful by all members in the local community, must not conflict with the governance norms of the government at the higher level.

CONCLUSION

Most of the issues related to sustainability are due to the mismanagement of CPRs. The discipline of economics and its theory have eminently contributed to the understanding and management of CPRs. Hardin made the first-ever attempt in this regard through the conceptualization of 'tragedy of the commons'. His theory underscored the challenges involved in implementing non-exclusion concerning the use of scarce CPRs. Ronald Coase suggested that allocative efficiency was achievable by bargaining among concerned parties if transaction costs were small. Elinor Ostrom emphasized that instead of privatization, the collaboration between local people and public officials could achieve sustainability of CPRs. These theories have given rise to the emergence of new principles in international environmental law.

REFERENCES

Balagopal, Bindu, and Chacko Jose. 2015–2016, June–May. 'Exploitation of Ground Water Resources by MNCs and Resistance by the Local People: A Study of Plachimada in Kerala'. *EPRA International Journal of Economic Growth and Environmental Issues* 3. Available at: https://eprawisdom.com/jpanel/

upload/articles/159pm3.Bindu%20Balagopal.pdf (accessed on 12 February 2020).

Beggs, J. 2019, 17 January. 'Introduction to the Coase Theorem'. Available at: https://www.thoughtco.com/introduction-to-the-coase-theorem-1147386 (accessed on 12 February 2020).

Cardenas, Juan Camilo, and Rajiv Sethi. 2016, 12 September. 'Elinor Ostrom: Fighting the Tragedy of the Commons'. Available at: https://booksandideas. net/Elinor-Ostrom-Fighting-the-Tragedy-of-the-Commons.html (accessed on 26 February 2020).

Coase, R. H. 1960. 'The Problem of Social Cost'. *The Journal of Law and Economics* III (October): 1–44. Available at: https://www.law.uchicago.edu/files/file/coase-problem.pdf (accessed on 26 February 2020). Reprinted as Chapter 5 in Coase 1988.

Felice, Flavio, and Massimiliano Vatiero. 2012, 27 June). 'Elinor Ostrom and the Solution to the Tragedy of the Commons'. Available at: https://www.aei.org/articles/elinor-ostrom-and-the-solution-to-the-tragedy-of-the-commons/ (accessed on 26 February 2020).

Haiduk, K. 2015. 'Hayek and Coase Travel East: Privatization and the Experience of Post-socialist Economic Transformation'. In *Hayek: A Collaborative Biography*, edited by Robert Leeson, Part VI, Good Dictators, Sovereign Producers, and Hayek's 'Ruthless Consistency', 249–280. New York, NY: Palgrave Macmillan.

Hardin, G. 1968. 'The Tragedy of the Commons'. *Science*, n.s., 162 (3859): 1243–1248. Available at: https://pages.mtu.edu/~asmayer/rural_sustain/governance/Hardin%201968.pdf (accessed on 26 February 2020).

Ostrom, E. 1990. *Governing the Commons*. Cambridge: Cambridge University Press.

Ponce, Victor M. 2010, 10 October. 'Hardin's "Tragedy of The Commons" Revisited'. Available at: http://tragedy.sdsu.edu/ (accessed on 26 February 2020).

Schlager, E., and E. Ostrom. 1992, August. 'Property-Rights Regimes and Natural Resources: A Conceptual Analysis'. *Land Economics* 68 (3): 249–262. doi:10.2307/3146375.

Walljasper, J. 2011, 2 October. 'Elinor Ostrom's 8 Principles for Managing A Commons'. Available at: https://www.onthecommons.org/magazine/elinor-ostroms-8-principles-managing-commmons (accessed on 26 February 2020).

Chapter 2
What International Law Can Teach Us about the Commons

Julien Cazala

We all know what the term 'commons' refers to: publicly available resources, which are freely usable but limited in supply. The most basic illustration consists of land areas used collectively by a community. What the difficulties could be, is widely known, and can be easily understood. If one member of the community uses a common resource, or over-exploits it, less of it is available to the other members of that community. Community members may thus be self-incited to exploit the resource to the fullest possible extent, as fast as possible, in a way to secure the maximum possible share and profits. The basic premise of the commons lies in the term *res communis*. The idea can easily be presented: some areas are open for the benefit of each and every member of a community and, as such, members share a common interest in their preservation and exploitation. This means that these areas are common to all; they are used and exploited by everyone but cannot be exclusively acquired by anyone.

How does international law interact with the commons? International law (meaning *public* international law) establishes and is grounded on, cooperation between states. The very gist of international law is to share, govern in commons, implement common rules, etc. We can then easily understand why and how international law can refer to the issue of the commons.

In 2002, Professor Joe Verhoeven of Louvain University in Belgium taught the general course of international law at The Hague Academy of International Law. The title of his general course was in French *considérations sur ce qui est commun* which could be translated into English as 'Reflexions on What Is Common' (or 'What We Have in Common'; Verhoeven 2008). One of the main aspects of his lecture was to discuss the concept of *common heritage of mankind* that was incorporated within the 1982 United Nations Convention on the Law of the Sea, mainly in recognition of the fact that mineral resources of high seas are non-renewable and that fisheries and flora, although renewable, can be quickly depleted to extinction.

Professor Joe Verhoeven stated that we could question the components of international heritage and the legal regime applicable to it. He added that in so far as we could not say anything very 'positive' on this point, the international 'community' still remains, in many ways, ghostly (Verhoeven 2008, 400). It is true that in many aspects, it is hard to say that the international community does exist: There is only an international society, not a community. This is to say that there are barely any common projects, common values or interests. However, this does not mean that states have never tried to give corpse to the concept of international community. The notion of common heritage of mankind, sometimes called 'common heritage of humanity' is the main contemporary aspect of this question (Baslar 1998 ; Noyes 2011).

It is sometimes quite hard to understand the meaning of a reference to this common heritage. We can mention the Preamble of the Rome Statute of the International Criminal Court (1998) states that 'all peoples are united by common bonds, their cultures pieced together in a shared heritage and concerned that this delicate mosaic may be shattered at any time'. In the same way, the recommendation for the Safeguarding and Preservation of Moving Images, adopted by the UNESCO in 1980, states:

> Considering that moving images created by the peoples of the world also form part of the heritage of mankind as a whole and consequently

that closer international co-operation should be promoted to safeguard and preserve these irreplaceable records of human activity and, in particular, for the benefit of those countries with limited resources. (UNESCO 1980)

Those indications are far from clear and we must admit that we really do not know what could be the legal consequences of such a qualification.

Some try to apply the concept of global commons extensively, sustaining that the rain forest should be qualified as such because of its positive contribution in favour of the climate (Wilson 1996, 244). This kind of argument is far from convincing and hurts the very essence of international law that posits sovereign equality among States. If you declare that the rainforests in Brazil or Indonesia are global commons, you radically negate the sovereignty of these two countries on a specific part of their territory (except, of course, if the States specifically agree with such a declaration; PCIJ 1923). Such a qualification clearly interferes with the well-established principle of sovereignty over natural resources according to which, be it good or not, a State has the right to exploit the resources located on its territory freely unless it has made an international commitment for an exception. This example illustrates the tension that can emerge from the confrontation of the commons and international law.

On some occasions, international law instruments give us a clear, and apparently less controversial indication about what we have in common. As it has very often been outlined, the international law of the sea is the most established frame of the identification of what could be the legal consequences of the common heritage of mankind qualification.

A sea, or at least parts of it, is a common resource. It means, very basically, that the seas do not belong to individuals but are available to the whole community. Under general international law, the principle applicable in the high seas is freedom. The navigational issues on the high seas are not a major difficulty as everyone can freely navigate in this area. However, the resources in the sea are finite; they can be exhausted if overexploited, and it is now common knowledge that the disappearance of several species is accelerating. Many authors consider that the high seas are still free in the most anarchic sense of the word; it would be an area beyond authority, outside the effective reach of law (Langewische 2004, 236). We can add that if the high seas outside of national jurisdiction could really be 'commons'; fish species, pollution and other effects of economic development do not respect these human-made legal boundaries.

Relying on the principle of freedom, all nations can fish at will in the high seas. Of course, selfish-interest is the problem. It would be futile if one country, individually, decided to refrain from fishing or from discharging pollutants into the sea, while other States (other members of the community) were to continue fishing or discharging pollutants. These two very basic examples illustrate that the use of the commons needs cooperation among members of the community. The open access model creates a structural lack of adequate incentives for regulatory cooperation.

In the early 1970s, two corporations, Kennecott and Deep Sea Ventures applied to the US, Canada, UK and Australia to obtain exclusive rights to explore the seabed. They were denied, with regard to the application made to the United States, on the ground that, 'the State Department does not recognize exclusive mining rights to the mineral resources of an area beyond the limits of national jurisdiction' (Statement on Claim of Exclusive Mining Rights, 1975). However, a few years later, the Reagan administration introduced the argument that freedom of the high seas, universally recognized as far as navigation is concerned, could be extended to the exploitation of minerals, ensuring that seabed minerals were open to all on a 'first come, first served' basis (Hasjim 1981, 42). Of course, developing countries and most of the developed States as well, which lacked the technology to exploit the deep seabed mineral resources, refused this idea. This is a clear illustration of the controversies to which this issue can give rise.

As early as 1970, the United Nations General Assembly adopted a resolution in which it outlined that the area of the seabed and ocean floor and the subsoil thereof, beyond the limits of national jurisdiction, as well as its resources, are the 'common heritage of mankind', the exploration and exploitation of which shall be carried out for the benefit of mankind as a whole, irrespective of the geographical location of States (United Nations 1970).

It is quite uncontroversial to say that the common heritage of mankind concept incorporates five principles (Joyner 1986, 190–199): (a) The areas are not owned by anyone, they cannot fall under any sovereign control and are to be managed by the community as a whole. (b) Priority is given to universal popular interest, not to national interest. (c) All benefits from the economic exploitation of these global commons are shared among the parties. (d) The use of the commons is limited to peaceful activities. (e) It promises reservation for future generations. This principle and its characteristics are clearly integrated within the 1982 United Nations Convention on the Law of the Sea (UNCLOS 1982), Article 136 of which states that 'the Area and its resources are the common heritage of mankind'. The areas beyond national jurisdiction include both the high seas and the Area (with a capital A). Despite apparent proximity, their legal regimes are, as of 22 November 2018 (Ricard 2017), to be distinguished. In the high seas, as has been previously mentioned, freedom is the core principle. Nevertheless, stating that the areas and its resources are the common heritage of mankind leads to the applicability of a very specific international legal regime. This is embodied in Articles 137–191 of the 1982 United Nations Convention on the Law of the Sea.

The main element of this legal regime is identified in Article 137 of the Convention. It states that 'No State shall claim or exercise sovereignty or sovereign rights over any part of the Area or its resources, nor shall any State or natural or juridical person appropriate any part thereof. No such claim or exercise of sovereignty or sovereign rights nor such appropriation shall be recognized'. It continues with 'All rights in the resources of the Area are vested in mankind as a whole, on whose behalf the Authority shall act. These resources are not subject to alienation. The minerals recovered from the Area, however, may only be alienated in accordance with this Part and the rules, regulations and procedures of the Authority'.

This is precisely what the commons are about. There is no possibility of appropriation and everyone can exploit the resources to the benefit of the whole. It is then easy to understand that we are confronted here with a situation that could lead to the realization of what is usually designated as the tragedy of the commons. This formula is customarily attributed to Garrett Hardin (Hardin 1968, 1243–1248 and UN General Assembly [UNGA], First Committee Debate, UN Docs A/C.1/PV.1515-1516, 1 November 1967), but the phenomenon has been presented long before. In 1833, William Forster Lloyd (Lloyd 1833) described the problem of overgrazing of cattle on the common areas of villages. It was a description of the problem generated by the sharing of a limited common resource (reprinted in Hardin 1964). We all know what the problem is: optimizing for the self in the short term is not optimal for anyone in the long term. To ensure the shared long-term exploitation of the resources, you have to regulate individual behaviours by promoting the use of coercive social arrangements.

Therefore, when States taking part to the negotiations of the United Nations Convention on the Law of the Sea decided to qualify the Area and its resources as common heritage of mankind, they had to find a way to avoid the realization of 'tragedy of the commons' phenomenon, 'to legislate temperance' (Hardin 1968). The developing countries claimed the establishment of an international organization with wide powers to regulate seabed mining, where the industrialized countries argued for a simple international registry for deep-sea claims (Ellingsen-Tunold 1984).

A new international organization, the International Seabed Authority (the Authority), has been created. The Authority is the organization through which States Parties to the Convention shall, in accordance with the regime for the Area established in Part XI, organize and control activities in the Area, particularly with a view to administering the resources located in the Area. The Authority is at the heart of the implementation of the United Nations Convention on the Law of the Sea regarding the Area designed as a common heritage of mankind. Many provisions of the convention illustrate this central position.

According to Article 144 of the International Seabed Authority, the Authority shall take measures in accordance with the Convention to acquire technology and scientific knowledge relating to activities in the Area; and, to promote and encourage the transfer to developing

States of such technology and scientific knowledge so that all States' Parties benefit therefrom. The article also mentions that the Authority and States Parties shall cooperate in promoting the transfer of technology and scientific knowledge relating to activities in the Area so that the Enterprise (which is the organ of the Authority which shall carry out activities in the Area directly) and all States Parties may benefit therefrom.

The Authority shall also adopt appropriate rules, regulations and procedures for the protection and conservation of the marine environment. The goal is to make sure that the exploitation of the Area will not be or the less possible be, harmful to the environment (UNCLOS Article 145). It is also of the jurisdiction of the Authority to control and make sure that the installations used to conduct activities in the Area respect the terms of the convention (especially regarding the non-appropriation of the Area).

What is really of interest for us is that, having due regard to their special interests and needs, the Convention promotes the effective participation of developing states in activities in the Area (UNCLOS Article 148). As a common heritage of mankind, the Area and its resources shall be exploited in such a way as to foster 'healthy development of the world economy and balanced growth of international trade, and to promote international cooperation for the overall development of all countries' (UNCLOS Article 150). To ensure that the principles are respected, the activities in the Area are organized, carried out and controlled by the Authority on behalf of mankind as a whole. These few selected provisions show us that during the negotiations of the United Nations Convention on the Law of the Sea, states had clearly in mind that the commons need regulation and proper enforcement mechanisms.

However, the evolutions of the Convention illustrate the idea that this kind of mechanism could be drafted and imposed on a small community. But when it comes to global commons, you have to deal with the world community, and it is, of course, way more complex and the outcome full of uncertainty. The informal power of shame might sometimes suffice in small groups. When there are many more users, there is much less incentive for regulation.

Global commons may not, as their name would logically imply, equally share resources. Common resources are, under international law, exploited to the benefits of select parties. It is particularly true because of the opposition of many high-income countries towards the convention's Part XI (dealing with the common heritage of mankind). This opposition led to an amendment of this part, which eventually allowed the entry into force of the convention in 1994. We can easily understand why some of the industrialized countries see the common heritage of mankind concept as an impediment to investment in the prospection and exploitation of the deep seabed resources. The amendments include: allowing free market principles to control deep seabed mining; eliminating mandatory transfer of technology and production control; recognizing established seabed mining claims; guaranteeing a seat for the United States on the executive body (even if it is not a party to the United Nations Convention on the Law of the Sea) and allowing states to apply the agreement provisionally in accordance with their domestic laws and regulations. We are far from the initial philosophy that led to the recognition of the common heritage of mankind. The 1994 amendments clearly lower the place and impact of the common heritage of humankind concept (Duff 1995, 1–66). This is the consequence of the initial opposition of the United States to the United Nations Convention on the Law of the Sea. On 9 July 1982, the US delegation stated that, even though the Convention contained many positive features, the deep seabed mining provisions did not meet US objectives.

Even if the Area's resources are still qualified as the common heritage of mankind, the legal regime attached to it shows the difficulty to effectively implement a conservation and exploitation regime in favour of a whole community. The Council on Foreign Relations (2013; a 'nonpartisan' US think tank) identified the serious limitations to a global governance regime in its publication on *The Global Oceans Regime*: (a) The world's leading power (the US) is not a party to the United Nations Convention on the Law of the Sea. (b) The Convention is

30 years old and does not adequately address a number of emerging issues (such as fishing on the high seas, widespread maritime pollution, transnational crime committed at sea). (c) Weak Surveillance and enforcement mechanisms. (d) The system is horizontally fragmented and fails to harmonize domestic, regional and international policies. (e) There is no global evaluation framework to assess progress. Five years later, there is nothing to withdraw from this list.

Some states have tried to identify some components of their common heritage and to build a legal regime associated with it. Commons need regulation; Global commons need global regulation. However, the issue is still very controversial. Whatever the size of the community, as long as you have free riders, that is, states staying outside of the global regime, it cannot be really under control or efficient. It is particularly true when the free rider is a major power.

Due to its well-identified lacunas, the common heritage of mankind concept has been rejected to guide the international regimes applicable to the international preservation of biodiversity and climate change. During the negotiations of the 1992 UN Convention on Biological Diversity, a proposal has been made to declare the global climate system as a part of the common heritage of mankind but this was rejected (mostly by lower-middle income countries) and the adopted version of the convention only acknowledges 'that change in the Earth's climate and its adverse effects are a common concern of humankind' (UNFCCC 1992). In the very same way, States did not admit the use of the term 'common heritage of mankind' in the 1992 UN Convention on Biological Diversity (Convention on Biological Diversity 1992).

The international law of the sea regime has shown the rise and decline of the common heritage of mankind concept. Nevertheless, it cannot be ignored and denied that human beings face a common global destiny regarding climate change, global pollution, management of non-renewable natural resources, etc. If the 'common heritage of mankind' concept is not the appropriate legal vehicle to manage such issues efficiently, the future is open to legal imagination and political efforts to build an efficient legal regime to manage and protect the global commons.

REFERENCES

Baslar, K. 1998. *The Concept of the Common Heritage of Mankind in International Law*. Dordrecht: Martinus Nijhoff.
Convention on Biological Diversity. 1992, 5 June. *United Nations Treaty Series*. Vol. 1760, I–30619. Rio de Janeiro: Convention on Biological Diversity.
Council on Foreign Relations. 2013. *The Global Oceans Regime*. Available at: https://www.cfr.org/report/global-oceans-regime (accessed on 23 April 2020).
Duff, J. A. 1995. 'UNCLOS and the New Deep Seabed Mining Regime: The Risks of Refuting the Treaty'. *Suffolk Transnational Law Review* 19 (1): 1–66.
Ellingsen-Tunold, B. M. 1984. *The UNCLOS III Negotiations on the Deep Sea-bed Regime: The Common Heritage of Mankind for the Benefit of Mankind as a Whole?*. Oslo: Institute of Political Science, University of Oslo.
Hardin, G. 1964. *Population, Evolution, and Birth Control*. San Francisco, CA: Freeman.
———. 1968. 'The Tragedy of the Commons'. *Science* 162 (3859): 1243–1248.
Hasjim, D. 1981. 'Law of the Sea Conference: Other Alternatives for Seabed Mining?' *New York Law School Journal of International and Comparative Law* 3 (1): 42.
Joyner, Chr. C. 1986. 'Legal Implications of the Concept of Common Heritage of Mankind'. *International and Comparative Law Quarterly* 35: 190–199.
Langewische, W. 2004. *The Outlaw Sea: A World of Freedom, Chaos and Crime*. London: Granta Books.
Lloyd, W. F. 1833. *Two Lectures on the Checks to Population*. Oxford: Oxford University Press. These two lectures have been reprinted in Garrett Hardin's book, Population, Evolution and Birth Control.
Noyes, J. 2011. 'The Common Heritage of Mankind: Past, Present, and Future'. *Denver Journal of International Law & Policy* 40: 447–471.
PCIJ. 1923. *The S.S. 'Wimbledon'*. Judgment of 28 June 1923. PCIJ series A no. 1, 25.
Reagan, Ronald. 1982, 29 January. Statement on United States Participation in the Third United Nations Conference on the Law of the Sea. Available at: https://www.reaganlibrary.gov/sspeeches/12982b (accessed on 23 April 2020).
Ricard, P. 2017. 'La conservation de la biodiversité dans les zones maritimes internationales'. (Marine Biodiversity Conservation Beyond National Jurisdiction) PhD Thesis. France: University of Paris I.
Rome Statute of the International Criminal Court. 1998, 17 July. 'Preamble § 2'. *United Nations Treaty Series*. Vol. 2187, I–38544.
Verhoeven, J. 2008. 'Considérations sur ce qui est commun'. *Recueil des cours de l'Académie de droit international* ('Reflexions on what is common', Collected Courses of the Hague Academy of International Law) 334: 9–434.
UNCLOS (United Nations Convention on the Law of the Sea). 1982, 10 December. *United Nations Treaty Series*. Vol. 1833, I–31363. Montego Bay.

UNESCO. 1980, 27 October. 'Recommendation for the Safeguarding and Preservation of Moving Images'. Preamble § 12. Available at: http://portal.unesco.org/en/ev.php-URL_ID=13139&URL_DO=DO_TOPIC&URL_SECTION=201.html (accessed on 23 April 2020).

UNFCCC (United Nations Framework Convention on Climate Change). 1992, 9 May. 'Preamble § 1'. *United Nations Treaty Series*. Vol. 1771, I–30822.

UN General Assembly (UNGA). 1967, 1 November. First Committee Debate. UN Docs A/C.1/PV.1515–1516.

United Nations. 1970, 12 December. 'Declaration of Principles Governing the Sea-Bed and the Ocean Floor, and the Subsoil thereof, beyond the Limits of National Jurisdiction, UN General Assembly, Res. 2749(XXV), § 1'. Available at: http://www.un-documents.net/a25r2749.htm (accessed on 23 April 2020).

US Department of State Statement on Claim of Exclusive Mining Rights by Deepsea Ventures. 1975. *International Legal Materials* 66.

Wilson, P. E., Jr. 1996. 'Barking Up the Right Tree: Proposals for Enhancing the Effectiveness of the International Tropical Timber Agreement'. *Temple International and Comparative Law Journal* 10: 244.

Chapter 3

The Precautionary Principle
An Instrument at the Service of Sustainable Development

Didier Guével

Two quotations illustrate, in my opinion, the evolution that the idea of precaution[1] could undergo and its ambivalence: 'I'd rather be too cautious then too secure,' declares Bartholo to Rosine in *The Barber of Seville, or the Useless Precaution* (ACT II, Scene 3), to which Voltaire (1878, Chapter XXIV) responds by saying: 'Nothing proves alarms better than excessive precaution'.

Works of research that relate to the precautionary principle are innumerable, scientific, epistemological, technical or polemical and often more sociological than legal in nature.[2] It is clear that the question leaves nobody indifferent and continues to be debated.

Let us first take up the term 'precaution' alone. It is etymologically derived from Latin *praecautionem*, meaning 'to be careful', 'to be

---

[1] An earlier version of this chapter was presented at the conference on 'Environmental Responsibility: Review and Perspectives' held at the University of Tokyo on 9 July 2017.

[2] There are about thousand articles depending on the database. For a select list of printed books in the French language, see the Works Cited section.

on guard' (*cavere*). It is notable that in Rome the word (already) had a legal meaning. It is found again in our modern idea of caution. It is a question of getting a guarantee, of preserving oneself legally. In this sense, the taking into account of unforeseeability is also a manifestation of legal precaution (New Article 1195 of the French Civil Code; see also Guével 2017).

Undoubtedly, there needs to be a separation between prevention and precaution. Prevention is for proven risk and leads to permanent measures. Precaution concerns a potential risk and results in provisional measures.

Since Montaigne, dictionaries have agreed that precaution is a provision taken to avoid harm or mitigate the effects of such harm. Beyond that, it seems that a consensus is emerging gradually to distinguish (probably within a broader category that could be called 'prudence'; Kourilsky and Viney 2000, 21) precaution from prevention. It is necessary, as in economics, to distinguish the (known, proven) risk that leads to preventive measures from protection, mere prudence and uncertainty (unknown risks, potential risks in the state of science [Kourilsky and Viney 2000, 42] that result in precautionary measures [Baghestani-Perrey 2005, 92; Kourilsky and Viney 2000, 18; Larceneux and Boutelet 2005, 24]).

Prevention leads to permanent measures, and precaution to provisional measures (Kourilsky and Viney 2000, 150). For some scholars, there would be, in addition, a difference in the mainspring of these notions (prudence being perceived as egocentric, even selfish, whereas precaution would apprehend the world in its globality and would be altruistic (Grison 2012, 51). As one author has pointed out, whereas insurance can relate to damages provoked by others or external factors, precaution refers to a fear of the effects of our own action (Ewald, Gollier, and Sadeleer 2001; 2009, 30), or at least of human action. Finally, in the chronology of the history of ideas, prudence and prevention occur earlier than precaution. It is true, however, that the boundary between the two is fluctuating: the more scientific research advances, the more we move, brutally or little by little, from uncertainty to risk and from precaution to prevention (Larceneux and Boutelet 2005, 57). Between the perfectly known and assessed and the totally unknown and never witnessed, there is room for a multitude of cases in which uncertainty can relate to the phenomenon itself, its gravity, its own characteristics, its intensity, etc. Moreover, it is especially in the matter of prevention that we can use the rule of reason and can balance the advantages against the disadvantages, since the risk is known there; thus, for DDT (dichlorodiphenyltrichloroethane), we know how harmful it may be, but we also know how primordial its action has been in the fight against malaria (Besancenot 2005, 57). Sometimes, it is a question of comparing a beneficial universal action with harmful individual effects (the risk of explosion of gases replacing CFCs [Chlorofluorocarbons] that destroyed the ozone layer [Besancenot 2005, 60]). The whole question is one of what triggers uncertainty. There is a significant risk of individuals or interest groups casting doubt without any reason on any novelty to paralyze its advancement, considered harmful to their own preoccupations. 'A minimum of doubts or suspicions must exist' (Belaïdi 2005, 84). The existence of scientific research on the concerned innovation ('the mere fact that studies exist in this area prove [sic] that suspicions exist and that is enough to implement the precautionary principle' [Belaïdi 2005, 84]) has been proposed as a criterion. However, it may be difficult to distinguish studies aiming at the creation of innovation (which also generally include an understanding of its possible adverse effects) from those tending only to highlight a possible harm. Finally, it is obvious, as we shall see, that we cannot implement the precautionary principle for minor or minimal and/or curable (they must be serious and/or irreversible) risks (Belaïdi 2005, 86). But how can the principle be determined if, by definition, we do not know what the risk is or whether any risk exists at all?

The separation between prevention and precaution cannot be as clear-cut as a simplified approach could let it appear; everything is, in reality, a question of degrees.

As for the term 'principle', it is subject to caution but, in any case, includes an element of moral value. Its meaning is far from being as obvious as it may seem on the face of it. Without going back to the long debates, in particular philosophical ones, devoted to what can be a principle in general (and not only what can be a legal principle

[Caudal 2008] or a general principle of the law), it seems useful to recall the fact that the reference dictionaries consider that there is an element of moral value in any principle.[3] The precautionary principle cannot, therefore, be tried on the ground that it is moralistic. It is interesting to note that the erection into a principle of the rule was a political gesture in France. The Coppens commission, which spearheaded the text of the French Charter for the Environment, did not want precaution to become a general principle (Baghestani-Perrey 2005, 93, 95).

The definitions of the 'precautionary principle' are numerous, both in doctrine and in various texts; they are all long, thus manifesting obvious uncertainties (for, what is conceived well should be expressed briefly). Jurists, economists and philosophers have their own definitions, even if there does not seem to exist, within each specialty, a distinct definition for each researcher concerned. For the European Union, this is 'a general principle of Community law requiring the competent authorities to take appropriate measures to prevent specific potential risks to public health, safety and the environment by giving precedence to these requirements related to the protection of those interests over economic interests' (Judgment of 26 November 2002—Joined cases T–74/00, T–76/00, T–83/00 to T–85/00, T–132/00, T–137/00 and T–141/00). For Thierry Martin, it would be 'a collective norm prompting us to take anticipated preventive measures with regard to serious and/or irreversible risks, but which are only suspected and about which there is insufficient scientific knowledge' (Martin 2005, 11) According to French law,

> 'The precautionary principle {is that} according to which the absence of certainty, taking into account of current scientific and technical knowledge, should not lead to the postponement of the adoption of effective and proportionate measures aimed at averting the risk of serious and irreversible damage to the environment, at an economically

---

[3] 'Rule of conduct, moral precept' according to *Littré*; 'rule of action based on value judgement' according to *Le Robert*; 'maxim, motive, rule of conduct, {...} principle of conscience, honour, justice and integrity' according to the *Dictionnaire de l'Académie* (8th edition).

acceptable cost' (Article L. 110–1, Section II, Paragraph 1, Charter for the Environment.), a definition described by a commentator as 'contrived'. (Sadeleer 2001, 91)

This convoluted formula shows, in any case, that the principle is active and not passive in France; it is a question of taking measures and not stopping any process. Article 5 of the Charter for the Environment goes in the same direction. For economists, the precautionary principle could constitute 'a principle of behaviour and management in the face of an uncertain environment' (Ewald, Gollier, and Sadeleer 2001; 2009, 104). The length of the definition proposed by Mrs Viney and Mr Kourilsky indicates a certain malaise:

> The precautionary principle defines the attitude to be adopted by any person who makes a decision about an activity that can reasonably be expected to pose a serious threat to the health or safety of current or future generations or the environment. It is especially binding on public authorities who should make health and safety requirements prevail over the freedom of trade between individuals and between States. It demands all measures to be taken to detect and assess the risk, to reduce it to an acceptable level and, if possible, to eliminate it, inform the persons concerned, at an economically and socially acceptable cost and gather their suggestions on the measures envisaged to treat it. This precautionary device must be proportionate to the extent of the risk and can be revised at any time. (Kourilsky and Viney 2000, 151)

When trying and establishing a definition of the precautionary principle that could bring about a consensus, it could be said that it is mainly a matter of justifying sustainable development policy decisions, abstentions or actions, when a product or service is potentially dangerous for the living beings in the long run. However, the expression is most often understood in a more restrictive sense than that of a general rule of life.

It is the calling into question of the beneficial effects of progress and an awareness of the risks incurred because of the sorcerer's apprentice activities of certain scientists that have justified the recent success of the precautionary principle.

Admittedly, fear is probably rooted in the collective unconscious: since the Promethean myth, man has learnt to be wary of the theft of divine knowledge. However, it has long been thought that progress could solve everything, even if it meant making some sacrifices. Now, the relationship has been reversed; it is considered that progress can sometimes have more negative than positive effects. You have to be in a city with a badly polluted atmosphere to understand the indignation of being caught in a deadly trap. Chernobyl and Fukushima are not considered mere accidents, as could be the explosion of a locomotive in the 19th century. However, in many areas, the religion of the majorities has not been established: in the case of shale gas, electromagnetic waves, genetically modified organism (GMO), nanocomponents or vaccinations (Besancenot 2005, 56), doubts persist for many. However, in the Anthropocene (or the anthropization of nature [Larceneux and Boutelet 2005, 5]), innovations are constantly being multiplied: We know what CRISPR Cas9 now allows for genetic manipulation in the whole set of living beings and things, that gene drives, modifying the genetic heritage, could destroy species that are deemed harmful (for instance, mosquitoes) and that the brand new RNA (ribonucleic acid) pesticide would allow the destruction of insects, thanks to a 'genetic-biological' method.[4] Added to these observations, the fact that the cost of curative treatment of the difficulties likely to arise often exceeds traditional financial capacities (supported by local authorities: insurance and reinsurance, taxes [Larceneux and Boutelet 2005, 5]). In particular, we are beginning to regain the understanding of the global interdependence of the living and even the molecular, for 'we are witnessing the end of great sharing, between nature and technology, nature and culture, nature and society' (Grison 2012, 35).

Gradually, the concept of precautionary principle tends to be a part of legal norms (I: progression in the reception of the concept) and progresses in the modalities of its implementation (II: progress in its implementation).

---

[4] By vaporizing small interfering RNA (ribonucleic acid) on the plants (the plants are not genetically modified, but the harmful insects approaching the plants are genetically modified).

PROGRESSION IN THE RECEPTION OF THE CONCEPT

Gradually, the principle has shifted from a simple standard behaviour, from a sort of philosophical choice to a real legal rule.

A Philosophical Choice

Perhaps, at the beginning, we only find the intellectualized and renewed image of an innate sense of the resilience of the living.

Before specifically speaking about the precautionary principle, it must be remembered that precaution constitutes a general human attitude. Even beyond humanity, it is likely that the idea of prudence is specific to all life, a guarantee of survival and resilience of species. Anyone who has ever seen an animal's attitude towards food, or a creature that they do not know, will understand the meaning of what I am trying to get across. The precautionary principle could constitute, in this perspective, the return of a religious gesture of humility and respect for life and nature. The most pessimistic thinks that man will disappear or even self-destruct in the near future, perhaps for having lost that innate sense of precaution that one is trying to reinstil, culturally this time. Foresight, circumspection—we are in the domain of forecast, but with an approach that is opposed to that of speculation.

For some, the precautionary principle would be but a moral and indeed even a spiritual principle. An author, in a beautiful formula, has advanced, that the principle of precaution was, in a way 'to be prepared to be surprised' (Grison 2012, 71). But if the expression is, literally, interesting, it remains very fuzzy, practically speaking. This principle could be used as a general rule of life in society like, for example, the principle of subsidiarity. One could even, as we have seen, go further by invoking morality, behavioural ethics (Jonas 1971; 2013) and a global paradigm change related to the awareness of the unity and interdependence of the living, indeed even of the molecular. One author has gone so far as to evoke a new spirituality, a 'spiritual conversion' (Ewald, Gollier, and Sadeleer 2001; 2009, 32, 40).

As it has been mentioned earlier, it would be more of an 'ethical' question (Icard 2005, 122), 'a philosophy of action' than a 'decision model' (Larceneux and Boutelet 2005, 29). The expression would then be essentially 'incantatory' (Besancenot 2005, 47) as if it were the ritual of a new doxa.

Above all, we are touching on fundamental philosophical choices: Must man control nature for his own benefit or is he an element of nature and should regard it as such? The precautionary principle is difficult to conceptualize in that it borders on these two theoretically irreconcilable concepts. The precautionary principle must not prohibit creativity and the modification of natural elements. Life is made only of often failed, sometimes achieved, attempts. Similarly, it is probably wrong to lock oneself in a debate that would oppose the benefits and misdeeds of science and try to determine which ones would prevail.

The question gets more complicated when one considers that the relations of cause and effect are no longer considered simplistically as in the early days of triumphant science. We have introduced the theory of chaos, the notion of complex systems (Grison 2012, 40; Kourilsky and Viney 2000, 46) and the principle of instability, all of which render random the results of any therapy. The consequences of an act may be unexpected and worse than the supposedly fought harm or evil.

Very quickly, a contrary doctrine that sneers at 'precautionism', which has become according to it, a form of 'neopopulism', and stigmatizes its negative effects of blocking scientific research, mainly in medical matters, has been established.

The precautionary principle has strong detractors (Bronner and Géhin 2010). They fear 'a dangerous drift towards the model of a society that is overcautious and hostile to innovation (Kourilsky and Viney 2000, 211) out of a fear of risk'. The precautionary principle would flatter what is the most cautious in Man (Grison 2012, 19), bordering on catastrophism, even if it is 'enlightened' (Grison 2012, 21). The precautionary principle would hinder (or indeed even block) innovation and any intervention (particularly medical) that is a bit risky. The evaders of the precautionary principle want it 'deconstitutionalized'

(Bronner and Géhin 2010, 1), speaking of 'precautionism' (Bronner and Géhin 2010, 2; which would constitute a 'neopopulism' [Bronner and Géhin 2010, 182]), sometimes using arguments as excessive as those who see dangers everywhere in industrial production, some of them getting close to conspiracy or conspirationist theses.[5]

'Precautionism thus comes down to populism in so far as it attempts to find a political end for some common errors of judgment,' they say (Bronner and Géhin 2010, 178). Some are more moderate but remain sceptical and circumspect.[6] It is true that, for vaccinations and probably for electromagnetic waves, their critical reasoning can be sometimes justified (Bronner and Géhin 2010, 161). As for GMOs, we can say that the religion of the French has not been made and that they remain expectative, contrary to what the enemies of the precautionary principle would have us believe. Detractors of the precautionary principle suggest that it can lead only to prohibitions of use, only to 'a suspicious principle of abstention' (Bronner and Géhin 2010, 14, 94) 'having become a fundamental rule, precaution may lead to a proliferation of moratoria and prohibitions that are harmful to innovation and, consequently, to health and environment' (Bronner and Géhin 2010, 21, 170), while the texts, on the contrary, refer to positive acts. Ultimately, if the remarks on the precautionary excesses are founded as well as those concerning the perverse role of the Internet in the dissemination of approximate but enticing information and the risks that any experimentation might include, especially with regard to drugs, or new therapy (Bronner and Géhin 2010, 36), indeed even regarding established therapy, excesses in the opposite direction do not serve to bring about a balanced debate. We can approve neither those who denounce the precautionary principle as a pseudo-will to return to primitive ages nor those who stigmatize it as an industrial conspiracy.

---

[5] Each party has websites of questionable value as main references. Without being too candid, one could say that the objective of the food industry is to reduce costs.

[6] I have noticed that doctors working in hospitals are allergic to any reference made to the principle of precaution.

Without adhering to these excessive and biased opinions, we could indeed think that the precautionary principle should only be used cautiously, so to speak. The tenants of the precautionary principle, unanimously, put the accent (a little too much, perhaps, to be always convincing) on the positive and active aspect of their approach. It must be admitted that if they are so obstinate about repeating it, it is perhaps because reality does not show it with such clear evidence.

To put things simply, it can be said that the authorities must (and companies can) ask the question of precaution before any action and especially, if such is the case, benefit from making it known. But one could think that things will go further and that the 'new principle will be able to be progressively affirmed as a rule of direct and autonomous application, but of a special type' (Ewald, Gollier, and Sadeleer 2001; 2009, 103).

The principle tends, little by little, to be more than a philosophy in order to become an original rule.

For some, it would only be a standard, which would already give it a peri-legal status.

Precaution would, therefore, be especially 'an inspiring principle {having} vocation to guide the parties' (Belaïdi 2005, 81). We would then be, in that case, close to a standard (Boy 1997; Cornu 1987; Kourilsky and Viney 2000, 22, 125), of one of these legal topics or places of rights (Perelman 1976, 87). However, we could challenge this qualification, which remains quite variable (Ewald, Gollier, and Sadeleer 2001; 2009, 95). We have gone, at least in French law, very probably beyond. It is clear, in any case, that even if the precautionary principle is only a general principle, its application can irrigate many legal fields, as we shall see again.

The whole question is to know whether and how this general principle can become a real legal rule. The jurists, accustomed as they are to litigation, always tend to see, in every fact or every act, what could be perverse about it. This professional deformation logically inclines them to support a precautionary attitude. They should, therefore, welcome the concept.

An Established Rule of Law

France, as we shall see again, is at the forefront in my subject; it is the first country to have constitutionalized the precautionary principle. The European Union is also at the forefront of this area. But making it an established rule of law can also have concrete translations with far-reaching consequences (hundreds of thousands of ducks have been slaughtered in France to prevent a possible spread of bird flu). The risk is also that the precautionary principle serves as a pretext for some states to conceal measures that are actually protectionist in nature (Kourilsky and Viney 2000, 12 and 75).

At first, we can notice that we have moved from the philosophical to the political. Decisions, justified by the precautionary principle, fall under the order of governance first and are taken after recourse to the rule of reason (and not according to any—real or fantasized—juridical syllogism).

Moreover, even when the precautionary principle may have become a legal rule, in some countries, it must be recognized that it has led to mainly political decisions, after a process of not a juridical syllogism, but a rule of reason. In particular, 'the determination of environmental goods and services to be protected from risks does not proceed {...} strictly from legal inferences but from a political choice' (Belaïdi 2005, 87). We are here (as, for example, with regard to concentrations of companies) in the face of eminently political decisions that must nevertheless be 'dressed in the legal attire'. It has even been possible to write that it was 'a major social phenomenon {involving} many aspects of the functioning of democracies' (Kourilsky and Viney 2000, 11).

The transition to the legal comes up against some obstacles. The Anglo-American world is reluctant to give a legal qualification to the precautionary principle, preferring the freedom to act and possibly, only action (in liability) a posteriori. The precautionary principle is especially in symbiosis with Continental Law and the emphasis it puts on preserving the security of legal relations.

Here again, two systems are in conflict: the Anglo-American system, based on freedom, which leads only to an a posteriori action in liability

(Kourilsky and Viney 2000, 34) and the continental system, which favours security and tends to intervene upstream. It is clear, therefore, that the precautionary principle is primarily a model of Romano-Germanic law. But everywhere in the world, it seems obvious that if they have one day the will, judges can overcome the absence of a legislative text and establish the precautionary principle themselves, through a multitude of substantive and procedural rules (except, probably, in criminal procedures, where a text is needed).

If we go further, and if we accept that there is here, 'law, it is necessary to determine whether to prefer soft law or hard law and if we opt for traditional law, whether it is a question of introducing suppletive or imperative provisions.

The first question to be asked is whether 'hard' law or 'soft' law is needed to better frame the principle. One is, of course, tempted to affirm, here as elsewhere, that a disarmed justice is no longer justice and that the sword of coercive law is needed. But we know that 'hard' law is not effective and that 'soft' law significantly influences economic actors (with the help of the sword of the media). It is also essential to determine whether, when there are legislative texts, the stakeholders concerned 'may' or 'must' act.

If the principle is elevated to the rank of rule of law, it necessarily affects the legal regime of evidence. Is it harmlessness or harmfulness that is presumed?

The precautionary principle could seem to fall under the purview of the law of evidence (Hautereau-Boutonnet and Truilhé-Marengo 2017, 827, 830) and more precisely, in the ambit of a set of presumptions (Guével and Dupichot 1997), which would be rebuttable here (Article 1354, paragraph 2, Civil Code). Even philosophers say it: It is first a question of the burden of proof (Ewald, Gollier, and Sadeleer 2001; 2009, 64). It seems out of the question to not only require a reversal of this burden, but also impose an irrebuttable presumption as in the case of hidden defects (it would then be up to the professional to prove the total safety of his product or service (Kourilsky and Viney 2000, 139)). Either it is presumed, until proven to the contrary, that any innovation is beneficial or, on the contrary, it is presumed to be harmful, except when its innocuousness is demonstrated. And this would be the very object of the precautionary principle we are studying. 'Whereas in the past it was up to a complainant to have a product or process banned by bringing proof of its harmfulness, the new situation would require the designer of that product or process to prove its harmlessness before putting it on the market' (Grison 2012, 13). But locking yourself in such a dilemma is to fall under sophism and *probatio diabolica*, because, in the matter of precaution, one can never truly provide, by definition, either of the contrary proofs.

The precautionary principle can only have a significant influence on civil liability (in particular by changing the causing factor and the causal relationship).

We find ourselves in the well-known framework of a theory of risk (here the fault lies first and foremost in the absence or insufficiency of the search for information and its dissemination, in the lack of vigilance (Sadeleer 2001, 98). Instead of contributing to the powerful comeback of responsibility for misconduct, the precautionary principle could, by its upstream requirements, contribute to widening strict liability, as the risk theory envisaged it (Kourilsky and Viney 2000, 184). The damages to be paid could also evolve by the systematic acceptance of possible damage (Kourilsky and Viney 2000, 180). Finally, the causal relationship can be transformed, by the recourse to simple indices (CJEU 21 June 2017, C–621/15, in order to establish the link between certain illnesses and vaccinations). In any case, it will be generating new mistakes (in the information, the follow-up of research, alerts [Kourilsky and Viney 2000, 188], etc.). This being the case, even if non-abidance with the precautionary principle is likely to be invoked a posteriori to initiate actions in liability, it is necessary to distinguish precaution from compensation, which is curative. Finally, it must be pointed out that a major criticism is that, in addition to being inoperative, the precautionary principle might entail the possible multiplication of actions for damages on the basis of non-compliance with an unfulfilled precautionary obligation (Besancenot 2005, 47).

The texts evoking or invoking the precautionary principle are numerous, a sign of a real fascination, but also a symptom of a lack of coherence and perhaps inversely proportional efficiency. Some allude to it only tacitly or implicitly. This is the case, for example, with the duty of vigilance imposed in France on public limited companies (Law No. 2017–399 of 27 March 2017 with reference to parent companies and contracting companies).

There are texts that express the precautionary principle, without expressly stating it (Kourilsky and Viney 2000, 119). French law has adopted a very interesting provision by Law No. 2017–399 of 27 March 2017 on the duty of care, by imposing a vigilance plan concerning not only respect for human rights (child labour, etc.) but also the health and safety of the people and the environment on large public limited companies (including subsidiaries and sub-subsidiaries). This is typically a provision for applying the precautionary principle.

Many texts, moreover, are only indicative and persuasive (white papers) and, when they are real legal texts (conventions, treaties, etc.), they often quote the precautionary principle as a form of simple advice, of indication of behaviour to uphold. It is, therefore, often difficult to know whether one is dealing with soft law or hard law. Besides, the precautionary principle, often confined to a specific area, is seldom mentioned alone (Ewald, Gollier, and Sadeleer 2001; 2009, 26).

Other texts constitute genuine legal creations, both internationally and at the European level.

At the international level, various texts evoke necessary precautionary measures. The World Conservation Charter of 1982, then, from 1984 onwards, the discussions between the states bordering the North Sea (especially Second conference on the North Sea 1987), in 1990, the United Nations Economic Commission, in 1992, the Convention on Biological Diversity allude to it (Ewald, Gollier, and Sadeleer 2001; 2009, 8). The Rio Declaration of 13 June 1992, devoted to the environment and development, envisages it in Article 15.[7] The same is true

---

[7] In order to protect the environment, the precautionary approach shall be widely applied by States according to their capabilities. Where there are threats of serious or irreversible damage, lack of full scientific certainty shall not be used as a reason for postponing cost-effective measures to prevent environmental degradation.

of the United Nations Framework Convention on Climate Change of 9 May 1992.[8] The Convention on Biological Diversity (CBD) adopted at the Earth Summit in Rio de Janeiro on 5 June 1992 applies the rule without naming it.[9] The World Trade Organization (WTO) takes up the principle tacitly in its Sanitary and Phytosanitary (SPS) Agreement, which entered into force on 1 January 1995.[10] The WTO cannot but be cautious in this matter: the precautionary principle running the risk of coming up against the very foundation of the organization that advocates increased freedom of commerce.

At the European level, this is dealt with in Article 191, 2 (1) TFEU (Treaty on the Functioning of the European Union).[11] The text of the European Union, as it has been interpreted, deals with the protection of

---

[8] Article 3, paragraph 3: The Parties should take precautionary measures to anticipate, prevent or minimize the causes of climate change and mitigate its adverse effects. Where there are threats of serious or irreversible damage, lack of full scientific certainty should not be used as a reason for postponing such measures, taking into account that policies and measures to deal with climate change should be cost-effective so as to ensure global benefits at the lowest possible cost. To achieve this, such policies and measures should take into account different socio-economic contexts, be comprehensive, cover all relevant sources, sinks and reservoirs of greenhouse gases and adaptation, and comprise all economic sectors. Efforts to address climate change may be carried out cooperatively by interested Parties.

[9] Preamble: Noting also that where there is a threat of significant reduction or loss of biological diversity, lack of full scientific certainty should not be used as a reason for postponing measures to avoid or minimize such a threat.

[10] Article 2, paragraph 2 of the WTO Sanitary and Phytosanitary Agreement: Members shall ensure that any sanitary or phytosanitary measure is applied only to the extent necessary to protect human, animal or plant life or health, is based on scientific principles and is not maintained without sufficient scientific evidence, except as provided for in Article 5, paragraph 7: In cases where relevant scientific evidence is insufficient, a Member may provisionally adopt sanitary or phytosanitary measures on the basis of available pertinent information, including that from the relevant international organizations as well as from sanitary or phytosanitary measures applied by other Members. In such circumstances, Members shall seek to obtain the additional information necessary for a more objective assessment of risk and review the sanitary or phytosanitary measure accordingly within a reasonable period of time.

[11] TFEU, Article 191, paragraph 2: European Union policy on the environment shall aim at a high level of protection taking into account the diversity of situations in the various regions of the Union. It shall be based on the precautionary principle

the environment, but also consumerism, food and 'human, animal and plant health' (European Commission Communication dated 2 February 2000). But there is also Article 174, paragraph 2 (former Article 130 R) of the Treaty of Rome of 25 March 1957, as amended by the Single European Act of 1986 and the Maastricht Agreements of 1992[12] and European Regulation No. 178/2002 of the European Parliament and of the Council dated 28 January 2002, on food security (Ewald, Gollier, and Sadeleer 2001; 2009 17). This is all the more interesting since it is likely, again, to run counter to the founding principles of the European Union, which are the great freedoms of movement (Icard 2005, 110). To this must be added the Nice European Council Resolution of December 2000 on the precautionary principle (Ewald, Gollier, and Sadeleer 2001; 2009, 15).

At the French level, the most remarkable text is that of Article 5 of the Charter for the Environment, which itself was introduced in 2005 in the preamble to the French Constitution.

First of all, there was the 'Barnier law', No. 95–101 of 2 February 1995 (on the strengthening of the protection of the environment), drafting a new article L. 200–1 of the Rural Code expressly providing for the precautionary principle.[13] But there is, mainly, Article 5 of the

---

and on the principles that preventive action should be taken, that environmental damage should as a priority be rectified at source and that the polluter should pay.

[12] Community policy on the environment shall aim at a high level of protection taking into account the diversity of situations in the various regions of the Community. It shall be based on the precautionary principle and on the principles that preventive action should be taken, that environmental damage should as a priority be rectified at source and that the polluter should pay.

[13] Article L. 200–1: Natural areas, resources and environments, sites and landscapes, animal and plant species, the biological diversity and balance to which they contribute are part of the common heritage of the nation. Their protection, enhancement, restoration, rehabilitation and management are of general interest and contribute to the objective of sustainable development which aims to satisfy the development needs of the current generations without compromising the ability of future generations to meet their own needs. They draw their inspiration, within the framework of the laws that define their scope, from the following principles:
- the precautionary principle, according to which the absence of certainty, based on current scientific and technical knowledge, must not delay the

Charter for the Environment of 2004,[14] introduced in the preamble to the French Constitution in 2005 (Versailles Congress, 28 February 2005); the French constitutional text evokes scientific knowledge. The precautionary principle in the Charter for the Environment is only one among the many principles set out. However, as Article 5 did not use the phrase 'within the framework of the laws defining its scope', it could be considered to have direct application (even if, on the other hand, it only concerned public authorities (Ewald, Gollier, and Sadeleer 2001; 2009, 93, 95). The conditions for its application are clear: risk assessment procedure and proportional and provisional character of the measures undertaken. The Rural and Maritime Fisheries Code provides, on its part, repeatedly for the opportunity to take 'measures of order and precaution' (Articles L. 912-7, L. 921-2–1 and L. 922-2).

By constitutionalizing the precautionary principle, France has been doubly innovative: by giving a legal and textual endorsement to the principle, which many countries have not yet done, but also and especially, by giving it the rank of constitutional rule, at the top of the hierarchy of standards. But France stayed at the environmental level, without generalizing the rule.

By doing so, France has regained the innovative and precursory legal spirit that was once its own. Admittedly, as Yves Jégouzo (2004) writes, this constitutional insertion is a source of many uncertainties. But what an impetus! The Environmental Code reproduces the statement in its Article L. 110-1 Section II, Paragraph 1[15] (copy of Article

---

adoption of effective and proportionate measures aiming to prevent a risk of serious and irreversible damage to the environment at an economically acceptable cost.

[14] Article 5: When the occurrence of any damage, albeit unpredictable in the current state of scientific knowledge, may seriously and irreversibly harm the environment, public authorities shall, with due respect for the principle of precaution and the areas within their jurisdiction, ensure the implementation of procedures for risk assessment and the adoption of temporary measures commensurate with the risk involved in order to preclude the occurrence of such damage.

[15] Article L110-I. Natural areas, resources and habitats, sites and landscapes, air quality, animal and plant species, and the biological diversity and balance to which they contribute are part of the common heritage of the nation.

II. Their protection, enhancement, restoration, rehabilitation and management are of general interest and contribute to the objective of sustainable development which aims to satisfy the development needs and protect the health of current generations without compromising the ability of future generations to meet their own needs. They draw their inspiration, within the framework of the laws that define their scope, from the following principles:

1. The precautionary principle, according to which the absence of certainty, based on current scientific and technical knowledge, must not delay the adoption of effective and proportionate measures aiming to prevent a risk of serious and irreversible damage to the environment at an economically acceptable cost;
2. The principle of preventive and corrective action, as a priority at source, of damage to the environment, using the best techniques available at an economically acceptable cost;
3. The polluter pays principle, according to which the costs arising from measures to prevent, reduce or combat pollution must be borne by the polluter.
4. The principle of participation, according to which everybody has access to information relating to the environment, including information relating to hazardous substances and activities, and whereby the public is involved in the process regarding the development of projects that have a major impact on the environment or on town and country planning.
5. The principle of participation whereby all persons are informed of public decisions having an impact on the environment under conditions allowing them to comment, which are taken into account by the competent authority.
6. The principle of ecological solidarity, which calls for taking into account, in any public decision-making having a significant impact on the environment of the territories concerned, the interactions of ecosystems, living beings and natural or built habitats.
7. The principle of sustainable use, according to which the practice of uses can be an instrument that contributes to biodiversity.
8. The principle of complementarity between the environment, agriculture, aquaculture and sustainable forest management, according to which agricultural, aquacultural and forest surfaces carry a specific and varied biodiversity and agricultural, aquaculture and forestry activities can to be vectors of ecosystem interactions that ensure, on the one hand, the preservation of ecological continuity and, on the other hand, environmental services that use the ecological functions of an ecosystem to restore, maintain or create biodiversity.
9. The principle of non-regression, according to which the protection of the environment, ensured by the legislative and regulatory provisions relating to the environment, can only be the object of a constant improvement, taking into account the scientific and technical knowledge of the environment available at the moment.

L. 200-1 of the former Rural Code).¹⁶ Law No. 61-842 of 2 August 1961 implicitly referred to it.¹⁷

The analysis of case-law decisions is interesting, even if this type of investigation is subject to caution, since judgments and rulings obviously respond to specific legal actions and may be conditioned by motives that are more processual than factual.

Even the International Court of Justice has been led to mention the precautionary principle with regard to a dam project (ICJ 25 September 1997, Hungary/Slovakia, with reference to the Gabcíkovo-Nagymaros project). At the level of the European Union, the ECJ, then the CJEU, have frequently used it (Ewald, Gollier, and Sadeleer 2001; 2009, 83). At the European level, it is case law that has given the principle a real normative force (Icard 2005, 104; Larceneux and Boutelet 2005, 9).

In France, it is above all the decisions rendered by the administrative courts that have implemented the principle (and this, in the matter of

---

III. The objective of sustainable development, as indicated in II, is sought, concomitantly and coherently, through the following five commitments:

1. Fight against climate change
2. Preservation of biodiversity, environments and resources, as well as the safeguarding of services they provide and the uses associated with them.
3. Social cohesion and solidarity between territories and generations.
4. The development of all human beings.
5. Transition towards a circular economy.

IV. Agenda 21 is a territorial project of sustainable development.

¹⁶ Article L110, Section 1, Paragraph 1: The precautionary principle, according to which the absence of certainty, based on current scientific and technical knowledge, must not delay the adoption of effective and proportionate measures aiming to prevent a risk of serious and irreversible damage to the environment at an economically acceptable cost.

¹⁷ Buildings, industrial, commercial, craft or agricultural establishments, vehicles or other movable objects owned, operated or owned by any natural or legal person, shall be constructed, operated or used in such a way as to comply with the provisions of this Act in order to avoid pollution of the atmosphere and smells that inconvenience the population, jeopardize public health or safety, or hinder agricultural production, the conservation of buildings and monuments or the character of sites.

the review of legality), and it is they who have forged a real corpus of case-law in this area.

Although many appeals to the French Supreme Court (Court of Cassation) evoke the precautionary principle, the Court takes it very rarely into account (Civil Case 07-16.449, First Chamber Decision 22 January 2009, with regard to the alleged effects of a vaccine). In 2003, it took care to set it aside, to recall that it is not (which was then true) a legal principle (Civil Case 01-18.056, 26 November 2003 Vitamin C sales points). Instead, it rather relied on a 'duty of vigilance' (Civil Cases: 04-16.179 and 04-16.180, First Chamber Decision 7 March 2006, Distilbène [Diethylstilbestrol] case). When it took up the content, it was to consider that the judges at the lower level had taken into account the different elements to reject the claim made (Civil Case 08-19.108, 3rd Chamber Decision, 3 March 2010, about drilling near a source of mineral water). This was the case with regard to the alleged harmful effects of very high-voltage lines (Civil Case 10-17.645, 3rd Chamber Decision, 18 May 2001)[18] where, finally, doubt led to a refusal of compensation.

Since 1995, many decisions of the Council of State have mentioned the precautionary principle. The Council of State mentioned it, first of all, with reference to the article of the Rural Code, and then, and especially with regard to the article of the Charter for the Environment (but also health (Council of State, Decision of 29 December 1999,

---

[18] Quotation from the decision:

Having correctly stated that the Charter for the Environment and the precautionary principle did not call into question the rules according to which it was for the person claiming compensation for the damage against the easement holder to establish that this prejudice was the direct and certain consequence of the defendant's action and that this demonstration, without requiring scientific proof, could stem from serious, precise, reliable and consistent presumptions, the Court of Appeal, which had noted that serious, divergent and contrary elements were opposed to existing indices as to the possible impact of electromagnetic currents on the condition of the livestock, so that there were significant uncertainties about this impact, and which had analyzed the factual circumstances in which the damage had occurred, was able to accept, without reversing the burden of proof, that, given all the explanations and data provided, the existence of a link of causality was not sufficiently characterized.

Rustica Prograin Company, cases 206687 and 207303). This had to do with control of legality mainly. The reading and analysis, since 1998, of the judgments mentioning the precautionary principle (originally provided for in the former Article L. 200-1 of the former Rural Code[19] and then incorporated into the Constitution) is particularly instructive. These are more questions of the validity of acts than liability as such (Kourilsky and Viney 2000, 152). Some have granted the claims: suspension of execution granted for an order listing three varieties of genetically modified corn (Council of State decision dated 25 September 1998, Case 194348) in the official French catalogue. Mostly, the petitions were dismissed (Council of State decision dated 5 July 1999, Case 194834, establishing a list of protected plant species and Council of State decision dated 28 July 1999, Case 184268 with regard to the installation of a power line), including those filed on the basis of the 1961 Act (against opponents of ecology, Council of State

---

[19] Article L.200-1, repealed in 2000: Natural spaces, resources and environments, sites and landscapes, animal and plant species, the diversity and the biological equilibrium in which they participate are part of the common heritage of the nation. Their protection, enhancement, restoration, restoration and management are of general interest and contribute to the goal of sustainable development that aims to meet the development needs of the current generation without compromising the ability of future generations to meet theirs. They draw inspiration, within the framework of the laws which define their scope, from the following principles:

- The precautionary principle, according to which the lack of certainty, taking into account the scientific and technical knowledge of the moment, must not delay the adoption of effective and proportionate measures aimed at preventing a risk of serious and irreversible damage to the environment at an economically acceptable cost;
- The principle of preventive and corrective action, as a priority at source, of damage to the environment, using the best techniques available at an economically acceptable cost;
- The polluter pays principle, according to which the costs arising from measures to prevent, reduce or combat pollution must be borne by the polluter;
- The principle of participation, according to which everybody has access to information relating to the environment, including information relating to hazardous substances and activities, and whereby the public is involved in the process regarding the development of projects that have a major impact on the environment or on town and country planning.

decision dated 20 March 2000, cases 202713 and 203229, rejecting a petition for cancelling a decision refusing the reopening of a nuclear station for abuse of power). With the methodological reservations recalled, it is interesting to make two observations: the judgments granting, in one way or another, a claim going in the direction of an application of the principle are very minor. And when these requests are granted, it is almost exclusively a matter of suspension or process stoppages. This observation pleads, it must be admitted, in favour of the critics of the principle who see it as a brake and not a new way of acting positively. But it is nevertheless certain that the principle is, henceforth, a rule of law.

The juridization of the principle has thus been accepted, even if, as Nicolas Sadeleer writes, one is perhaps confronted with an application of what is called "Post-modern or neo-modern law" (Sadeleer 2001, 75). This legalization is manifested in concrete measures.

PROGRESS IN THE IMPLEMENTATION OF THE PRECAUTIONARY PRINCIPLE

If there is a rule of law, several questions arise and not the least. According to the texts and according to the authors, there is still a debate as to which is the exact field of application of the precautionary principle and who are the persons in charge of its application.

It is, therefore, necessary to distinguish what are the conditions of implementation of the precautionary principle and what are the means of action that can be used to apply it Larceneux and Boutelet 2005, 6).

Complex Conditions

It is difficult to know how to harmonize the precautionary principle with other major principles: freedom of movement of persons and goods, freedom of commerce, freedom of establishment, freedom of competition (Sadeleer 2001, 77). The implementation of the precautionary principle is likely to conflict with the right of ownership, without necessarily calling it totally into question.

It is obvious that, in certain occurrences, precaution will lead to the prohibition of *abusus*[20] (Grison 2012, 6).

One might conceive that the precautionary principle is more recent than the others, so it prevails over others. It could, nevertheless, be more general (unless it is confined to the environment) and the special derogates from the general. If the precautionary principle is to prevail over all others, there is a big risk that a state will use it to actually implement a protectionist measure.

As to the fields of application of the principle, if we start with environmental questions, we see the rule gradually extending to the area of health in general and even, more generally, to the protection of life. It would then exceed the scope of a special environmental law.

The determination of the areas and fields of application of the precautionary principle is delicate. Everything started in Germany, around the 1970s, with the *Vorsorgeprinzip*, risks for the environment (Ewald, Gollier, and Sadeleer 2001; 2009, 6). It is obvious that the environment is both at the origin and the heart of the area concerned. The French Charter does not directly target human health, but the administrative case law seems to have taken the step (Baghestani-Perrey 2005, 95). The Treaty of the Union targets only the environment, but European case law has extended the principle to the sanitary field (Icard 2005, 104). There would also be health, human health, then animal and plant health, and finally and undoubtedly, security in general, including the case when the cause is not necessarily of human origin (for instance, disasters). Beyond that, there is the preservation of living things (biodiversity) and even inert natural bodies (non-renewable resources, remarkable landscapes). But as it has been written, 'nothing precludes, a priori, the extension of the principle' (Martin 2005, 11). A decision of the Court of First Instance of the European Communities in 2002 stated that the precautionary principle should apply in all areas of the EEC at the time (Court of First Instance of the ECJ, 26th November 2002, Artegodan case T–74/00 and others, See Ewald, Gollier, and

---

[20] Latin term meaning 'the right to dispose of a property'.

Sadeleer 2001; 2009, 16, 85). The human activities involved are multiple: agriculture, industries, research, waste, etc. At the extreme, it could concern any security policy (Ewald, Gollier, and Sadeleer 2001; 2009, 3).

Could one go so far as to intervene in artistic matters (Bronner and Géhin 2010, 121), if an installation or an exhibition could be considered as potentially harmful to the mental health of the youth? Some even went so far as to want to apply it in cultural matters. Indeed, it has happened that the precautionary principle was invoked in cultural or religious matters, to censor a show (Grison 2012, 10) about the removal of the staging of an opera of Mozart which was contested).

In any case, the general movement seems to be going in the direction of a constant widening of the area of application of the principle. As to who is in charge of its implementation, again, enlargement has been gradual: initially it was only the administration; then it was imposed, little by little, on businesses and finally on every citizen. The problem is to know who is in charge of its implementation: public authorities and administrations, private companies, any citizen. Originally, it was only States (this is what the French Charter provides), then States and their administrations. Hence the considerable place of administrative litigation. But as soon as the principle was extended to the field of health, private companies (pharmaceutical laboratories, chemical industries, etc.) could no longer be excluded. So, little by little, we have widened the circle of entities that must respect the principle. Ultimately, any individual may have to respect the principle.

'The precautionary principle must be binding on all "decision-makers," that is, on anyone who has the power to initiate or stop an activity that may pose a risk to others' (Kourilsky and Viney 2000, 143).

Who benefits from the principle? Certainly, humanity. But beyond that, future generations and nature, even life on earth or the earth itself, including its non-living elements (Guével 2017, 30–32).

The conditions of application of the precautionary principle are of two kinds.

First, there must be a potential (non-imaginary) risk, most often considered to be serious and irreversible. It is necessary to determine the conditions of application of the principle. 'The precautionary principle must govern the implementation of precaution' (Kourilsky and Viney 2000, 21) and the precautionary principle itself! Because 'precaution {in itself} presents risks' (Kourilsky and Viney 2000, 19). We do not need a purely imaginary risk (Kourilsky and Viney 2000, 145). In the name of a potential risk, it is not necessary to prohibit a product which has beneficial effects (case of DTT, vaccinations, etc., already mentioned). The difficulty comes from the fact that the principle resembles Ouroboros: it necessarily requires a preliminary analysis of a risk that which, by definition, we do not really know yet. We are close to contradiction, insofar as it is necessary at the same time for scientific knowledge to be inadequate to give answers, but adequate enough to leave space for serious doubts. But no human activity can be considered to be totally secure and reliable. It is, therefore, a matter of degree of severity or frequency. Moreover, you need a doubt. But, if we stick to a Cartesian approach, does not there always exist (and must not there always exist) a doubt? Is there not, in addition, a danger that doubt is fabricated, hijacked, manipulated (Larceneux and Boutelet 2005, 30) discussing weapons of mass destruction attributed to Iraq)? To put it in a nutshell, there must be an existence of threats and an absence of certain scientific knowledge (Baghestani-Perrey 2005, 96; Martin 2005, 13).

Many authors and texts argue that one can or must act only if the uncertain risk is serious and irreversible. Here again, we are close to a logical flaw, because it is rather difficult to determine whether a risk is serious and even more to say whether it is irreversible, while the risk is, if not unknown, very uncertain at the least.

Thus, a risk, but only a potential risk, is a kind of 'risk of risk', as two eminent specialists (Kourilsky and Viney 2000, 16) write: The precautionary principle presupposes a prior measurement of the importance of a risk which is (by definition) unknown. It has been said: 'we are {here} in the imaginary, the virtuality of risk' (Ewald, Gollier, and Sadeleer 2001; 2009, 36). There lies, probably, the major difficulty in the implementation of the mechanism.

A very low probability of occurrence of a major risk (destruction of humanity) may require a stronger response than a significant probability of minor risks (Jonas 1971, quoted by Bronner and Géhin 2010, 54). But it is essential to determine what risk we are talking about. Often the risk is not so much sanitary as political (private appropriation of an innovation). Opponents of the precautionary principle also argue, rightly or wrongly, that environmentalists abusively mix environmental defence and anti-capitalism (Jonas 1971, quoted by Bronner and Géhin 2010, 133). Appreciating possible damage is logically impossible, in any case very complex, especially because it has to be understood in terms of 'its location {…}, the time of its occurrence {…}, its frequency {…}, its duration {…} and its magnitude' (Belaïdi 2005, 77).

Then, one must arrive at a subtle calculation of several proportionalities; proportionality of financial cost/effectiveness, human cost/benefit, risks to be avoided/possible risks induced by the measure itself.

'We do not respond to the uncertain by the irrational' (Maurice Toubiana, quoted by Grison 2012, 12). It is often said that precautionary measures must meet the principle of proportionality (Belaïdi 2005, 87; Grison 2012, 69); we do not fight against a fly by crushing it with a tank. The principle is known, both in law and in many other fields, especially in medicine where it is known that any medicine has undesirable effects. The principle of proportionality is applied by European Union Law (Court of First Instance of the ECJ, 11th September 2002, Case T-13/PP, Pfizer) in matters of precaution. Again, we are close to a syllogism: how to take proportionate measures with regard to an unknown or uncertain risk (Larceneux and Boutelet 2005, 27)? And, beyond that, how to establish a reliable 'cost-effectiveness' ratio (the reference to an economically acceptable cost is not always mentioned)? It would be necessary, moreover, to undoubtedly wonder also about the social, human cost of the envisaged measures. There are, in fact, several types of proportionality to be respected (financial, social, etc. [Kourilsky and Viney 2000, 149]). First of all, there is a proportionality of means and costs (the economists' cost–benefit analysis (Ewald, Gollier, and Sadeleer 2001, 108), which sometimes seems shocking when it leads to managing the earth as a firm, to sacrificing a few human lives if the cost of the measure is too big or refusing any measure dealing with very long term risks, the investment being then likely to be more expensive if it is realized now than if it is delayed (Gollier 2001, 113). The French example of the vaccination of an entire population for a threat that disappeared before the very end of the operation is obvious in this respect.[21] But there is also a proportionality to be respected between the risk which one intends to protect oneself from and the risks that the measure itself, when taken, can cause. In the area of health, if it is a question of intervening in research and innovation, it is also, in the case of therapeutic action, to determine whether one dare or not take an unknown but possibly deadly risk, to heal, even to try to save by using an unexplored technique; there is then a kind of balancing of the hoped-for advantages against the imagined inconveniences (Besancenot 2005, 55). Moreover, as it has been pointed out, and more generally, we find ourselves caught 'between the too much and the too little' (Ewald, Gollier, and Sadeleer 2001; 2009, 31). We must, therefore, use the 'rule of reason' and proceed, not legally, but socio-economically by putting advantages and disadvantages into perspective. Again, these are political decisions.

Finally, it is often forgotten that at least in France, the principle is not considered as isolated but presented as the first among a rather long list of principles sometimes difficult to harmonize. For the record, one could cite the principles of 'preventive and corrective action', 'polluter pays', 'right of access to information', 'participation', 'ecological solidarity', 'sustainable use', 'complementarity', and 'non-regression', without it being always clear whether one of these different principles can be invoked separately.

It is often added that the measure taken must be reversible (as opposed to the preventive measure) (Kourilsky and Viney 2000, 46). But this is already a way of evoking the means of action available to the precautionary principle. The need for revisable, reversible provisions is also mentioned (Grison 2012, 69). This condition is probably easier to fulfil.

---

[21] The 2009 vaccination campaign against the H1N1 virus cost many hundreds of millions of euros to the taxpayers.

Tangible Means of Action

What are the precautionary techniques and procedures?

Of course, first, there exist abstentions.

As for the means of implementation of the principle, its champions always argue that it is to advocate actions and not, as stated by its opponents, to be equated with abstentions or renunciation. 'Precaution expects that technological power be implemented differently and with other objectives, without undermining development and prompting abstention' (Belaïdi 2005, 78). The precautionary principle must not be interpreted as a systematic recommendation for abstention (Kourilsky and Viney 2000, 12). However, we need to recognize that, above and beyond the mere affirmation, the practical modalities of these actions remain vague and that very often it is a stoppage (of research, production) that will happen, even if it is conceived to be provisional. Indeed, one intervenes in the name of the precautionary principle as a rule while waiting for scientific research to say that it is harmless or on the contrary, it is harmful. If one takes absolute uncertainty with regard to risk (a totally unknown risk) as a condition for precaution, it is obvious that only abstention is to be envisaged, at least provisionally. No positive action tending to protect us against the unknown could be programmed or the realization of objective, independent, multidisciplinary (Kourilsky and Viney 2000, 61) and public expertise.

It is obvious that the place of expertise is fundamental and primordial here. A system of objective, highly scientific, but academic and well-paid expertise is needed. Decision-makers (executive or jurisdictional) are not aware of the phenomena that they have to combat or have only an approximate or partial knowledge of them. It is, therefore, the experts who will actually assume, not the responsibility for the decisions taken, but the responsibility for their basis. The question arises then of the method retained in the choice of experts and their deliberative modes. The risk is high, at this stage of the process, of an influence of various lobbies (private companies funding research, associations having to justify their existence).

It is also advisable to set up dedicated agencies, big coordinated national agencies or, better, supranational agencies.[22] As long as they are in reciprocal relationships and have common statuses, mission, and powers,[23] national or, better, supranational agencies could prove to be useful tools at the service of the precautionary principle.

We could still talk about prior authorizations for release into the market, maximum thresholds to be respected (exposure, issuance, etc.) expropriations for public use, criminal (Sadeleer, 2001, 100) and civil liability adapted to serve as a deterrent for those who would not like to abide by the principle (Ewald, Gollier, and Sadeleer 2001; 2009, 60).

Beyond that, there exist still many precautionary techniques; labelling, traceability (Kourilsky and Viney 2000, 51,81), standardization (Kourilsky and Viney 2000, 72), the different modalities of access to information, intervention funds, the right of interference (Kourilsky and Viney 2000, 55), referenda and the various means of making the population participate in the decision-making processes, the restriction of business secrecy and industrial secrecy (Kourilsky and Viney 2000, 58), the bringing together of the so-called exact sciences and the so-called human sciences, the preservation of species and knowledge (e.g., the Svalbard global seed reserve in Norway or the Traditional Knowledge Digital Library [TKDL] in India), granting legal personality to entities to be protected (river, nature, mother earth (Guével 2018), and, of course, the creation of the 'commons' (Guével 2017) (including terrestrial areas or maritime protected areas) with a view to avoiding appropriations or destructive uses of the resources.

In France, however, the assessment of the application of the precautionary principle remains mixed. Thus, recently, a law has

---

[22] It is perhaps worth the while to harmonize the powers, missions and structures of several French agencies, as it has been attempted recently in 2017 with regard to independent administrative authorities, and gather several bodies in one agency as has been done in the case of the French Agency for Biodiversity.

[23] One could foresee a significant common text, indeed even a common code. A recent law on independent administrative authorities (law no 2017-55 of 20 January 2017) on independent administrative authorities and independent public authorities has shown that, little by little, we could move towards such harmonization.

strengthened the protection of business secrecy cases that may hinder the implementation of precaution (Law no 2018-670 dated 30 July 2018 on the protection of business secrecy). Similarly, the recent delays of the French public authorities in prohibiting the use of glyphosate have shown how much pressure groups could manage to paralyze the application of the precautionary principle.

At the international level, as we have seen, with the example of genetically modified organisms, the precautionary principle is sometimes misguided in that it is used to try to protect a national market, which may be commendable, but which is not the purpose of the rule. Last but not the least, the return of ultra-liberal policies around the world, based solely on the idea of necessary economic growth, tends, de facto, to reduce precaution to the rank of an inefficient principle.

It is not forbidden to think that a simple principle of humility (Guével 2018) could have been as appropriate (one also thinks of the phronesis of Aristotle, combining prudence and practical wisdom (Aubenque [1962] 2014). Perhaps it is the choice (deliberate or implicit) of some countries that have not adopted the precautionary principle. As Grison says, 'we need humility in the Socratic sense', and we must 'consider hesitation as a value' (Grison 2012, 80).

The merit of the precautionary principle consists indeed, in our view, first of all, in constituting, for the first time, an awareness, on the part of the Western human, of both his fragility and his indignity and the need for him to abandon his position of 'domineering externality' (Grison 2012, 28). The human being is in the process of grasping that he has no right to behave like a dictator of nature, but especially how many 'interactions' exist between 'natural systems' and 'humanized systems' (Larceneux and Boutelet 2005, 23). Undoubtedly, only those countries which have never stopped understanding this interdependence (if there are any left) need no legalized precautionary principle.

Translated from French by Geetha Ganapathy-Doré

REFERENCES

Printed Books and Articles

Aubenque, P. (1962) 2014. *La prudence chez Aristotle* (Prudence in Aristotle). Paris: PUF, coll. Quadrige.

Baghestani-Perrey, L. 2005. 'Le Principe de précaution en droit positif' (The Precautionary Principle in Positive Law). In *Le Principe de précaution. Débats et enjeux* (Principle of Precaution. Debates and Challenges), edited by A. Larceneux and M. Boutelet, 91. Actes du colloque du 4 juin 2004 (Proceedings of the Colloquium held on 4th June 2004). Dijon: éd. Universitaires de Dijon, Coll. Sociétés.

Beaumarchais, P. A. C. 1776. *The Barber of Séville or the Useless Precaution. A Comedy in Four Acts. With Songs.* London: J. Chouquet.

Belaïdi, N. 2005. 'Les enjeux de la formulation du principe de précaution pour une politique globale de l'environnement' (The challenges of formulating the precautionary principle for a global environmental policy). In *Le Principe de précaution. Débats et enjeux* (Principle of Precaution. Debates and Challenges), edited by A. Larceneux and M. Boutelet, 77–90. Actes du colloque du 4 juin 2004 (Proceedings of the Colloquium held on 4th June 2004). Dijon: éd. Universitaires de Dijon, Coll. Sociétés.

Besancenot, J.-P. 2005. 'Le principe de précaution devant le risque sanitaire' (The principle of precaution when confronted with the health risk). In *Le Principe de précaution. Débats et enjeux* (Principle of Precaution. Debates and Challenges), edited by A. Larceneux and M. Boutelet, 47–67. Actes du colloque du 4 juin 2004 (Proceedings of the Colloquium held on 4th June 2004). Dijon: éd. Universitaires de Dijon, Coll. Sociétés.

Boy, L. 1997, 8 January. 'La référence au principe de précaution et l'émergence de nouveaux modes de régulation' (The reference to the precautionary principle and the emergence of new modes of regulation). *LPA* 4: 4.

Bronner, G., and É. Géhin. 2010. *L'inquiétant principe de précaution* (The worrisome precautionary principle). Paris: PUF, Collection Quadrige.

Caudal, S., ed. 2008. *Les principes du droit* (Principles of Law). Paris: éd. Economica, Coll. Études juridiques (Legal Studies Collection).

Cornu, G. 1987. *Vocabulaire juridique* (Legal Vocabulary). Paris: PUF.

Ewald, F., C. Gollier, and N. De Sadeleer. (2001) 2009. *Le Principe de précaution* (Principle of Precaution). 2nd ed. Paris: PUF, Collection Que sais-je? (What do I know?).

Grison, D. 2010. *Vers une philosophie de la précaution* (Towards a philosophy of precaution). Paris: L'Harmattan.

———. 2012. *Qu'est-ce que le principe de précaution?* (What is the principle of precaution?). Paris: J. Vrin, Coll. chemins philosophiques.

Guével, D., and J. Dupichot. 1997. *Contrats et Obligations: Présomptions* (Contracts and Obligations: Axioms). Jurisclasseur civil, Articles 1349–1353. Fascicule 155. Paris: Editions techniques.

———. 2017. 'Les communs hors du commun. Propos Introductifs' (Out of the Ordinary, The Commons, Introductory Remarks). Colloque Montréal CDRP-IRDA, 1 and 2 May 2017. Available at: https://www.youtube.com/watch?v=X9U346k96kw (accessed on 23 April 2020).

———. 2018. *Du principe de modestie (éloge de l'expression d'une vraie ou fausse humilité)* (The principle of modesty [praising the expression of a true or false humility]). Paris: Dalloz.

Hautereau-Boutonnet, M. 2005. *Le Principe de Précaution en droit de la responsabilité civile* (The Precautionary Principle in Civil Liability Law). Paris: LGDJ.

Hautereau-Boutonnet, M., and E. E. Truilhé-Marengo. 2017. *Quel modèle pour le procès environnemental?* (What model for environmental lawsuits?). D 2017. 827.

Icard, P. 2005. *Le principe de précaution façonné par le juge communautaire* (The precautionary principle shaped by the community judge). In *Le Principe de précaution. Débats et enjeux* (Principle of Precaution. Debates and Challenges), edited by A. Larceneux and M. Boutelet, 103–123. Actes du colloque du 4 juin 2004 (Proceedings of the Colloquium held on 4th June 2004). Dijon: éd. Universitaires de Dijon, Coll. Sociétés.

Jégouzo, Y. 2004. 'Quelques réflexions sur le projet de Charte de l'environnement' (Some reflections on the Draft Environmental Charter). In *Cahiers du conseil constitutionnel* (Constitutional Council Notebooks) 15. Available at: https://www.conseil-constitutionnel.fr/nouveaux-cahiers-du-conseil-constitutionnel/quelques-reflexions-sur-le-projet-de-charte-de-l-environnement (accessed on 23 April 2020).

Jonas, H. (1971) 2013. *Le principe de responsabilité. Une éthique pour la civilisation technologique* (The Principle of Responsibility. An Ethical Code for the Technological Civilization). Paris: Champs Essais. Translated from the original German title *Das prinzip Verantwortung, Versuch einer Ethik für die technologiche Zivilisation.*

Kourilsky, P., and G. Viney. 2000. Rapport au Premier ministre. *Le principe de précaution* (Report submitted to the Prime Minister. The Principle of Precaution). Paris: éd. Odile Jacob – La Documentation française.

Larceneux, A., and M. Boutelet, eds. 2005. *Le Principe de précaution. Débats et enjeux* (Principle of Precaution. Debates and Challenges). Actes du colloque du 4 juin 2004 (Proceedings of the Colloquium held on 4th June 2004). Dijon: éd. Universitaires de Dijon, Coll. Sociétés.

———. 2005. 'Incertitude, information et principe de précaution' (Uncertainty, Information and the Principle of Precaution). In *Le Principe de précaution. Débats et enjeux.* Actes du colloque du 4 juin 2004 (Proceedings of the Colloquium held on 4th June 2004). Dijon: éd. Universitaires de Dijon, Coll. Société: 21–38.

Martin, T. 2005. 'Le principe de précaution et l'aversion au probable' (The Principle of precaution and the aversion to the probable). In *Le Principe de précaution. Débats et enjeux*, edited by A. Larceneux and M. Boutelet, 11–19. Actes du colloque du 4 juin 2004 (Proceedings of the Colloquium held on 4th June 2004). Dijon: éd. Universitaires de Dijon, Coll. Sociétés.

Perelman, C. 1976. Logique juridique. Nouvelle rhétorique (Juridical Logic. A New Rhetoric). Paris: Dalloz 47: 87.

Sadeleer, N. 2008. 'Le statut juridique du principe de précaution' (The legal status of the principle of precaution). In *Le Principe de precaution*, edited by F. Ewald, C. Gollier, and N. Sadeleer, 73–103. Paris: PUF, Collection Que sais-je? (What do I know?).

Voltaire. 1878. *Précis du siècle de Louis XV* (The Concise Handbook of Louis XV's Century).

Legal Decisions

Council of State

Case 194348, decision dated 25 September 1998, on modified corn seeds.

Case 194834, decision dated 5 July 1999, establishing a list of protected plant species decision.

Case 184268, decision dated 28 July 1999, with regard to the installation of a power line.

Cases 206687 and 207303, decision dated 29 December 1999, Rustica Prograin Company.

Cases 202713 and 203229, decision dated 20 March 2000, against the reopening of a nuclear station.

Cassation Court

No. 07-16.449, 22 January 2009 (after-effects of vaccination).
No. 01-18.056, 26 November 2003 (vitamin C sales outlets).
No. 04-16.179 and No 04-16.180, 7 March 2006 (Distilbène).
No. 08-19.108, 3 March 2010 (drilling near a mineral water source)
No. 10-17.645 18 May 2001.

Court of First Instance (ECJ)

T–74/00, 26 November 2002, *Artegodan* v Commission.

Court of Justice of the European Union (CJEU)

C–621/15, 21 June 2017, N. W. and Others v Sanofi Pasteur MSD SNC and Others.

International Court of Justice, ICJ

25 September 1997, Hongrie c/Slovaquie, regarding the Gabcíkovo-Nagymaros project.

Laws

French Constitutional Law

French Charter for the Environment 2004.

French Statute Law

Law no. 61-842 of 2 August 1961 (fight against atmospheric pollution).
Barnier Law no. 95-101 of 2 February 1995 (strengthening environmental protection).
Law no. 2017-55 of 20 January 2017 (on independent administrative authorities).
Law no. 2017-399 of 27 March 2017 (regarding the duty of vigilance of parent and contracting companies).
Law no. 2018-670 of 30 July 2018 (protecting business secrecy).
French Environmental Code (2000, amended in 2005 and 2007).
French Rural and Maritime Fishing Code, updated 2019.

EU Treaties

Treaty of Rome, 1957.
Single European Act, 1986.
Treaty of Maastricht, 1992.
Treaty on the Functioning of the European Union, 2007.

EU Secondary Legislation

European Commission, COM (2000) 1 final, 2 February 2000 on the precautionary principle.
European Regulation no. 178/2002 of EU Parliament and Council, 28 January 2002 devoted to food security.

International Conventions

World Charter for Nature, 1982.
Second International Conference on the Protection of the North Sea, 1987.
UN Convention on Biodiversity 1992.
Rio Declaration 1992.
UN Framework Convention on Climate Change, 1992.
WTO Sanitary and Phytosanitary Agreement, 1995.

Unpublished Conference Papers

Guével, D. 2017. 'Le principe de précaution, instrument au service du développement durable' (The Principle of Precaution, Instrument at the service of Sustainable Development). Presented in the Colloquium entitled 'La responsabilité environmentale: bilan et perspectives' (Environmental Responsibility: Review and Prospects) organized by the University of Wassseda in Tokyo on 9 July 2017.

Guével, D. 2017. *L'imprévision dans le Code civil français: une réforme, deux révolutions* (Unpredictability in the French Civil Code: One Reform, Two Revolutions). Presented at Pontifica Universidad del Perù in Lima on 9 June 2017 and in the colloquium entitled La réforme du droit des contrats. Regards croisés franco-argentin (Contract Law Reform, Franco-Argentinian Exchanges of Viewpoints) in Mendoza co-organized by A. Kemelmajer, Fr. Bicheron (MIL) and M. Mekki (IRDA) on 23 October 2017.

PART II

Climate Change and Governance

Chapter 4

The Global Commons and the Climate Governance Regime
Effectiveness and Challenges

Anju Lis Kurian and C. Vinodan

INTRODUCTION

Climate change impacts are felt worldwide and present more vulnerabilities in developing countries than in the developed world. The past few years have witnessed an emergence of interest in climate change negotiations and governance regimes across the globe. The predictions and assessments on climate change emphasize grave aftermaths for humanity and nature (Stavins et al., 2014). It should be noted that there exist perplexed interrelations between stakeholders as well as societal coordination processes that are categorized as 'governance' (Pachec, Vasconcelos, and Santos 2014). In the governance articulation, the role of the stakeholders, economy, civil society, political parties as well as the state, needs to be aligned with sector-specific perspectives on varied policy areas and allied spheres.

Climate change governance comprises a pack of regulatory as well as structural forms across a multitude of stakeholders. The global climate change articulation began creatively during the past few years but lacks essential modalities to combat climate change maladies (Gupta

2016). Presently, the climate change regime is engendering a myriad of challenges for existing administrative or political systems, as these have emerged to cope with various sorts of issues. For developing economies, far-reaching climate governance is needed to overcome institutional inactiveness that cramps the evolution of an effective and timely response (Held, Nag, and Roger 2012; Maikasuwa 2013). Moreover, conflicts of power and interest are inevitable in climate negotiations. Indeed the complexities are intensified and more ironic when dealing with the global commons (Marquardt 2017).

The global commons constitute a larger area of the planet than do sovereign territories, which are critical zones for global connectivity and a source of global military power. Nations have used international airspace to project force since they began to use aircraft as instruments of war. The outer space links closely to the cyber domain and has become, thanks to advanced technology, a force multiplier capable of enabling complex military operations on a global scale. In addition, the global commons comprise vital environmental resources. Moreover, it can be contended that several of world's natural assets such as the sunshine, air, water, winds, climate system as well as seeds are considered as global commons in the perspective of the crucial ecological roles that they accomplish for life on Earth.

THE GLOBAL COMMONS AND CLIMATE CHANGE

The global commons are enormously vast and inherently assailable, as they are open access resource domains without a central governing articulation. Countries defend their national sovereignty and territory as essential to their legitimate existence, but the global commons lack a comparable existential stakeholder or custodian. Open access to the global commons is intrinsic to the existent liberal world order, which functions by virtue of its ability to generate interdependencies through a global nexus. Thus, the global commons exist within the current international system without strong and effective institutions for governance (Freeman 2016). The international law recognizes four global commons such as the outer space, the high seas, Antarctica and the atmosphere that are manoeuvred by the doctrine of the common heritage of humanity. The remarkable advancements in technology as well as science in the last decades and the hike in resource utilization induce burgeoning of all categories of anthropogenic activities. Planet Earth is confronting stunning ecological threats, significantly global warming and climate change, together with the diminution of natural resources and commons (Anand 2013; Sand 2017).

The catastrophe of the commons represents a Herculean task for an array of environmental issues and serves to drive efficient mitigation strategies (Engel and Saleska 2005). However, the climate change mitigation challenge is witnessing several hurdles and pitfalls. Climate change requires that countries do not abridge but entirely stop greenhouse gas (GHG) releases. It is, therefore, essential to put in place a clean energy system that will satisfy basic needs (Patt 2017).

THE CLIMATE GOVERNANCE REGIME AND THE GLOBAL COMMONS

The current global system and interdependence, along with global governance, including global economic governance as well as the governance of the global commons under the pressure of climate change, is appropriate for attaining sustainable development and outcomes. Globalization led to an increase in migration, commercial as well as financial flows. Climate change affects global commons and incites individual states, which have become susceptible to a greater extent, to new policy frameworks. Thus, coordination and concerted agenda setting at the international level, anchored in human rights standards and equity, are the need of the hour. The governance of the global commons is considered as the basis of global environmental governance (Cottier et al. 2014). The global commons are driven by the doctrine of the common heritage of humanity (Berkes 2008). The execution of the common heritage doctrine combined with mutual obligations links straight to the cardinal enabling factors that are identified as cornerstones of the post-2015 development agendas, namely, environmental sustainability, inclusive economic development, inclusive social development, and peace and security.

The United Nations Framework Convention on Climate Change (UNFCCC), the Kyoto Protocol and the 2015 Paris Agreement are the pillars of climate change governance. Thus, there is more to climate change mitigation efforts than international obligations and state-based climate change policies and commitments. Solutions by non-state actors also exist in the form of a nexus rather than hierarchies or markets. They exhibit the dispersion of authority and the vertical differentiation parallel. It should be noted that the dimension of governance solutions is the path in which climate change governance egresses from the bottom-up due to voluntary collective action or bargaining or as a result of processes assigned top-down.

Effective and practical policies battling global warming and incentivizing diminution of GHGs meet with significant impediments to concerted action. The exclusion of international commitments, by states for short-term interests, keeps also at abeyance international obligations in return for getting benefits out of programmes to combat global warming. In this scenario, the commons have emerged as a principal international environmental legal arena for dealing with collective action problems relating to them. The commons open up new avenues for international cooperation and individual actions at the national level. They allow the extraterritorial impact to be distributed while addressing the challenges of global warming, climate change and mitigation effectiveness. It should be noted that unilateral measures chiefly translate into measures of trade policy. The doctrine of Common Concern is implicitly colligated and fixed by subsisting legal disciplines (Schrijver, 2016).

EFFECTIVENESS AND CHALLENGES

Under the purview of both scholarship and policy, a global framework is prognosticating an institution for dealing with an international issue like climate change and global commons. The espousal of the Kyoto Protocol was scarcely extolled as a nostrum to the global climate concern either at its inception or later. The Kyoto Protocol on climate change is a fundamentally blemished agreement that set back solutions on climate change over the years. The efficiency and effectiveness of Kyoto Protocol is a clear case of institutional failure. Its very design bears liability for the incriminated outcome (Rosen 2015). Various frameworks and targets set by the protocol within the negligible time frame for action have resulted in default by member states and failed to attain targets enshrined therein. Moreover, proposals for specific management of global commons are also absent.

The historic Paris Agreement adopted in 2015 represents a significant victory for global diplomacy, which was tailored as a globally coordinated but nationally navigated long-term action plan that will guide countries in addressing climate change concerns from 2020. The Paris Agreement offers a novel epitome inside the climate governance regime by institutionalizing a flexible and nationally driven bottom-up approach. The success of the Paris Agreement will be based on how signatories follow up with their ambitious targets, goals and binding responsibilities of conduct with regard to mitigation. This will vary from country to country, as they are engaged in climate protection initiatives like investing in renewable energy and energy efficiency. However, the Paris Agreement offers only a basic framework for the new climate change management regime. The governance architecture enshrined in Paris Agreement is expected to work as a principal governing authority to pressure actors in the global common domains.

The Paris Agreement does not furnish an effective mechanism for attaining stabilization of climate change mitigation strategies, especially with regard to the global commons. However, it is ultimately the trust, though small, that a primal and nippy energy transition is doable; that should alter political and social behaviour and policies in the forthcoming years. Likewise, the Paris Accord is an ambitious international treaty that will spark and legitimize profound climate mitigation and adaptation programmes across the globe. However, it is doubtful whether this will happen quickly or within an expected time frame to forefend calamitous global temperature inversion. Such an outcome cannot be accomplished without determined and far-reaching policy interventions by concerned governments in the energy markets, particularly in developed countries. It can be concluded that the global commons are laboratories for innovational international law-making and global governance. At best, it will have brought about an irreversible deviation from the fossil fuel age towards quick de-carbonization of the global economy. Otherwise, the opportunity offered by the Paris Accord will be another missed chance for international leaders, who made dim and wispy assurances. An unclear management of the global commons will have devastating effects on the planet, the commons and the inhabitants.

CONCLUSION

Climate change adversely affects global commons in a multidimensional manner with a myriad of repercussions, as lack of clear borderlines and GHGs emissions in the atmosphere contribute to the difficulties. The global commons are a public good. It is difficult to exclude users from it once it has been provided. It should be noted that there is a need to introduce a more equitable cost- and benefit-sharing framework for effective outcomes. The global climate governance articulation under the aegis of the UNFCCC has to guarantee the conservation of the global commons for future generations. Innovative governance architecture is pivotal to achieve leapfrogging from narrow national interests to an international regime. The global commons issue reflects a major part of the challenges in climate governance. Costs of and benefits from the global commons remain unequal. The actors directly affected by the overuse of the commons and by climate change, are not able to participate in decisions about their use and governance. The efforts for a climate change governance regime, grounded on equitable cost- and benefit-sharing via carbon taxation, cap and trade for GHGs emissions, damages for climate change reverberations and support for adaptation to the climate change impingements, contribute to the protection of global commons in a remarkable manner. An arrangement of global mechanisms to bring about a sea change in demeanour across sectors and jurisdictions in an equitable and effective way will be crucial to the triumph of not only climate change regime, but also of the management of the global commons.

REFERENCES

Anand, S. V. 2013. 'Global Environmental Issues'. *Open Access Scientific Reports* 2: 632. doi:10.4172/scientificreports.632.
Berkes, F. 2008. 'Commons in a Multi-level World'. *International Journal of the Commons* 2 (1): 01–06. doi:10.18352/ijc.80.
Cottier, T., P. Aerni, B. Karapinar, S. Matteotti, J. de Sépibus, and A. Shingal. 2014. 'The Principle of Common Concern and Climate Change'. *Archiv des Völkerrechts* 52 (3): 293–324. doi:10.1628/000389214X14186502494027.
Engel, K. H., and S. R. Saleska. 2005. 'Subglobal Regulation of the Global Commons: The Case of Climate Change'. *Ecology Law Quarterly* 32 (2): 183–233.
Freeman, C. P. 2016. 'The Fragile Global Commons in a World in Transition'. *SAIS Review* 36 (1): 17–28.
Gupta, J. 2016. 'Climate Change Governance: History, Future, and Triple-loop Learning?' *WIREs Climate Change* 7 (2): 192–210.
Held, D., E.-M. Nag, and C. Roger. 2012. *The Governance of Climate Change in Developing Countries: A Report on International and Domestic Climate Change Politics in China, Brazil, Ethiopia and Tuvalu*. LSE-AFD Climate Governance Programme. Available at: https://www.afd.fr/en/ressources/governance-climate-change-developing-countries-report-international-and-domestic-climate-change-politics-china-brazil-ethiopia-and-tuvalu (accessed on 21 April 2020).
Maikasuwa, S. A. 2013. 'Climate Change and Developing Countries: Issues and Policy Implication'. *Journal of Research and Development* 1 (2): 15–24.
Marquardt, J. 2017. 'Conceptualizing Power in Multi-level Climate Governance'. *Journal of Cleaner Production* 154: 167–175. doi: 10.1016/j.jclepro.2017.03.176.
Pachec, J. M., V. V. Vasconcelos, and F. C. Santos. 2014. 'Climate Change Governance, Cooperation and Self-organization'. *Physics of Life Reviews* 11(4): 573–586. doi:10.1016/j.plrev.2014.02.003.
Patt, A. 2017. 'Beyond the Tragedy of the Commons: Reframing Effective Climate Change Governance'. *Energy Research & Social Science* 34: 01–03. doi:10.1016/j.erss.2017.05.023.
Rosen, M. A. 2015. 'The Wrong Solution at the Right Time: The Failure of the Kyoto Protocol on Climate Change'. *Politics & Policy* 43 (1): 30–58.
Sand P. H. 2017. 'Accountability for the Commons: Reconsiderations'. In *The Role of Integrity in the Governance of the Commons*, edited by L. Westra, J. Gray, and F. T. Gottwald, 3–21. Cham: Springer.
Schrijver, N. 2016. 'Managing the Global Commons: Common Good or Common Sink?' *Third World Quarterly* 37 (7): 1252–1267.

Stavins, R., J. Zou, T. Brewer, Grand M. C., M. Den Elzen, M. Finus, J. Gupta, N. Höhne, M. K. Lee, A. Michaelowa, M. Patterson, K. Ramakrishna, G. Wen, J. Wiener, and Winkler, H. 2014. *International Cooperation: Agreements & Instruments, Climate Change 2014: Mitigation of Climate Change*. Contribution of Working Group III to the Fifth Assessment Report of the Intergovernmental Panel on Climate Change, edited by O. Edenhofer, R. Pichs-Madruga, Y. Sokona, E. Farahani, S. Kadner, K. Seyboth, A. Adler, I. Baum, S. Brunner, P. Eickemeier, B. Kriemann, J. Savolainen, S. Schlömer, C. von Stechow, T. Zwickel, and J. C. Minx, 1005–1082. Cambridge: Cambridge University Press.

Chapter 5

Polycentric Approach in Climate Change Mitigation and Adaptation Programme
Effectiveness and Challenges

Sisira K. G., Govind N. and
Mohanan Bhaskaran Pillai

INTRODUCTION

Sustaining a stable climate by reducing greenhouse gas (GHG) emissions into our atmosphere is the most urgent common problem of the time that seeks the attention of all the stakeholders. We need to develop ways and means to overcome the problems that we have been facing from the phenomenon of climate change. We need to evolve strategies to reduce carbon dioxide emissions by 2020. In other words, radical collaboration by all stake holders is the strategy to bend the emissions curve by Mission 2020. Thus the pertinent question is how do we prevent a 'tragedy of commons' and overcome hurdles to cooperation?

Climate change has been annoying us for quite some time now. This challenge is purely global in nature and dimension, and there are, in fact, some national and regional solutions to this problem. However, climate change governance is a complex task and it poses challenges of many magnitudes. The governance of climate change must, therefore, be altered in such a way that it can address emerging issues of climate change mitigation and adaptation. Apart from these adaptation and mitigation, many cross-cutting issues require global collective action.

Even though climate change governance system is in existence for more than 30 years, it is still like a work in progress. As stated by Victor, 'the international climate regime centred on the 1992 United Nations Framework Convention on Climate Change (UNFCCC), has been heavily criticized for being too slow to produce results' (Victor 2011, 10). The international regime has experimented many ways to reduce GHGs emissions. However, still, there is a significant gap between current emissions and what is required to be achieved.

Various ideas and suggestions focusing on different ways in which governance could be made have been floated around for many years (Rayner 2011). For instance, Elinor Ostrom introduced Polycentric Governance for Climate Change in the late 2000s. This new and more active form of governing climate change emphasizes careful designing of all the aspects of governance by international negotiators. Thus, polycentric governance is a bottom-up approach providing multi-level pattern of governance.

In the light of the above, we have encapsulated our arguments in four distinct sections. The first section highlights the significance of polycentric approach in climate change governance. The second section ruminates about the institutional diversity and arrangements in polycentric governance. The third section cogitates the existing system of adaptation and mitigation policies at the local level. Finally, this chapter reviews the effectiveness and challenges in the planning and implementation of polycentric governance in climate change policy.

DELVING INTO THE MEANING OF POLYCENTRIC GOVERNANCE

Vincent Ostrom, Charles Tiebout and Robert Warren argued in an article on municipal government that the traditional pattern of government in metropolitan areas with their multiplicity of political jurisdictions may more be conceived as a Polycentric Political System (Ostrom,

1999). It is an experimental enquiry whether they work freely or not is instead an associated system of connections. They consider business connections somewhat and go into different authoritative and shared endeavours to determine clashes with one another. In this manner, distinctive political specialists will work reliably with unsurprising examples and interfacing conduct in metropolitan territories. So one might say it works as a device (Cole 2011).

Thus, polycentricism as an approach in which several entities are capable of making reciprocal adjustments, through a structured set of rules, to order their relationships with each other, yet each element behaves regardless of the other elements (Ostrom 1999).

The polycentric approach is bottom-up in nature where diverse elements look for various benefits at different scales in a phenomenon like climate change. This implies that global benefits, as a result of mitigation and adaptation measures, will not only be generated by reducing GHGs emissions. However, it will also provide extra help such as enhanced air quality and decreased reliance on fossil fuels, resulting in shorter knowledge of fluctuating prices and enhanced energy security.

Polycentrism is not just about the number of levels of government. It is more about the combination of various perspectives by which respondents can establish or dissolve connections between distinct collective institutions. Respondents will, therefore, be able to select those suppliers or manufacturers that are best suited to the particular problem at hand (McGinnis, 1999).

A precise polycentric scheme is one in which distinct units of government compete and collaborate, learn and interact with each other instead of a monocentric scheme in which units at higher levels make all the choices, and units at the lesser levels must follow those instructions. This will help to tailor the duties to suit the scale of the public services at each stage (Ostrom 2014).

Some of the underlying assumptions of the polycentric approach—as summarized by Elinor Ostrom (2009) are—differences between public goods and services based on their production function and their scale of effects; homogeneous policy preferences among smaller units as opposed to an entire metropolitan area; multiple jurisdictions giving citizens more clear understanding about the functions of each jurisdiction; presence of large number of producers of goods and services empowering the elected officials to make effective choices; multiple jurisdictions allowing officials and citizens to choose active modes of providing and producing public goods that utilize the best technology available and improving their performance over time; enabling producers to compete for contracts leading to searching for innovative technologies and enhancing their capable team production.

So far, no institutional arrangement has been able to diminish opportunistic behaviour. Metropolitan areas, however, appear to have decreased opportunistic behaviour with the polycentric strategy. Thus, a polycentric strategy enables people to create small-scale collective consumption units that encourage them to engage in face-to-face conversations and thus help them to reach a common knowledge. On the other hand, establishment of bigger units decrease the chances of wealthy's dishonest conduct, helping them escape into tax havens, free riding in other jurisdictions on the tax contributions of people. They can also deal efficiently with public goods and services that have significant impacts (Ostrom 2009).

From the above, it is clear that the polycentric approach incorporates multi-level, bilateral, formal and informal communication and interactions that increase trust and potential for cooperation. Moreover, this approach also provides for an excellent opportunity to experiment, choose and learn. In the absence of a world government, providing a stable collective action calls for a stable climate. However, we should mobilize collective action on a small scale, where climate change stands as a severe problem for humanity.

INSTITUTIONAL DIVERSITY IN POLYCENTRIC APPROACH

As said above, the polycentric approach is required to tackle climate change problems. Therefore, there is a need for polycentric governance research to explore the institutional arrangements and informal rules that seem to have the significant impact on both curbing GHG emissions and making progress on adaptation and mitigation projects.

Climate change governance itself has multi-level governance and diverse institutional designs. Dissimilar governance functions, such as provisioning, monitoring and execution, have different scales of operation. For instance, collective environmental choices can be taken at a higher level, whereas resource provision can best be made at a lesser level. Thus, there is a horizontal dispersion of authority in the institutional arrangement of climate change governance. This multitude of governance solutions, prevailing in the polycentric approach, necessarily leads to polycentrism in a broader sense.

Polycentric governance of climate change includes a variety of actors in distinct combination and roles, including local governments, communities, non-governmental organizations and governmental organizations. Most of these organizations are voluntarily adopted and have voluntary membership. These non-state actors and sub-national governments collaborate across borders without the involvement of their national governments.

S. No.	Type	Hybrid	Voluntary
1	Global	Carbon markets	Business sector initiatives
2	National	Carbon markets and public–private partnerships	Adaptation networks of local government
3	Local	Public–private partnerships	Communities, cities and local action

Source: (Paavola 2012).

In a broader polycentric governance strategy, there are two forms of climate change governance: Hybrid and Voluntary governance. They function as internal policy and financial decision-makers, engaging in mitigation operations and increasing pressure to advance conformist state-based forms of governance for climate adjustment. These hybrid and voluntary forms of climate change governance, which are composed of a more extensive policy of polycentric governances offer us a decentralized, flexible and encouraged way of reducing GHGs emissions.

Stakeholders' participation is essential in a polycentric governance approach. It does not entail that every stakeholder is included in this process, but those who are concerned about the climate change problem actively participate in it. The same logic can be applied to the local level as well, where those who are concerned shall participate. Climate change adaptation is a multi-level process where local initiatives may create some benefits at other places, for example, calamity polders and up-stream–down-stream relations. There is also scope for governmental intervention in guaranteeing a transparent and fair process for the implementation of benefits transfer schemes.

Every developed and developing country has its programmes and policies for reducing GHS emissions on a large scale. However, through the polycentric approach, various line-ups have been recognized at different levels of government to mitigate GHG emissions.

Role of National and Sub-national Governments in Climate Change Governance

Each country has its programmes to mitigate GHGs emissions. However, at the national level, the European Union (EU) has established its internal programme called the European Union-Emission Trading Scheme (EU-ETS). The United States (USA) is in the process of establishing The Environmental Protection Agency (EPA) for green house gases (GHGs) regulation under the Clean Air Act. At the same time one should take cognizance of the fact that USA and China have not ratified the Kyoto Protocol. Both these countries have assured to diminish the carbon emissions from their economic production to an extent.

At the sub-national level, California has established a mitigation programme of its own, including emissions trading. In 2002 itself, California was a part of the Western Climate Initiative, a consortium of US states and Canadian provinces which established a regional emission trading programme. The US has another emission trading programme which is called the Regional Greenhouse Gas Initiative (RGGI). Other important climate change mitigation programmes are Carbon Development Mechanisms (CDM) and Reducing Emissions from Deforestation in Developing countries (REDD) from international climate change negotiations.

The Role of Local Governments in Climate Change Governance

There is an increasing responsibility for local governments to prepare and adapt to global climate change through climate adaptation planning. Tackling the climate change challenge requires urgent action, which involves the engagement of local governments and communities.

A local government with other actors plays an essential role in:

- Creating a community vision
- Developing appropriate strategies
- Implementing efficient policies
- Developing activities

Government alternatives to reduce GHGs emissions in their jurisdiction have been actively created and enforced by local governments. One such effort is the Cities for Climate Protection (CCP) programme. It is intended to enlist 100 municipalities globally, with one billion metric tons of CO_2 in joint emissions. The programme also aimed at strengthening local GHGs emissions reduction obligation and to develop best practices and strengthen the connection between municipalities at a global and domestic level (Paavola 2012).

The programme aims at developing an action plan by each of its members to reduce the emission of GHGs from municipal buildings and vehicles. It also expects the members to organize climate change public awareness campaigns and undertake climate-friendly products and services-based initiatives. There is an emphasis to connect with the local government for developing and emerging economy of countries to promote the growth of technological and financial transfers.

Role of Private Actors in Climate Change Governance

The polycentric approach is related to governance and not about governments. Cooperation between public officials at distinct levels is not exclusively worried. It included both private and public actors. Private officials include GHG emitters. NGOs and tiny groups of worried people, including households like those who have installed a solar system at home (Cole 2015).

When we talk about the role of private actors in polycentric governance for climate change, we cannot ignore the activities of the World Business Council for Sustainable Development (WBCSD). Cement Sustainability Initiative (CSI), is a programme under the WBCSD and this was seen as a model for a sectoral approach to mitigation of climate change. Another example of a private voluntary collective action for climate change mitigation is the Chicago Climate Exchange (CCX), a private emissions-trading market, established in 2003.

The role of private actors in the process should not be underestimated, as the cultivation of levels of confidence and collaboration between people who are decision-makers within private enterprises as well as supporters of strategies and those who set and enforce public policies could be beneficial for climate policy (Cole 2015).

ADAPTATION AND MITIGATION AT LOCAL LEVEL

According to Elinor Ostrom, polycentric systems are the organization of small, medium and large-scale democratic units that each may exercise considerable independence to make and enforce rules within a circumscribed scope of authority for a specific geographical area. Adaptive management suggests that there should not be a single centre of power, but a system dividing power to multiple centres, or a polycentric governance system (Ostrom 2014).

Adaptation Strategies are less expensive that result in mitigation effects. For example, promoting to save energy mitigates the causes, and saves financial resources to enable better adaptation to the inevitable impacts of change. Adaptation involves helping their constituents to cope with and adjust to any changes in their climate regime or natural resources' base. This might involve targeted asset building, planning for early warning and disaster response planning.

Mitigation can be investment intensive. Therefore, countries can only make efforts according to their means. However, less expensive mitigation mechanisms such as land use planning and carbon pricing bring high returns on investment, including climate stabilization. Mitigation involves helping their constituents to reduce their GHGs emissions. This might include forest management or energy conservation interventions.

Local climate change fighting needs government to develop local-level climate change mitigation plans. An efficient strategy is a combination of indigenous knowledge and scheduled adaptation strategies. It results in community-wide ownership and dedication to the process of adaptation, thus ensuring stronger climate reactions. Climate change preparedness is only useful if it is integrated into the current plans for local growth. This investment in social capital enhances the local government's capacity building in human resources, abilities, expertise, planning and negotiations in an efficient way for the local climate change plans (Deri 2008).

Urban Local Bodies (ULBs) in Mitigation and Adaptation

Urban regions have a distinct kind of situation as far as the reasons for environmental change emergency and its belongings. Urban communities represent 30–70 per cent of worldwide GHGs emissions and devour about 60 per cent of the world's vitality. Simultaneously, the anticipated environmental change impact demonstrates that urban populaces and framework over the world are at impressive hazard. Therefore, ULBs have risen as critical players in worldwide endeavours to decrease GHGs emanations and receive enhanced approaches and projects to secure the two individuals and properties.

About 75 per cent of urban areas around the globe revealed taking part in both adaptation and mitigation. Over 24 per cent was exclusively founded on mitigation. Most urban areas still carry out moderation planning as opposed to making autonomous environmental change techniques. Urban communities' report says that they are executing environmental change increasingly more on other neighbourhood government techniques (UN-Habitat 2016).

ULBs follow adaptation and mitigation policies on climate change governance. There are several motivations for initiating climate change governance:

1. To demonstrate leadership globally, nationally and regionally
2. To promote sustainable urban development
3. To improve community quality of life
4. To understand the expected local climate-related risks and vulnerabilities
5. Creating green jobs and green economic development

Institutional Structures and Integration

The vast majority of the relief and adjustment plans of the urban areas are created through a joint arranging process, including various neighbourhood government offices and divisions. The essential duty rests with the associations that contribute most to the structures and usage of atmosphere moderation strategies and projects. The improvement of casual channels of correspondence and individual contacts, and certainty between the individual liable for climate change planning and staff in other nearby government organizations is positioned as the best method to incorporate environmental change commitment (UN-Habitat 2016).

In urban local governance, there are numerous institutional arrangements for making collective choice decisions about climate change adaptation. It includes a change in policy and legal frameworks, changes in policy instruments for implementations, change in organizations to meet new objectives and change in coordination arrangements between different actors. These changes have the potential to enhance adaptive and mitigating programmes in urban governance systems. They provide an institutional innovation that can be promptly observed in an urban governance system (Patterson and Huitema 2018).

In the process of developing adaptation and mitigation strategies, the responsible decision-making actors are local- and higher-level organizations which are aiming to find a balance between decentralized and centralized control.

EFFECTIVENESS AND CHALLENGES

A polycentric strategy to climate change governance can provide opportunities to accelerate progress towards global climate stability by offering numerous and diverse possibilities for significant emitting parties to participate in face-to-face communications in bilateral and multilateral fora. These interactions, facilitated by the UN, could inspire a kind of confidence that seems necessary to increase. A broader focus on bilateral and multilateral agreements could, therefore, be a needed prerequisite for more productive negotiations in the UN-based worldwide system (Cole 2015).

In a polycentric administration framework with a coordinated foundation and complete guidelines, projects on environmental change are increasingly successful. For instance, a global counselling firm Booz published a paper saying that nationally-based, base up environmental change relief and adjustment procedures, taking into account every nation's specific needs and resources, establish a progressively authentic and conceivable way to deal with battling the impacts of environmental change than a top-down, universally coordinated methodology (Filho 2015).

The ongoing advancements inside the UNFCCC-likewise affirm the pattern towards more prominent polycentricism. World leaders consented to establish a more bottom-up arrangement of administration at the 2015 Paris Climate Conference (COP21). Through this, the states would promise to make outflow decreases and bit by bit ratchet them up as a component of a procedure of progressing evaluation and audit (Keohane and Oppenheiner 2016). The Paris Agreement additionally offered substantial support to the current just as new atmosphere activities by non-state and subnational retainers (Hale 2016), thus underlining the importance of the general trend towards greater polycentricism.

Local NGOs, church-based organizations, voluntary institutions such as CCP and CSI are being more supportive of climate change policies. Furthermore, local governments are also receiving support from local businesses of industries.

The benefit is, however, distributed across scales from households to the globe. Because, units smaller than the globe have sought to reduce emissions, at least some marginal reduction of GHGs emissions is likely to result from projects undertaken at multiple scales while waiting for global policies to evolve. Only doing nothing would lead to increase in the level of GHGs, emitted at an ever-greater rate. While the number of reductions that climate scientists estimate is needed to avert calamity, reduction levels do appear to be growing in at least some parts of the world, which may provide examples to other regions of what can be done and what these actions cost. Better technologies for tracking CO_2 emissions are also being developed that will help evaluate the effectiveness of all policies in the future (Ostrom 2012).

However, there are some loopholes and challenges in the polycentric approach to climate change policy. They are:

1. Difficulty in acquiring finance for hiring enough staff for climate-related planning.
2. Competing priorities (health, housing, sanitation, economic growth).
3. Difficulty in mainstreaming climate change into existing departmental functions and organizing collaborative action across local government.
4. Problem with monitoring, verification, and enforcement.
5. The problem of 'hot air'—excess emission credits that do not represent actual emission reduction.

'The sub-global negotiations and agreements might not reduce GHG emissions rapidly enough to anticipate the need for adaptation is no reason to maintain an exclusive focus on global policies that have failed and global negotiations that remain stalled' (Cole 2015).

From another viewpoint, if there are a higher number of projects and activities to be operated at multiple scales, then that system will become chaotic. Sometimes projects will be costly and ineffective, and those that are rewarded are not genuinely interested in reducing climate change problems.

Hybrid and voluntary forms of climate change governance can play a significant part in legitimizing and integrating climate change among stakeholders and internal political and economic decision-makers by reducing the limits for involvement in mitigation operations and growing pressure for advancement in standard forms of climate change governance based on the state (Paavola 2012).

On the contrary, being a part of broader polycentric governance, hybrid and voluntary forms provide a decentralized, flexible and induced way to learn, innovate and experiment with reducing GHGs emissions.

Lamentably, global moderators do not seem, by all accounts, to be discussed to determine the proper scale and scope of emissions trading let alone conducting comparative cost-benefit analyses. The absence of due thoughtfulness regarding the flaws in the current global lawful mechanism and the presence of better institutional components at lower levels of government just shows that we have not yet arrived at the sort of tipping point as proposed in Heal and Kunreuther's model. From the polycentric point of view, the result of worldwide exchanges throughout the following two years may have less long haul significance for the state of worldwide atmosphere approach than what occurs in the EU, USA, China, and other major nations both locally and through littler scale universal courses of action (Cole 2011).

CONCLUDING OBSERVATIONS

In recent years, the question that has been continuously asked is regarding the relevance of the polycentric approach for the analysis of climate change and global public goods. They have also questioned the effectiveness of polycentrism or bottom-up approach to climate change programmes. The answer to this question would be that there is an urgent need for polycentric governance research to explore the institutional arrangements and informal rules that seem to have the most impact on both curbing GHGs emissions and making progress on adaptation and mitigation programmes. Elinor Ostrom has introduced this polycentric approach as a 'global solution' to the climate change problems and proposed an alternative approach to the climate change policy. She has derived this concept from the famous slogan 'Think globally and act locally' which necessitated an active collaboration of various actors in this system.

ULBs are pursuing adaptation and mitigation arranging in an integrated model and mainstreaming it across the local government agencies.

They are conducting their planning in a collaborative manner that incorporates multiple governmental and non-governmental actors. Urban cities are expanding the scope of local greenhouse gas emissions inventories and expanding the scope of local networks of climate change governance, including the civil society and private sector actors. (UN-Habitat 2016).

There is a cross-cutting finding that a lack of engagement of economic actors (private and public) in the design and implementation of urban response to climate change. Even though climate change governance's hybrid and voluntary forms have their loopholes. In general, voluntary initiatives are not representative, and their account remains unclear.

Another important and most significant contribution of polycentric governance is building mutual trust through collective action. This approach is facilitating communication that ultimately leads to trust-building and cooperation among actors. Therefore, mutual trust among resource users can be created over the period through communication.

It is suggested that in order to bring about initiatives to tackle the challenges faced by polycentric climate change governance, the evidence base on the efficiency of non-conventional forms of climate change governance and the interaction of distinct kinds of governance alternatives that are component of a broader polycentric governance approach needs to be improved. The central government should support the development of local government climate change plans that incorporate both adaptation and mitigation elements. In the case of acute vulnerability and weak central government, ULBs should have recourse to international support through global or multilateral mechanisms and bilateral development assistance. Above all, it helps to build carbon-friendly products' markets and to subsidize technologies that over time reduce the marginal carbon subsidy costs.

REFERENCES

Cole, D. H. 2011. 'From Global to Polycentric Climate Governance'. *Climate Law* 2 (3): 395–413. doi:10.3233/CL-2011-042.

———. 2015, 28 January. 'Advantages of a Polycentric Approach to Climate Change Policy'. *Perspective: Nature Climate Change* 5 (2): 114–118. doi: 10.1038/nclimate2490

Deri, M. Alam A. 2008. 'Local Governments and Climate Change'. Available at: gsdrc.org/document-library/local-governments-and-climate-change/?cv=1 (accessed on 22 April 2020).

Filho, W. L. 2015. *Handbook of Climate Change Adaptation*. Heidelberg: Springer Verlag GmbH. doi: 10.1007/978-3-642-38670-1

Hale, T. 2016, 22 August. 'All Hand on Deck: The Paris Agreement and Non-state Climate Actors'. *Global Environmental Politics* 16 (3): 12–22.

McGinnis, M. D. 1999. 'Introduction'. In *Polycentricity and Local Public Economies*, edited by M. D. McGinnis. Ann Arbor, MI: University of Michigan Press.

Ostrom, E. 2009, October. 'A Polycentric Approach for Coping with Climate Change'. World Bank Policy Research Working Paper no. 5095. Available at: http://documents.worldbank.org/curated/en/480171468315567893/pdf/WPS5095.pdf (accessed on 22 April 2020).

———. 2012. 'Nested Externalities and Polycentric Institutions: Must We Wait for Global Solutions to Climate Change before Taking Actions at Other Scales?' *Economic Theory* 49 (2): 353–369.

———. 2014. 'A Polycentric Approach for Coping with Climate Change'. *Annals of Economics and Finance* 15 (1): 97–134.

Ostrom, V. 1999. Polycentricity Part 1. In M. D. McGinnis, *Polycentricity and Local Public Economies: Readings from the Workshop in Political Theory and Policy Analysis* (52–74). Michigan: University of Michigan Press.

Paavola, J. 2012. 'The Climate Change: The Ultimate "Tragedy of the Commons"?' In *Property in Land and Other Resources*, edited by Daniel Cole and Elinor Ostrom, 417–431. Cambridge: The Lincoln Institute for Land Policy.

Patterson, James J., and Dave Huitema. 2018, 21 December. 'Institutional Innovation in Urban Governance: The Case of Climate Change Adaptation'. *Journal Of Environmental Planning and Management*: 374–398. doi: 10.1080/09640568.2018.1510767.

Rayner, S. 2011, 15 June. 'How to Eat an Elephant: A Bottom-up Approach to Climate Policy'. *Beyond Copenhagen* 10 (6): 615–621. doi: 10.3763/cpol.2010.0138.

Keohane, Robert, and M. Oppenheimer. 2016, 8 September. 'Paris: Beyond the Climate Dead End through Pledge and Review?' *Politics and Governance* 4 (3): 142–151. doi: 10.17645/pag.v4i3.634.

UN-Habitat, U. N. 2016, October. *Addressing Climate Change in National Urban Policy: A Policy Guide for Low-Carbon and Climate-Resilient Urban Development*. Available at: http://www.acclimatise.uk.com: http://www.acclimatise.uk.com/wp-content/uploads/2017/08/Addressing-Climate-Change-in-National-Urban-Policy.pdf (accessed on 10 November 2018).

Victor, D. G. 2011. *Global Warming: Gridlock: Creating More Effective Strategies for the Planet*. Cambridge: Cambridge University Press.

Chapter 6

International Legal Challenges of Climate Refugees

S. Chemmalar

INTRODUCTION

The climate refugee is an emerging concept which has far-reaching impact on economic, legal and social activities at both national and international levels. The problem of climate refugees, in a general sense, refers to human displacement caused by climate change at a large scale. Climate change is the global factor that affects all living beings in the world. Ironically, the consistency of the impact varies from one human to another and from one region to another. While discussing the consistency of impact resulting from climate change, the concept of 'common but differentiated responsibility' comes into play.

The issue of climate refugees is increasingly discussed in recent days. Nonetheless, this concept lacks international legitimacy despite the fact that this is a human rights issue. Till now, there has been no clear definition for the term 'climate refugee' because none of the conventions, documents, treaties or resolutions of the General Assembly mentions the term. Whereas the term has been in public discourse since 1985, when Essam El-Hinnawi, an expert of UN Environment Programme (UNEP) defined 'environmental refugees' as people who have been forced to leave their traditional habitat, temporarily or permanently, because of environmental disruption that jeopardized their existence or seriously affected the quality of their life (Apap 2018).

The purpose of this article is to discuss how climate change and other environmental factors contribute to the displacement of people. It will try to answer the following questions: What are the rights affected by these factors? Are the rights of these people internationally protected? What is the prevailing law in India that protects the right of climate refugees? Are the provisions contained in the Refugee Convention 1951 applicable to climate refugees? What distinguishes environmental refugees from other refugees or other migrants? What is the responsibility of developed nation with respect to the protection of climate refugees?

FACTORS INDUCING THE DISPLACEMENT OF PEOPLE

The relation between climate change and displacement is complex and it has occurred throughout human history. There are various environmental factors that contribute, directly or indirectly, to the displacement of people worldwide. The following are the generally accepted factors of displacement: (a) low-lying islands, (b) littoral areas and (c) regions affected by land degradation.

The Intergovernmental Panel on Climate Change (IPCC) has released its *Special Report on Global Warming of 1.5 °C*. The report states that global warming of 2°C will be considerably more challenging for the planet's climate than 1.5°C by 2100 (IPCC 2018). This study is a way forward to measure and counter climate-related problems.

Rising sea level is one of the concerns of climate change. Sea level rising is due to various environmental factors such as the melting of Greenland glaciers and Antarctica ice sheets, and thermal expansion (Tim and David 2014). About 600 million people are likely to be affected by sea-level rising (People and Ocean 2017). Moreover, two-thirds of the world's densely populated cities are located in risk-prone areas. If this scenario continues to exist, then the cities located in these areas need to be relocated. Appropriate measures need to be taken either to combat climate change or take alternative steps for the well-being of the people who live in these areas. Otherwise, the situation will lead to a massive exodus of climate refugees, complicating the current legal framework. Sea level rising produces a visible impact on environmental degradation. But there are a few more factors that are associated with sea level rising such as salinization, sand erosion, unavailability of fresh water, etc. In these situations, people displace gradually in search of secure areas.

INTERNATIONAL PERSPECTIVES

Climate refugees cannot rely on any legal basis in international law. Climate change was initially considered as an environmental challenge. Therefore, the conventions and other international frameworks concentrated on the scientific aspects of environmental change and its impact on species and humans. Climate impacts on forced displacements were given less importance in the international sphere. However, in recent years, the impact of the environment on economic and social aspects received more attention. There is a gap in contemporary international law as to the interchanging of terms such as refugees, migrants, displaced persons. However, from an international legal perspective, we could say that these words are used to describe people from a political perspective and not an economic or social perspective. For instance, the Refugee Convention 1951, which underpins the refugee rights against persecution, has nothing to say about environmentally displaced persons. Various international frameworks such as the United Nations Framework Convention on Climate Change (UNFCCC), IPCC and other instruments are dedicated to the political as well as the economic impacts of environmental changes. Apart from these instruments, the UN High Commission for Refugees (UNHCR) is a global organization that deals with statelessness and forcibly displaced communities. Most importantly, the Nansen Conference 2011 was a huge step in managing climate change induced displacements.

THE UNFCCC FRAMEWORK

The UNFCCC is a significant component of International Environmental Law on climate change. The multilateral treaty has been adopted to provide a plausible solution to the present problem. The UNFCCC was formally adopted in Rio de Janeiro, Brazil, in 1992 and was ratified by 196 countries. Article 2 of the UNFCCC provides that the 'ultimate objective' of the UNFCCC is to achieve stabilization of greenhouse gas concentration in the atmosphere in accordance with the provisions of the convention. The first paragraph of Article 3 lays down the principle of 'Common but differentiated responsibility and respective capabilities' (UNFCCC 1992).

The Paris Agreement, adopted in 2015, brought together all the states parties to the UNFCCC to address the climate change problem. Strengthening the global response to the threat of climate change by keeping the global temperature below 2°C is the main objective of the agreement.

The IPCC is a body of experts that makes an assessment of climate change. It released its special report on global warming, sustainable development and climate change. The report demonstrates how a 0.5°C difference could impact the global population and ecosystem. The report highlighted the fact that by limiting global warming to 1.5°C, fewer people are affected by global temperature rises compared to 2°C. The IPCC has set a stringent target by reducing global warming to 1.5°C. However, the main objective of the Paris Agreement is to reduce global warming below 2°C and try to reach 1.5°C (IPCC 2018).

THE REFUGEE CONVENTION 1951

The convention dealing with the status of refugees (commonly referred to as Refugee Convention 1951) is a UN convention. This Convention is the only framework that provides a legally binding definition for the term 'refugee'. The Convention entered into force on 22 April 1954. It has been amended only once. An amendment was made in 1969 to incorporate the adoption of a protocol. This protocol removed geographical and time limitations, which was the major drawback of the 1951 Convention (UNHCR 1951). The Convention comprises seven chapters and 46 articles.

The Refugee Convention 1951 is the primary document that defines the term 'refugee'. Article 1 of the Convention states that a refugee is 'someone who is unable or unwilling to return to their country of origin owing to a well-founded fear of being persecuted for reasons of race, religion, nationality, membership of a particular social group, or political opinion'. The definition given in the convention for refugees requires three conditions for acquiring the refugee status: (a) unwillingness and inability to return to their country of origin, (b) there should be fear that is considered as well founded (fear based on strong reasons) and (c) the reasons given are limited to political reasons only. Hence, it is clear from the definition given by the convention that to establish refugee status for environmentally displaced persons, only the first condition is fulfilled, for example, inability to return to their country of origin and the second condition, well-founded fear of persecution requires the unfair and cruel treatment by a person or a group. Environmental displacements do not meet the threshold of persecution. The third condition pertains to political and economic changes and is silent on climate or environmental factors. It is, therefore, obvious that climate or environmental refugees are not recognized under the Refugee Convention 1951.

Nevertheless, Article 33 (1) of the Refugee Convention made a special mention about the principle of non-refoulement, which is one of the fundamental principles of UN Convention on Refugees. It specifies that no one shall be expelled or returned (*refoulé* in French) against his or her will, from the country where they seek protection and unwilling to return to their own country. The term 'non-refoulement' is considered as *Jus Cogens* (peremptory principles of international law) for which derogation in any form is not allowed. Hence, even non-member states of the UN Refugee Convention 1951 cannot derogate from the said principle. Ironically, this principle is not applicable to climate refugees. The United Nations Convention is the only convention that addresses the issues of refugees. The issues of climate refugees are, nevertheless, left unaddressed. Hence, there is a need to amend the definition of refugees mentioned in the 1951 refugee convention.

A WAY FORWARD
Nansen Principles 2011

The Nansen Conference on Climate Change and Displacement, which was convened in Oslo by the Government of Norway, is a way-forward measure that addresses the issues of climate-induced refugees (UNHCR 2011). A group of international experts and delegates discussed the ways in which climate change-induced displacement and other related challenges could be tackled. They came out with 10 principles to deal with the fundamental concern of unclear laws and policies to protect people displaced across international borders due to natural disasters (UNHCR 2011). Fridtjof Nansen, the first High Commissioner of Refugees in 1922 devised and issued a 'passport for stateless persons'. The passport was referred to as the 'Nansen Passport' which provided international protection for paperless refugees (Skran 1988). The Nansen passport contained the holder's identity, nationality and race with one-year validity of the refugee status. The passport was recognized by 52 countries. Nansen Principles and Nansen Initiatives are inspired by the name of the legendary Fridtjof Nansen, who made an innovative response to the refugee issue that arose as the outcome of the First World War (UNHCR 2000).

The Nansen conference was intended to strengthen the actions to prevent humanitarian crises at the international level and meet the needs of displaced peoples on a non-discriminatory basis. The conference came up with 10 principles, which are not formally adopted, but constitute guiding principles. It was the first conference in response to the problem. The following are the guiding principles recommended by the conference to respond to the complex challenges relating to climate-induced displacement (UNHCR 2011):

Principle I: Knowledge-based response to the problem
Principle II: State responsibility
Principle III: Stakeholder's responsibility
Principle IV: International cooperation at the national level
Principle V: Shared responsibility to implement the Hyogo Framework
    for Action 2005–2015
Principle VI: Local and national response to disasters
Principle VII: Adherence to International Law
Principle VIII: Implementation of the principles by the States
Principle IX: Coherent approach
Principle X: Equitable approach in making policies

The Nansen Initiative

The Nansen Initiative is a consultative process that seeks to build unanimity on the elements of the protection agenda. The Nansen Initiative was designed in 2012 by Switzerland and Norway. In the year 2015, the Nansen Initiative took place in Geneva, where 110 countries recognized the 'agenda for the protection of cross-border displaced persons in the context of disasters and climate change' (Goodwin-Gill and McAdam, 2017). The conference envisaged three core elements: (a) international cooperation; (b) standards for the treatment of affected people; (c) operational responses.

COMMON BUT DIFFERENTIATED RESPONSIBILITIES

The notion of 'common but differentiated responsibilities' is based on the idea that developed countries are expected to contribute more with respect to the investment in resources and also bear more responsibility towards the environment. This is a universally accepted principle that is based on the recognition of two concurrent needs, for example, the need for all states to take responsibility for environmental problems and the need to take into account the differences in levels of economic development between states. In general, global environmental responsibilities are different from the responsibilities which are purely regional or trans-boundary in nature such as air or river pollution. The concept of 'common concern' was first designated by the Rio declaration with the intent to include the environment as 'common heritage of mankind' and involve global responsibility (UNCED 1992). The term is of recent development in International law. Hence it lacks clarity with regard to legal sanctions under international law.

Global environmental responsibilities are *erga omnes* in nature, for example, legal obligations owed to the whole international community of states in contrast to the legal obligation owed to the affected state. International law acknowledges contextual differences, most importantly the varying capabilities of developed and developing nations. This differentiation of standards of conduct between developed and developing nations is more apparent in the provisions of environmental laws such as Climate Change Convention and Ozone Protocol Convention etc.

STATE RESPONSIBILITY IN INTERNATIONAL LAW

State responsibility refers to the accountability of the states for violation of international obligations. This is the principle that governs the extent to which the states are responsible for their acts in the international sphere. Initially, state responsibilities were determined based on customary international law and treaty law. However, with the adoption of Draft Articles on the Responsibility of States for International Wrongful Acts, the scope of state responsibility has been clarified (International Law Commission 2001). In the Chorzow Factory case, a case about state responsibility for the breach of an international agreement, Permanent Court of International Justice (PCJI) held that 'the violation of a commitment involves an obligation to make reparation in an adequate form is a basic principle of international law' (Germany v Poland 1926). German Interests in Polish Upper Silesia (Germ. v. Pol.), 1926 P.C.I.J. (ser. A) No. 7 (May 25)

According to the Draft Articles on State Responsibility, state obligation is established if two tests are met. Firstly, the conduct of the state must involve an act or omission. Secondly, the act or omission of a particular state should constitute a breach of an international obligation of that state.

All states contribute to climate change; most importantly, the developed states' involvement is much higher than the developing and least developed nations. Hence the conduct of the developed countries constitutes both an act and an omission concerning environmental degradation and resulting in the breach of an international obligation. Applying the principle of common but differentiated responsibility, developed countries have more responsibility in handling the climate refugee problem in its economic and social aspects.

JUS COGENS AND CLIMATE REFUGEES

Jus cogens falls within peremptory norms, which means that derogation in any form is not allowed. The notion of *jus cogens* was provided in

Article 53 of the Vienna Convention on the Law of Treaties, 1969 (United Nations 1969). *Jus cogens* is defined therein 'as a peremptory norm of general International law'. The provision stipulates that a treaty will be void, if it conflicts with *jus cogens*. Article 53 is declaratory in nature insofar as *jus cogens* overrides other sources mentioned in the article, even though *jus cogens* is not expressly stated in international law.

The principle of non-refoulement, which protects the persons from persecution, is now recognized as *jus cogens*. By applying this principle, protection for the climate refugees though not expressed in any convention acquires the status of *jus cogens*.

CONCLUSION

The Internal Displacement Monitoring Centre has published a report on displacement, stating that since 2008 nearly 26.4 million persons worldwide have been forcibly displaced due to natural disasters (Internal Displacement Monitoring Centre 2018). The refugee Convention 1951 and its optional protocol are used to address the issue relating to victims of persecution and do not address contemporary issues posed by environmental degradation. What is required is the coordinated effort among the nations towards finding a plausible solution for contemporary issues. An inclusive framework has to be prepared by the states keeping in mind the dictum of responsibility-sharing based on the capability of a state in terms of financial support and taking into account the contribution of the states to the environmental change faced today. Moreover, the principle of non-refoulement is now considered as *jus cogens* which could be applied to the status of climate refugees as well. Indeed a Draft Convention on the International Status of Environmentally Displaced Persons prepared by researchers at the University of Limoges in France in consultation with legal, scientific and philosophical experts working for regional and international organizations and NGOs and published in the *Revue européenne de droit de l'environnement* in 2008 has been made available on the internet in its French, English and Spanish versions. A comprehensive and ratified legal framework where the states are to be made treaty-bound is the need of the hour for the protection of climate refugees.

REFERENCES

Apap, J. 2018. 'The Concept of "Climate Refugee": Towards a Possible Definition'. European Parliamentary Research Service. Available at: http://www.europarl.europa.eu/RegData/etudes/BRIE/2018/621893/EPRS_BRI(2018)621893_EN.pdf (accessed on 22 April 2020).

Centre International de Droit comparé de l'environnement. 2013. 'Draft Convention on the International Status of Environmentally Displaced Persons (Third Version)'. Limoges. Available at: https://cidce.org/wp-content/uploads/2016/08/Draft-Convention-on-the-International-Status-on-environmentally-displaced-persons-third-version.pdf (accessed on 22 April 2020).

Goodwin-Gill, G. S., and J. McAdam. 2017. *Climate Change Disasters and Displacements*. UNHCR. Available at: https://www.unhcr.org/596f25467.pdf (accessed on 22 April 2020).

People and Ocean. 2017. *United Nations Fact Sheet*. The Ocean Conference, United Nations, New York. Available at: https://www.un.org/sustainabledevelopment/wp-content/uploads/2017/05/Ocean-fact-sheet-package.pdf (accessed on 22 April 2020).

Internal Displacement Monitoring Centre. 2018. *Global Report on Internal Displacement*. Available at: http://www.internal-displacement.org/global-report/grid2018/ (accessed on 22 April 2020).

International Law Commission. 2001. *Responsibility of States for Internationally Wrongful Acts*. Available at: http://legal.un.org/ilc/texts/instruments/english/draft_articles/9_6_2001.pdf (accessed on 22 April 2020).

IPCC (Intergovernmental Panel on Climate Change). 2018. *Special Report on Global Warming*. Available at: https://www.ipcc.ch/site/assets/uploads/sites/2/2019/06/SR15_Full_Report_High_Res.pdf (accessed on 22 April 2020).

Skran, C. M. 1988. 'Profiles of First Two High Commissioners'. *Journal of Refugee Studies* 1 (3–4): 277–296. doi:10.1093/jrs/1.3-4.277.

Stephens, T., and D. L. V. Zwaag. 2014. *Polar Oceans Governance in an Era of Environmental Change*. Northampton, MA: Edward Elgar Publishing.

United Nations. 1969. Vienna Convention on the Law of Treaties, 23 May 1969, United Nations, Treaty Series, vol. 1155, p. 331. Available at: https://www.refworld.org/docid/3ae6b3a10.html (accessed 17 May 2020).

UNFCCC (United Nations Conference on Environment and Development). 1998. *Agenda 21, Rio Declaration*. New York, NY: United Nations. Available at: http://www.unesco.org/education/pdf/RIO_E.PDF (accessed on 22 April 2020).

———. 1998. *Kyoto Protocol to the United Nations Framework Convention on Climate Change*. Available at: https://unfccc.int/resource/docs/convkp/conveng.pdf (accessed on 22 April 2020).

UN High Commissioner for Refugees (UNHCR). 2011, September. 'The 1951 Convention Relating to the Status of Refugees and its 1967 Protocol'. Available at: https://www.refworld.org/docid/4ec4a7f02.html (accessed 17 May 2020).

———. 2000. *The State of World Refugees 2000: Fifty Years of Humanitarian Action.* New York, NY: Oxford University Press.

———. 2011, June. *Climate Change and Displacement in 21st Century.* The Nansen Conference, Oslo, Norway. Available at: https://www.unhcr.org/afr/4ea969729.pdf (accessed on 22 April 2020).

Vienna Convention on the Law of Treaties. 1969, 23 May. Article 53 Opened for Signature. Available at: http://legal.un.org/ilc/texts/instruments/english/conventions/1_1_1969.pdf (accessed on 22 April 2020).

Chapter 7

Maritime Spatial Planning
A Means of Organizing Maritime Activities Measured in Terms of Sustainable Development Goals

Catherine Colard-Fabregoule

The world of the sea is traditionally an area of freedom, but states have long undertaken to extend their skills in maritime areas. The marine environment, a coveted area, faces multiple pressures. The interactions of maritime activities between each other and those between maritime activities and the environment can thus be conflictual. Subject to strong natural constraints, these human activities need to be regulated with a perfect knowledge of the environment in which they are exercised. Furthermore, global warming and other forms of pollution appear largely to be the result of human activities. The seas and oceans are central to the problem of climate change. Through studies and projections, experts from all disciplines are trying to assess the impact of global warming on marine areas, in terms of sea level rise, multiple coastal risks and marine biodiversity. Global warming appears largely to be the result of human activities on the planet to the point of constituting what one can call a kind of pollution, a source of modification of life on earth, generally speaking. As such, the production of clean renewable energies is an alternative to fossil fuels and a necessity. If the power of the oceans is legitimately frightening, this same force can become a positive element in the fight against climate change. While launching the *Grenelle de la Mer* at the end of February 2009, Jean-Louis Borloo, the French Minister of Ecology and Sustainable Development at that time, had said, 'it is the sea which will save the earth' (*Le Figaro* 2009). He emphasized the fundamental nature of the marine environment for the future of the planet.

We also know that times of crisis often create vast processes of creation and imagination. Many new 'clean' and renewable energy experiments are invented, tested and proven. The oceans are becoming theatres of experimentation and major technological and industrial daring. For example, there was a plan to capture and store CO_2 in the seabed; another idea imagined was to fertilize the oceans to allow greater absorption of CO_2. However, it is in the field of clean and renewable energy production (Schneider 2015, 594) at the very heart of the marine area that the achievements are most astonishing. They obviously involve massive investments and a perfect mastery of the environment in which they will be deployed. In all the cases considered, whether we are talking about wind energy, wave energy or marine currents, scientific feasibility and practical industrial achievements must be seen in the light of legal constraints. Legal science is put to test in the face of these new challenges. The use and sharing of the marine area, partially privatized by states but necessarily common, becomes crucial. Environment and economic activities often seem to be antithetical. Indeed all activities need to be regulated and coordinated. That is where the planning tool can help us and, as we can see, maritime spatial planning is a growing phenomenon throughout the world. It determines the right of using the sea, a common good, but taking into account the constraints and the necessity to coordinate activities and define priorities. In fact, all these activities are subject to strong natural constraints. They do need to be regulated and coordinated because several activities can coexist in the same area at the same time, in the light of sustainable development which has become a benchmark and a goal. Maritime spatial planning involves the idea of coordinating activities with one other through a state order and an adapted administrative framework. The European approach in this area embraces the goals, methodology, and concerns of a regional organization to coordinate national issues.

THE NECESSARY COORDINATION OF ACTIVITIES AMONG ONE ANOTHER: STATE ORDER AND THE ADMINISTRATIVE FRAMEWORK

The sea is the scene of multiple activities. The question of the administrative framework is central to both the maritime area itself and the coastal zone. The example of marine renewable energies is particularly convincing because it is through this axis that energy will be repatriated to the Earth, its final destination.

Many activities have been developed along coastal areas: navigation, defence, fishing, extraction and drilling, aquaculture but also tourism, and more recently, exploitation of new renewable energies. All the activities carried out at the seas are important, but their importance varies according to the point of view adopted. Defence activities, for example, traditionally appear to be at priority for states, while biodiversity, wildlife or flora will be essential for an environmental protector or activist. For the economic world, profitability and business will be of major interest. That is how the topic is connected to sustainable development because, as we all know, sustainable development corresponds to the idea that human societies must be organized in a long-term perspective and by taking into account multiple interests. Sustainable development endorses not only the idea that we need to take into account human activities on the environment but also the need to create a fairer society. A fairer society includes the combination of all elements of sustainable development: environment, of course, but also the social and economic aspects. However, it is not easy to implement such a combination.

The seas and oceans are the scenes of new technological activities of energy creation. The energies of the currents or the tidal streams concern very specific sites such as straits or capes and other places where one observes an increase in speed. Wave energy is also potentially interesting because, according to the World Energy Council,[1] 10 per cent of the world's annual electricity demand could be covered by the

---

[1] This Council was created by the United Nations to influence energy action around the world. Its current ambition is to achieve a sustainable and affordable energy situation for everyone.

so-called wave production. Wind energy can be exploited by windmills at the seaside (onshore) or at sea (offshore). The electricity produced at sea is then repatriated to the earth by cable networks. Its interest consists in taking advantage of marine winds by limiting inevitable noise and visual nuisances. Significant technological challenges have been tackled and the first floating wind turbines have recently seen the light of day.[2] They offer great prospects for yield because they can be installed far from the coast, where winds are strong and constant, and where the depths are appropriately profound. They also have the advantage of reducing visual and noise pollution. To these new technologies, we must add the thermal energy of the seas, tidal energy or the energy of salinity gradients, which involve strong technological (particularly in terms of maintenance and repair), economic but also regulatory constraints. Since 1991, when the first offshore wind farm was inaugurated in Denmark, investments have been launched in Europe and elsewhere in the world. The first offshore wind farm was decided in 2015 as regards India. India, the third-largest energy consumer in the world, has recently started a major renewable energy development plan, particularly at sea. India's assets are numerous because of its coastline of almost 7,000 km and the water depths rather low near the coast.

It is necessary to remember that in terms of renewable energies, the states give the impetus, but the role of the companies is crucial. They are the ones that produce the necessary Research and Development. They are the ones that engage in long-term and very costly investments. Obviously, they need predictability and legal certainty. These activities must also be linked to other activities in the maritime domain and, as a result, pressures on maritime areas are becoming more numerous. Environmental imperatives must, of course, be taken into account.

Generally speaking, the production of renewable marine energies began in the sea, but the energy will be brought back to the land (its final destination) via the coast. Of course, each country has its own regulatory framework. However, the constraints are almost everywhere the same. They are related to the physical environment, the need to

---

[2] France inaugurated the first wind turbine of this type in the Atlantic Ocean in July 2018.

protect the environment and biodiversity, landscape and all the uses of the maritime public domain. In France, for example, if we consider installing an offshore wind farm, we will have to consider whether the place falls within the framework of a specific regulation: Is it near or situated in a wildlife park? Is it a place classified under the European Birds Directive? Are there important archaeological sites nearby? Offshore wind projects can fall within the scope of the French law on preventive archaeology of 2001.[3] These are a lot of questions to consider. We understand that many constraints exist that are applicable not only to marine spaces but also to terrestrial spaces that are criss-crossed by several networks (telephone, electricity, water). The public domain also includes areas subject to special regulations that are related to military zones, for example, or maritime concessions such as aquaculture or navigation. All these delimitations are specified by administrative authorities endowed with competence in these areas. Near an airport, for example, we have easements of release, and we have concerns about the disruption of radars and electronic communications.

In short, the sea is a highly coveted area, the interactions between the environment and the activities, and activities between them can be conflictual. Planning is a tool, a means and a goal to coordinate activities in the maritime space.

Maritime spatial planning is a technique originating from state practices and proves to be a possible response to these constraints. If we consider the term 'planning', we can say it has many synonyms: provision, programme, schedule, organization, calculation, leadership, project etc. Planning places the state and public authorities at the centre of the process of reflection and decision making. The state bears the central responsibility for economic development. It is also in charge of general interest. General interest (Colard-Fabregoule 2012, 71–96) is a very complex concept that is difficult to define. Pursuing the general interest is an objective and a duty for a state, whatever the objective is. We can venture to say further that the state, therefore, has at its disposal economic indicators, but also another yardstick, for example,

---

[3] Preventive archeology is governed by the provisions of Book V of the French *Code du patrimoine*. The provisions were amended in 2003, 2009 and 2016.

general interest, which could be sustainable development. That is how the maritime spatial planning may become an appropriate answer because it contains the idea of coordinating and sharing the common space for activities at sea, while having sustainable development as a goal or standard, with an in-depth knowledge of the marine environment. More specifically, according to the European Commission and the Bureau of Maritime Affairs: 'Maritime Spatial Planning, a process that consists in regulating human activities in the waters bordering coastal areas in order to preserve marine' (European Commission and UNESCO 2017).

To sum up, we have an economic and technological component that responds to investors' risk concerns; we have an environment and sustainable development component that responds to the ecological risk; and we have science and knowledge of the site because to be able to forecast well, one must perfectly know the environment in which one is preparing to develop new activities. That is why planning is supposed to answer the question that can be roughly summarized as follows: who will do what, where, how and for how long? More than a tool, it can appear as a solution for the sound management of maritime spaces taking into account the interests of different actors and activities and the environment itself.

PLANNING: A TOOL AND A METHODOLOGY TO COORDINATE ACTIVITIES AMONG ONE ANOTHER AND PROMOTE INTERNATIONAL COOPERATION

Marine Spatial planning is a relatively new concept that the oceanographic commission of the UNESCO defines as 'a process of analyzing and allocating parts of three-dimensional maritime spaces … to specific uses or objectives, to achieve ecological, economic, and social objectives that are usually specified through a political process'. This is maybe the perfect definition of sustainable development. Sustainable development goals are intended to often balance competing sectoral interests with the objective of using space and marine resources efficiently and sustainably. Maritime spatial planning also helps make decisions based on reliable data and an in-depth knowledge of the marine environment. Furthermore, it can help enhance the legal security of investors and encourage economic development. It can appear as a zoning process, but it is much more than that. It is a territorial management tool which also contains a general vision, a reflection on constraints, an assessment, a forecast of the future, a research aspect and the participation of the public in a democratic process, which is very important. It can be an instrument to improve decision-making. It can also be an arbitration framework for conflicts on the use and management of the impact of human activities on the marine environment.

In Europe, an attempt at unification and impetus is being led by the European Commission in order to streamline its methods and meet the challenges of tomorrow (European Commission Integrated Maritime Social Policy). At the international level, several international forums are showing growing interest in Maritime Spatial Planning. This is the case of the International Oceanographic Commission or the International Council for the Exploration of the Sea.

At the European level, we can see that many states are engaged in the process of maritime planning: today the United Kingdom is the world's largest producer of offshore wind energy and its ambitions are to produce enough power to supply the entire country with electricity by 2020. For the first time in 2018, wind energy exceeded nuclear energy in this country, with almost 19 per cent of the energy produced. Denmark, Sweden, Norway, Spain, Poland, Germany are also involved in this process. In 2018, France confirmed the construction of six offshore wind farms.

Everywhere around the world, these projects are accompanied by planning regulations. Sometimes, it means adapting existing legislation. Poland, for example, had to change its planning law because of the legal status of offshore platforms, which were considered artificial islands and as it is, were authorized only for five years. As we know, investments are much longer, of course, for wind energy installations. They typically range from 20 to 25 years. Portugal, which has a large coastal area, is a pioneer by adopting, on 31 August 2007, the world's first 'Marine Occupation Plan', defining the legal regime for the use of maritime public domain property for the production of electricity. We have a great dynamism around the question of wind energies elsewhere too. India, for example, is the fourth more dynamic country in the world for wind energy today.

Despite those disparate practices, European countries are the target of an attempt to unify and stimulate, on the part of the European institutions. It is important to rationalize practices and respond to possible conflicts of tomorrow.

In Europe everything generally starts with a coloured book from the Commission: a *Green Book* in 2006 on maritime policies of the Union focused on the growth of maritime activities and the increasing competition. Its Chapter 4 on 'Spatial Planning for a Growing Maritime Economy' predicted that maritime activities would increase and competition would keep growing. Another *Green Book* in 2008 regretted that, in the member states, there was insufficient strategic planning and insufficient dialogue with the public. The Commission also pointed out the risks associated with a lack of planning on investment decisions. A *Blue Book* in 2007 proposed an integrated maritime policy for the European Union (EU). Subsequently, in November 2008, the Commission published its *Road Map for Maritime Spatial Planning*. Annex VI of Directive 2008/56/EC of the European Parliament and of the Council provides a list of examples of possible measures, including the regulation of spatial and temporal distribution and instruments for coordinated management. Let us also note that the United Kingdom has ensured that maritime spatial planning will support the implementation of the Marine Strategy Framework Directive. Finally, the Directive no. 2014/89/EU dated 23 July 2014 of the European Parliament and of the Council established a framework for maritime spatial planning (European Parliament and Council 2014). In its proposal for the directive, the European Commission remarked that:

> Such an approach to ocean management has been developed in the Integrated Maritime Policy for the European Union, including, as its environmental pillar, Directive 2008/56/EC of the European Parliament and of the Council of 17 June 2008 establishing a framework for Community action in the field of marine environmental policy. (European Commission 2013)

Maritime spatial planning appears as an integral part of the Europe 2020 strategy (European Parliament and Council 2008) on a smart growth strategy, which is connected to international instruments and specifically the United Nations Convention on the Law of the Sea (UNCLOS) of 1982. It aims to turn the EU 'into a smart, sustainable and inclusive economy delivering high levels of employment, productivity and social cohesion' by 'promoting a more resource-efficient, greener and more competitive economy' (European Commission Document 52010DC2020).

It is a practical tool in assisting the member states to comply with their obligations: The competences of the member states relating to maritime boundaries and jurisdiction are not altered by the Directive. The European Commission explains that global planning is not possible without taking into account the specificities of each marine region or subregion. The member states are responsible for the planning of the maritime area and the principle of subsidiarity applies in this case. But the European Commission believes that a common approach at the EU level and closer coordination between the member states could simplify administrative procedures and provide a stable legal framework for investors.

On the other hand, it is worth remembering that the sea does not take into account administrative boundaries, and activities in one state may affect other neighbouring countries. In the European vision, if each country of the Union is free to plan its own maritime activities, a set of minimum common requirements must make local, regional and national planning in shared waters more compatible with each other. In the minds of its European promoters, the planning of the maritime space makes it possible to: reduce conflicts between sectors and create synergies between different activities; encourage investment; introduce predictability, transparency and clearer rules, which can help stimulate the development of the sources and networks of renewable energy; encourage the creation of marine protected areas and facilitate investment in oil and gas; strengthen coordination between the administrations of each country through the use of a single instrument to balance the development of a range of maritime activities, which will be simpler and less costly; increase cross-border cooperation between EU countries, with regard to cables, oil and gas pipelines, shipping routes, wind energy production facilities; and finally, protect the environment by an early identification of the impact of the multiple uses of marine space and the opportunities it offers. Let us recall that for Europe, the global potential of marine renewable energies is significant thanks to the 32,000 km of coast and the 25 million km^2 of maritime area. Thus, maritime spatial planning is presented as a major instrument of this integrated marine policy. In an integrated area such as the EU, the idea of a coherent common vision is important, and planning falls within the overall coherence of such a vision. States must ensure that the pressure exerted by human activities does not jeopardize the ecological balance. Consequently, the member states have to co-operate where they share a marine region or subregion in common.

The EU is interested in varying degrees in a large number of areas to which fisheries must be added, since the common fisheries policy falls under the exclusive competence of the community. The Recommendation on Integrated Coastal Zone Management (ICZM) sets out common principles among which figures coherence of territorial planning. The European approach is likely to avoid problems of compatibility between the energy production of electricity at sea, and the application of specific legislative texts in the field of environmental protection.

In the background, since the beginning of the 2000s, major future community energy markets have been prepared in Europe, notably electricity and gas interconnection strategies and storage issues. In 2008, the European Commission stated that the connection of the remaining isolated energy markets in Europe is a priority and that a master plan for an energy network in the North Sea should be put in place with a view to mutually interconnecting national electricity grids in north-western Europe and connecting the many planned offshore wind energy projects. A key objective remains the construction at sea of a gigantic network encircling Europe and 'connecting the solar energy of the south, wave energy of the west and the wind or water power of the north to large centers of consumption' (COM 2008, 781).

It must be understood that the coordination of activities among one another adds to the problem of cross-border coordination. On an international level, the UNESCO Intergovernmental Oceanographic Commission discussed its strategies to promote this process worldwide on 9 June 2017 at the United Nations Conference on Oceans held in New York (UN, The Ocean Conference 2017). This international organization brings together policymakers, public and private actors, and citizens to coordinate and jointly design human activities in marine areas to achieve UN's Sustainable Development Goals by 2030, including in particular Goal 14 on the conservation and use of oceans, seas and marine resources. The organization likes to recall[4] that, when the International Oceanographic Commission organized the first-ever international workshop on Marine Spatial Planning in November 2006, only three countries had maritime spatial plans approved by their governments. At that time, they represented only about 0.3 per cent of the world's exclusive economic zones (EEZ). Since then, 15 countries have implemented Maritime Spatial Planning and another 25 have already completed or approved plans. By 2030, at least half of the world's EEZ area is expected to have government-approved maritime spatial plans. In 2009, the International Oceanographic Commission published the Guide for the Assessment of Maritime Spatial Plans, which has since become an internationally recognized standard. Its objective is to help states 'to foster the development of their technical and institutional capacities to reduce the loss of biodiversity and manage their marine ecosystems in a sustainable manner' (IOC 2014).

International cooperation seems underway. At the conference held from 15 to 17 March 2017, the Intergovernmental Oceanographic Commission and Directorate General for Maritime Affairs and Fisheries of the EU adopted the Common Road Map (UN-EU Joint Roadmap) to accelerate the processes of planning the maritime space in the world. Maritime spatial plans now cover nearly 10 per cent of exclusive economic zones in the world. This voluntary commitment of the two institutions, undertaken within the framework of a UN conference, aims at further encouraging the development of maritime planning in all the

---

[4] Retrieved from: http://www.unesco.org/new/en/member-states/single-view/news/la_coi_unesco_ouvre_la_voie_a_une_gestion_durable_de_loc/

seas and oceans of the globe in order to triple the surface of territorial waters by 2030. This common roadmap includes five priority areas that are, in addition to the ecosystem-based transboundary Marine Spatial Planning, blue economy, ecosystem-based Marine Spatial Planning, capacity building and building mutual understanding.

REFERENCES

Colard-Fabregoule, C. 2012. 'Les contours de la notion d'intérêt général en droit international public' (The contours of the concept of general interest in public international law). In *Liber Amicorum Darcy,* edited by Patrick Charlot and DOAT, 71–96. Brussels: Bruylant.

COM. 2008, 13 November. 'Communication de la commission au parlement européen, au conseil et au comité économique et social européen, et au comité des régions' (Communication from the Commission to the European Parliament, the European Economic and Social Committee of the Regions). Available at: https://www.senat.fr/europe/textes_europeens/e4140.pdf (accessed on 22 April 2020).

European Commission. Integrated Maritime Social Policy EUROPE 2020 A strategy for smart, sustainable and inclusive growth. Available at: https://eur-lex.europa.eu/legal-content/en/ALL/?uri=CELEX%3A52010DC2020 (accessed on 18 May 2020).

———. 2013, 12 March. *Proposal for a Directive of the European Parliament and of the Council.* Brussels: European Commission. Available at: http://ec.europa.eu/environment/iczm/pdf/Proposal_en.pdf (accessed on 22 April 2020).

European Commission and UNESCO. 2017, 15 March. 'The Governance of Maritime Space at the Heart of a Conference Organized by the European Commission and UNESCO. Brussels: European Commission. Available at: https://ec.europa.eu/maritimeaffairs/content/governance-maritime-space-heart-conference-organized-european-commission-and-unesco_en (accessed on 22 April 2020).

European Parliament and Council. 2008. 'Directive 2008/56/EC of the European Parliament and of the Council of 17 June 2008 Establishing a Framework for Community Action in the Field of Marine Environmental Policy (Marine Strategy Framework Directive)'. Available at: https://eur-lex.europa.eu/legal-content/EN/TXT/?uri=CELEX%3A32008L0056 (accessed on 23 April 2020).

———. 2014. 'Directive 2014/89/EU of the European Parliament and of the Council of 23 July 2014 Establishing a Framework for Maritime Spatial Planning. Available at: https://eur-lex.europa.eu/legalcontent/EN/TXT/?uri=uriserv:OJ.L_.2014.257.01.0135.01.ENG (accessed on 23 April 2020).

IOC (Intergovernmental Oceanographic Commission). 2014. *A Guide to Evaluating Marine Spatial Plans*. Paris: UNESCO. Available at: https://unesdoc.unesco.org/ark:/48223/pf0000227779 (accessed on 23 April 2020).

Le Figaro. 2009. 'Borloo lance le Grenelle de la Mer' (Borloo launches the Grenelle de la mer [roundtable on the sea]). *Le Figaro*, 27 February. Available at: http://www.lefigaro.fr/flash-actu/2009/02/27/01011-20090227FILWWW00418-borloo-lance-le-grenelle-de-la-mer.php (accessed on 23 April 2020).

Schneider, F. 2015. *Les énergies marines renouvelables, approche juridique en droit international, européen et comparé* (Marine renewable energies, a legal approach in international, European and comparative law). Paris: Pedone.

UNESCO. 2017. 'La COI-UNESCO ouvre la voie à une gestion durable de l'océan grâce à la planification de l'espace maritime' (IOC-UNESCO leading the way for sustainable management of the ocean through Marine Spatial Planning). Paris: UNESCO. Available at: http://www.unesco.org/new/en/natural-sciences/environment/water/wwap/display-single-publication/news/ioc_unesco_leading_the_way_for_sustainable_management_of_the/ (accessed on 22 April 2020).

United Nations-EU. 2017. 'Joint Roadmap to Accelerate Marine/Maritime Spatial Planning Worldwide'. Available at: http://www.unesco.org/new/fileadmin/MULTIMEDIA/HQ/SC/pdf/Joint_Roadmap_MSP_v5.pdf (accessed 18 May 2020).

UN, The Ocean Conference. 2017. 'Our oceans, our future: partnering for the implementation of Sustainable Development Goal 14'. Available at: https://oceanconference.un.org/about (accessed 18 May 2020).

Chapter 8

Views on Environmental Democracy in France

Jean-Jacques Menuret

Environmental Democracy, in France, is at the crossroads of human rights and environmental protection. It follows the same 'philosophy of life' that motivated the great republicans of the 1789 Revolution and later the members of the Constituent Assembly of 1946. This philosophy is that of a democracy in which participatory forms of government complement the general expression of political suffrage (Sauvé 2010).

Principle 10 of the 1992 Rio Declaration on Environment and Development proclaimed that:

> Environmental issues are best handled with participation of all concerned citizens, at the relevant level. At the national level, each individual shall have appropriate access to information concerning the environment that is held by public authorities, including information on hazardous materials and activities in their communities, and the opportunity to participate in decision-making processes. (UNESCO website)

Everything has been said in that principle: public information and the participation of the public in public decision-making processes constitute active principles of environmental law, which are at the same time, indispensable for the acquisition of greater legitimacy and universality (Naim-Gesbert 2011, 184).

French law gives a large place to these principles, which are the corollaries of a whole. The Charter for the Environment of 2004, which has constitutional value (*JORF* 2005, 3697), deals with them in its Article 7 ('Everybody has the right, in the conditions and to the extent provided for by law, to have access to any information pertaining to the environment in the possession of public bodies and to participate in the public decision-making process likely to affect the environment'), just like the law, in Article L. 110-1, Section II of the Environmental Code.[1]

These principles are also echoed by international standards, first and foremost by the Aarhus Convention of 25 June 1998,[2] ratified by France on 8 July 2002, which promotes environmental democracy in a tripartite manner, by linking information (Articles 4 and 5) and public participation (Articles 6–8) with access to justice (Article 9).

---

[1] The Environmental Code, after having united the two principles under the aegis of Article L. 110-1, Section II, Paragraph 4, which initially referred to a right of the citizens to participation involving a right to information (the earlier version of Article L. 110-1, Section II, Paragraph 4 provided: 'The principle of participation, according to which everyone must have access to information relating to the environment, including those relating to hazardous materials and activities'), seems to distinguish between them today, without, however, questioning the intimate connection between them. Article L. 110-1, Section II states:

> Paragraph 4: The principle according to which every person has the right of access to environmental information held by public authorities/Paragraph 5: The principle of participation whereby a person is informed of projected public decisions having an impact on the environment under conditions allowing him to make his observations, which are taken into consideration by the competent authority.

[2] Aarhus Convention of 25 June 1998 on Access to Information, Public Participation in Decision-making and Access to Justice in Environmental Matters. Adopted on 25 June 1998 by the United Nations Economic Commission for Europe (UNECE), the Convention entered into force on 30 October 2001. France ratified it on 8 July 2002. It entered into force in France on 6 October 2002 (Law No. 2002-285 of 28 February 2002 authorizing the approval of the Aarhus Convention and Decree No. 2002-1187 of 12 September 2002 on the publication of the Aarhus Convention).

The current environmental democracy in France is, therefore, a significant source of renewal of the social pact, and also of administrative democracy. It reflects the emergence of a new form of citizenship, whose purpose, somewhat paradoxically, is not so much the governance of the city as participation in the determination of public affairs (Sauvé, 2010).

Nevertheless, while the principles of citizens' participation and information have led to the creation or reinforcement of many participatory procedures, their effectiveness or real scope continues to remain, despite recent reform, a matter for discussion. The review of the main participatory instruments reveals that they remain imperfect: (a) citizens' information and participation still appear to be insufficient, and (b) the citizens' initiative limited when confronted with the public authorities.

CITIZENS' INFORMATION AND PARTICIPATION STILL INADEQUATE

While the reform resulting from the order of 3 August 2016 (Hélin 2016; Jamay 2016; Mozol 2018; Zarka 2016),[3] has proclaimed new rights to strengthen their effectiveness, information and participation of the citizens still remain insufficient in the main participatory procedures, whether they are located upstream or downstream of the decision-making process with an environmental impact.

---

[3] Ordinance of 3 August 2016 reforming the procedures to ensure information and public participation in the elaboration of specific decisions that may have an impact on the environment (*JORF* 2016). This ordinance been ratified by Law No. 2018-148 of 2 March 2018, ratifying Ordinances No. 2016-1058 of 3 August 2016 relating to the modification of the rules applicable to the environmental assessment of projects, plans and programmes and No. 2016-1060 of 3 August 2016 reforming the procedures to ensure information and public participation in the elaboration of certain decisions likely to have an impact on the environment (*JORF* 2018). The provisions of the ordinance were specified by Decree No. 2017-626 of 25 April 2017 on the procedures to ensure information and public participation in the elaboration of certain decisions likely to have an environmental impact and amending various provisions relating to the environmental assessment of certain projects, plans and programmes (*JORF* 2017).

Before the Decision-making Process

Before the decision-making process, two procedures deserve attention: public debate and prior consultation.

Public debate is an instrument that aims at informing the public about the desirability, the characteristics and the objectives of a project or programme, and also the largest possible expression of the citizens, to enlighten the project contractor and to discuss alternative solutions, including the non-implementation of a project.

The central element of this procedure is the National Commission for Public Debate (The NCPD or CNDP in French) was established by Law No. 95-101 of 2 February 1995 on strengthening the protection of the environment (*JORF* 1995, 1840), which is one of the 26 independent administrative authorities (IAA) now recognized by the French legislator (the commission is mentioned in the list annexed to the general status of IAA defined by Law No. 2017-55 of 20 January 2017 on the general status of independent administrative authorities and independent public authorities; *JORF* 2017a) who, while acting on behalf of the State, are not subordinate to the Government (*Independent Administrative Authorities*, State Council's 2001 report, 257).

The law (Article L. 121–1 of the Environmental Code) entrusts the legislator with the mission of ensuring respect for information and public participation throughout the proceedings.

Before the 2016 reform, the law provided for mandatory referral to the French National Commission for Public Debate only in the case of 'development or infrastructure projects of national interest' of public institutions, 'when they have high socio-economic stakes or have a significant impact on the environment or land use planning'.

Henceforth, and this is a novelty introduced by the Ordinance of 3 August 2016, which had been suggested by the commission itself, the NCPD shall also be open to review 'national plans and programmes' (e.g., a national transport infrastructure plan).[4]

---

[4] Article L. 122-4 of the Environmental code approximately defines the following terms: Paragraph 1: ' Plans and programmes': The plans, diagrams, schedules

However, even in these cases of compulsory referral, the complex conditions of which are defined by statutory instruments, the NCPD is not obliged to organize a public debate. It appreciates the necessity for the referral on the basis of the file by setting up a special commission for this purpose. In such a case, however, the NCPD determines the modalities of public participation in the decision-making process in an independent manner (Article L. 121-9 of the Environmental Code).

Anyhow, if the practical contribution of the public debate as well as the role of the NCPD, which is exerted totally independently, can hardly be disputed, the relevance of this procedure deserves to be discussed.

Let us take note of the fact that, in practice, the procedure is proving costly to organize. Over the 2002–2012 period, the NCPD found that the least costly debate amounted to 300,000 euros, and the most expensive involved more than four million euros. Out of the 55 debates analysed, 31 cost less than one million. Finally, the average cost of a debate is about 800,000 euros (NCPD 2012, 106). Let us also note that the procedure is mandatory only for some specific decision-making processes. Its major disadvantage is that its conclusions are drawn only from an appreciation of the completeness and sincerity of the debate.

However, at this early stage of the decision-making process, it is the question of the desirability of the project that should first and foremost be the subject of the NCPD's opinion. Furthermore, while the powers of the Commission have recently been expanded in so far as it can now establish a national list of people who are the guarantors of the consultation (Article L. 121-1-1 of the Environmental Code), exercise a conciliation mission, if the parties concerned so request (Article L.

---

and other planning documents adopted by the State, the local authorities or their groupings and the public establishments which depend on them, as well as their modification provided that they are provided for by law or regulations, including those co-financed by the European Union; Paragraph 2: 'Environmental Assessment': a process consisting of the preparation of an environmental impact report, the carrying out of consultations, the taking into account of the report and consultations during the decision-making process by the authority which adopts or approves the plan or programme, as well as the publication of information on the decision, in accordance with articles L. 122-6 and following.

121-2 of the Environmental Code) and make decisions about expertise, the Commission is still forbidden to comment on the merits of projects. Article L. 121-1 of the Environmental Code provides in fine: 'The National Commission of Public Debate and the special commissions do not pass judgment on the substance of the plans, programs or projects submitted to them'.

The consequence is that this question often comes back in force, sometimes in a very different way, especially during the public enquiry stage (Hélin 2016). That is precisely what happened during the uplifting affair of the Greater West Airport project in *Notre-Dame-des-Landes*. Initiated in 1963, then launched again in 2000, it was finally abandoned in January 2018, after a public debate that took place between 2002 and 2003, and even a declaration of public utility in 2008.[5]

This case—like others—revealed that public debate does not serve the issue of settling the appropriateness of the project once and for all. In this, the procedure fails to produce the expected results.

The second procedure that requires our attention at the upstream stage is prior consultation. Set up by the 2016 reform (Article L. 121-15-1 and the subsequent paragraphs of Environmental Code), it is an alternative to the lack of organization of a public debate. The modalities and effects of this procedure are close enough to those of a public debate. However, prior consultation differs from NCPD in the sense it does not oblige the contracting authority to publicly announce the consequences that the said authority reserves for its project. The prior consultation procedure does not operate under the control of the NCPD.

In fact, the French law is already rich with several mandatory or optional consultation procedures, which had initially been planned for urban planning and then extended to the environment.

---

[5] Decree of 9 February 2008, declaring of public utility the necessary works for the realization of the project of airport for the Great West–Notre-Dame-des-Landes and its road connection and carrying approval of the new provisions of the local plans of town planning of the municipalities of Fay-de-Bretagne, Grandchamp-des-Fontaines, Notre-Dame-des-Landes, Treillières, Vigneux-de-Bretagne in the department of Loire-Atlantique.

Thus, Article L.103-2 of the Town Planning Code aims at associating, on a mandatory basis, the persons concerned by a number of projects being developed (like PLU, the French Local Town Planning. Cf. Article L. 103-2 of the Environmental Code).

The newly created optional procedure can involve only a limited number of projects, which are particularly subject to environmental assessment and which do not always result in a referral to the NCPD, or which are not subject to the mandatory consultation procedure scheduled for urban planning.[6]

When the procedure is implemented at the request of the NCPD, it will be under the aegis of a 'guarantor', that is to say, a person responsible for ensuring the quality, sincerity and intelligibility of the information given to the public.

Beyond this last and undoubtedly the most interesting aspect, the reform multiplies the assumptions of consultation in a flood of laws and regulations with or without guarantee, with more or less information, mandatory or not.

In short, the procedure could benefit from being made mandatory, as in urban planning. On the contrary, what we are witnessing is a scattering of its terms and conditions, at the risk of damaging its readability.

---

[6] Article L. 121-15-1 of the Environmental Code states:

The prior consultation may concern:

1. The projects, plans and programs mentioned in Article L. 121-8 for which the National Commission for Public Debate has requested a prior consultation pursuant to Article L. 121-9;

2. The projects mentioned in Section II of Article L. 121-8 for which prior consultation is conducted by the developer under the same Section II;

3. Projects subject to an environmental assessment pursuant to Article L. 122-1 and not falling within the remit of the National Commission for Public Debate pursuant to Sections I and II of Article L. 121-8;

4. Plans and programmes subject to environmental assessment pursuant to Article L. 122-4 and not falling within the competence of the National Commission for Public Debate pursuant to Section IV of Article L. 121-8.

After the Decision-making Process

After the decision-making process, environmental democracy is mainly expressed through a public enquiry. This system dates back to the early nineteenth century. Designed to ensure the respect of the right of ownership during the expropriations carried out by the State, it has gradually changed to provide information to the public during the procedure. It is for this reason that it appears today in Article L. 123-1 of the Environmental Code. It states:

> The purpose of the public inquiry is to ensure the information and participation of the public as well as the taking into account of the interests of third parties when elaborating decisions likely to affect the environment which are mentioned in Article L. 123-2. Observations and proposals received during the investigation period shall be taken into consideration by the developer and the competent authority while taking the decision.

A public enquiry allows authorities, for a given period of time, and under the supervision of public investigators, to inform the public and gather their observations, so that the contracting authority can take them into consideration or even abandon the project.

It is the last moment in which environmental democracy can be expressed in the decision-making process. It can sometimes last several decades (as in the case of the high-speed *Lignes à grande vitesse* [LGV] rail projects). It precedes indeed the declaration of public utility of the project, which enables not only the expropriation of land and properties, but also the beginning of the works which will have an impact on the environment.

This procedure reveals few shortcomings in practice, if the contracting authority develops a sufficient portfolio of the project and draws the consequences of the public's comments and opinions and the recommendations of public investigators.

However, this does not deprive the procedure of the inconvenience of tardiness, since it comes at a stage where large sums of money have already been committed to studying the project and where, nevertheless, the lack of real utility of the project can still arise. Above all, the procedure may fail to mobilize citizen participation.

The 2016 reform rewrote many of the provisions of the public enquiry procedure, without, however, modifying the tested system. It has mainly sought to generalize dematerialization (digitization) to encourage public participation.

Thus, the reform provides access to a dematerialized version of the public enquiry file, while maintaining access to paper in one or more specific locations. It also allows the public to make observations over the internet, that is to say, without having to move. However, in the absence of the setting up of dematerialized discussion forums, public meetings can always be organized.

In general, despite their shortcomings, the proposed participatory processes undoubtedly encourage citizen participation and information. It is nonetheless necessary that such opportunities be offered to them.

This is not always the case, as we shall see in the second part of this article.

Citizens' Initiative Still Limited When Confronted with the Public Authorities

The review of the various procedures of environmental democracy indeed reveals, somewhat paradoxically, that the citizen does not really have the initiative and that the public authorities retain the control. Besides, it is only during the judicial trial that the citizen can find such a capacity, but in a limited way.

The Control of the Procedures Maintained by the Public Authorities

The control of the procedures by the public authorities is evident in each of the participatory procedures encountered.

Thus, if we take again into consideration the public debate procedures, the NCPD must be referred to by the manager of the development project or programme, when such projects or programmes meet some specific criteria or exceed some thresholds (Article L. 128-1 of the Environmental Code). When the referral is thus mandatory, the question of its author does not *a priori* raise any reservations. It is in complete independence that the NCPD may, if necessary, decide not to organize a public debate.

On the other hand, when referral to the NCPD is only optional, practice reveals that it is far from systematic. The public authority, in the person of the contracting authority or the responsible public institution, retains a real power of initiative.

The texts traditionally provide that the NCPD can also be seized by 10 MPs, or a local authority, an inter-municipality or an approved association for the protection of the environment (Article L. 128-1 of the Environmental Code). Nevertheless, this amounts to depriving the citizens of any initiative, and entrusting the exercise of their right to participation to intermediaries.

The 2016 reform has tried to overcome this problem by creating a genuine citizens' initiative procedure.

From now on, NCPD's referral to a project is open to 10,000 EU citizens residing in France. This referral is made on the basis of a petition written in French and presented in the same terms to all signatories (Article R. 121-28, Paragraph 1 of the Environmental Code).

And when the government wants to reform a public policy having a significant effect on the environment or regional planning, the NCPD can once again be seized, by 60 MPs or 60 senators and apart from them, by 500,000 EU citizens of legal age residing in France (Article L. 121-10 of the Environmental Code).

The future alone can tell us if this popular initiative can remedy the absence of mandatory or systematic referral to the NCPD. For the moment, however, this is the only initiative procedure that is in the hands of citizens, who can independently express the will of participation through public debate.

The consultation procedure comes across, as regards its implementation, similar obstacles.

If, in addition to the initiative left to the contracting authority, the responsible public authority, the authorized communities and associations, the law also provides for a citizen's right of initiative, the mobilization thresholds retained are too high to seriously consider the implementation of this right (National Council for Ecological Transition, Recommendation, 16 February 2016).

Indeed

A number of EU citizens residing within the perimeter of the declaration of intent, equal to 20% of the population counted in the communes of the same perimeter, or to 10% of the population counted in the department or departments, in the region or regions where all or part of the territory mentioned in the declaration of intent is located

are required to fulfil the legal conditions for the procedure to launched (Article L. 121-19 of the Environmental Code).

Moreover, if it materializes, this mobilization will be used only to be able to ask the prefect to organize a preliminary consultation. However, this representative of the State, after consulting the contracting authority, does not have the obligation to give a favourable reply.

Thus, the assessment of the appropriateness of participation does not belong to the citizens, although any decision to refuse on the part of the prefect must be substantiated. It would probably have been better for such power to return to the NCPD, which is independent of the State.

Finally, regarding the public enquiry procedure, it is hardly necessary to recall that, even when mandatory, it is implemented by the State representative.

Above all, the contracting authority can decide at any time to interrupt it, that is to say, even before the public enquiry, or before the public utility of the project (amended thanks to the observations of the public) is declared by a decision of the public authority. Thus, notwithstanding the cost of such a procedure, a project finding favour in the eyes of citizens can finally be abandoned.

Finally, the public authorities keep here and there, the stranglehold on all these procedures, notwithstanding the will of citizen participation. Undoubtedly, environmental democracy could benefit from strengthening the role of the NCPD, which could replace the public authorities, in all cases where it does not have to decide on the project's merits, but only to draw the consequences of the citizens' desire for more significant information and participation (Mozol 2017, 2123).[7]

THE LIMITS OF THE ENVIRONMENTAL LAWSUIT

Unsatisfied with the existing procedures, citizens today tend to seek information and participation by taking legal action.

Although it is not useful to consider the recent mock trials in some high-profile cases, like the Monsanto case,[8] which are organized in disregard to the fundamental rules of the trial, it is clear that trial at court is becoming more important and turning out to be the place where environmental causes can be heard, even the way to influence the direction of public decisions.

However, this form of expression of citizen participation is encountering some limitations (Hautereau-Boutonnet and Truilhé-Marengo 2017, 827).

---

[7] This idea has been further reinforced with regard to the new local consultation procedure created by Ordinance No. 2016-488 of 21 April 2016 on local consultation on projects likely to have an impact on the environment, Official Journal of the French Republic of 22 April 2016. Thus, according to the new Article L. 123-20 of the Environmental Code, it is provided that

> The State may consult the voters of a specific territorial area in order to obtain their opinion on an infrastructure or equipment project likely to have an impact on the environment, the realization of which is subject to the issue of an authorization falling within its competence, including the case where a declaration of public utility has been made.

Here again, the initiative belongs totally to the State, and the procedure appears more like a procedure of legitimation than like an enrichment of the project submitted for consultation.

[8] https://fr.monsantotribunal.org/

In order to be able to seize the judge, the applicant must obviously assert a sufficiently direct and personal interest or an injured right, behind which may appear the environmental interest.

Above all, depending on the procedures and jurisdictions, the trial is not always the best instrument to apprehend the scientific and technical data relating to the environment.

First, the burden of proof generally falls on the claimant, even though, in the administrative process, the public authority will often have to justify its decisions. Besides, if the mechanism of presumptions can exist when scientific or technical evidence is difficult to report, it is preferable to benefit from an inquisitorial procedure where the judge will conduct the instruction and order the parties to produce the elements necessary for the establishment of truth rather than an adversarial procedure where these tasks fall to the parties.

Then, expertise appears as a key element for the manifestation of truth. Without being a guarantee for the parties, it can be an adequate response to scientific uncertainty. It is, however, necessary to ensure the quality of the experts and the cost of such expertise that the parties will then have to bear.

Finally, the ultimate limit is the effectiveness of the court decision. Even on the basis of expertise, the judge may have some doubts about the right decision to make. For example, what measure should be ordered, from a scientific and financial point of view, to restore nature? France is already familiar with procedural agreements (mediation and conciliation in particular), and the contractualization of legal proceedings could then emerge as an effective way to address these difficulties inherent to the environmental field.

Anyhow, subject to these limitations, the trial is gradually becoming an instrument of expression of the participation of citizens because the initiative belongs to them.

Perhaps then we should think about creating a specialized jurisdiction, or better yet, an Independent Administrative Authority with environmental mediation and decision-making powers.

In conclusion, environmental democracy still has some distance to travel to be fully effective, even in France, where an important place has already been carved out. The inadequacies found in the existing procedures, such as the control of the initiative kept by the public authorities, call into question the political will in this area.

What to ask finally if, today, as yesterday, the rulers do not intend to keep the first and the last word in terms of environmental democracy?

Translated from French by Geetha Ganapathy-Doré

REFERENCES

Conseil d'état, Rapport public. 2001. *Les autorités administratives indépendantes*. Paris: La Documentation française (Independent Administrative Authorities, State Council's 2001 report, La Documentation française, 2001, 257).

Hautereau-Boutonnet, M., and E. Truilhé-Marengo. 2017. 'Quel modèle pour le procès environnemental?' (What model for environmental lawsuits?) *D.*, 827.

Hélin, V. J.-C. 2016. 'Le projet d'ordonnance relative au dialogue environnemental. Bien visé, mal tiré?' (The draft environmental dialogue order. Well aimed, but badly shot?) *Énergie-Environnement-Infrastructures*, Alert 261.

Jamay, F. 2016. 'L'ordonnance du 3 août 2016, un dialogue environnemental encore bien timide'. (The Order of 3rd August 2016, an environmental dialogue that is still timid) *Énergie-Environnement-Infrastructures*, Commentary 82.

Loi n° 95-101 du 2 février 1995, *relative au renforcement de la protection de l'environnement. Act no. 95–101 of 2 February 1995 on the reinforcement of environmental protection. JORF (Journal Officiel de la République Française)*. 1995, 3 February. 29, 1840.

Loi constitutionnelle n° 2005-205 du 1ᵉʳ mars 2005 *relative à la Charte de l'environnement. Constitutional Law No 2005-205 of* 1 March 2005 on the *Charter for the* Environment. 2005, 2 March. 51, 3697.

Ordonnance du 3 août 2016 *portant réforme des procédures destinées à assurer l'information et la participation du public à l'élaboration de certaines décisions susceptibles d'avoir une incidence sur l'environnement*. Order of 3rd August 2016 reforming the procedures intended to ensure information and public participation in the development of certain decisions that may have an impact on the environment. 2016, 5 August. 181.

Loi n° 2017-55 du 20 janvier 2017, *portant statut général des autorités administratives indépendantes et des autorités publiques indépendants*. Act no. 2017-55 of 20 January 2017, establishing the general statute of independent administrative authorities and independent public authorities. (2017a, 21 January. 18.

Décret n° 2017-626 du 25 avril 2017 *relatif aux procédures destinées à assurer l'information et la participation du public à l'élaboration de certaines décisions susceptibles d'avoir une incidence sur l'environnement et modifiant diverses dispositions relatives à l'évaluation environnementale de certains projets, plans et programmes.* Act no. 2017-626 of 25 April 2017 concerning the procedures intended to ensure information and public participation in the preparation of certain decisions that are likely to have an impact on the environment and modifying various provisions relating to the environmental impact assessment of certain projects, plans and programmes. 2017b, 25 April). 99.

Loi n° 2018-148 du 2 mars 2018, *ratifiant les ordonnances n° 2016-1058 du 3 août 2016 relative à la modification des règles applicables à l'évaluation environnementale des projets, plans et programmes et n° 2016-1060 du 3 août 2016 portant réforme des procédures destinées à assurer l'information et la participation du public à l'élaboration de certaines décisions susceptibles d'avoir une incidence sur l'environnement.* Act no. 2018-148 of 2nd March 2018, ratifying order no. 2016-1058 of 3rd August 2016 concerning the modification of the rules applicable to the environmental impact assessment of projects, plans and programmes and order no. 2016-1060 of 3rd August 2016 reforming procedures intended to ensure public information and participation in the development of certain decisions that are likely to have an impact on the environment. 2018, 3 March. 52.

Mozol, P. 2017, 2 May. 'La procédure de consultation locale issue de l'ordonnance du 21 avril 2016, un outil de rénovation du dialogue environnemental?' (The local consultation procedure resulting from the order of 21st April 2016, a tool for renovating environmental dialogue?) *JCP éd. A.*, 2123.

———. 2018, 26 March. 'Quelles modalités d'information et de participation du public pour les projets et les décisions ayant une incidence sur l'environnement? 'A propos du décret no. 2017–626 du 25 avril 2017 (What information and public participation methods for projects and decisions having an impact on the environment? 'About decree no. 2017-626 of 25th April 2017). *JCP éd. A.*, 2092.

Naim-Gesbert, E. 2011. *Droit général de l'environnement*. (General Environmental Law) Paris: Lexisnexis.

National Council for Ecological Transition, Recommendation, 16 February 2016. (https://www.ecologique-solidaire.gouv.fr/sites/default/files/CNTE%20-%20 Avis%202016.pdf)

NCPD 2012, self-publishing, 106 (https://www.debatpublic.fr/sites/cndp.portail/ files/documents/pratique-du-debat-public_2002-2012.pdf

Sauvé, J. M. 2010, 17 November. 'La démocratie environnementale aujourd'hui – (Environmental Democracy Today. Inaugural Lecture.) Conférence inaugurale'. Available at: https://www.conseil-etat.fr/actualites/ discours-et-interventions/la-democratie-environnementale-aujourd-hui

Zarka, J. C. 2016, 17 October. 'La réforme du dialogue environnemental' (The Reform of Environmental Dialogue). *JCP éd. A.*, 2271.

Chapter 9

The Cyberspace as a Distinct Domain of the Global Commons
An Analysis of Cyberspace Governance

Binu Joseph and
Mohanan Bhaskaran Pillai

INTRODUCTION

The existence of diverse natural resources is vital for the subsistence of plants and species on the planet. These resources are now becoming scarce and vulnerable. Now, an alarming situation has arisen in the world, as reported by many scientific studies, which reveal that common global resources are deteriorating at a fast rate. The degeneration of global resources is occurring because they are being excessively used and their habitat illegitimately occupied. Recent political debate in the world has tended towards addressing questions about the management of the common resources of the world. The commons are an area where limited resources are collectively shared by multiple groups (Soroos 1995, 2). The debate over the term 'global commons' emerged in the arena of global political debate during the post-Second World War era. Some global ecological regions were not part of the territorial jurisdiction of any nation-state or occupied/controlled by any state or community, and such regions became the 'global commons'. Mainly, there are four categories of the global commons, namely, Antarctica, the atmosphere, the high seas and space. Nowadays, cyberspace is also discussed under the category of 'global commons' (World Conservation Strategy 1980, Chapter 18), owing to its independent role and existence beyond the nation-state boundaries. However, of late, political claims are being made in some quarters for specific nation-state based laws to govern cyberspace.

THE SPECIALITY OF THE GLOBAL COMMONS

'Global commons' is a term that denotes the collection of many specific ecological regions beyond the sovereignty and jurisdiction of the states. These regions are usually very vulnerable and require special attention to their conservation. The positions of these areas usually make it difficult for human beings to explore and access them, which means that, for centuries, these areas had remained wholly outside the jurisdiction of the states (Salmon and Imber 1998). There are concrete definitions, which clarify the concept of global commons. For instance, the Organisation for Economic Co-operation and Development (OECD) defined global commons as 'natural assets outside national jurisdiction such as the oceans, outer space and the Antarctic' (United Nations 1997, 37). The existing definitions of global commons imply that these are 'territories which no person or state may own or control and which are central to life' (NATO Unclassified 2010).

The United Nations Convention on the Law of the Sea (1982, Part XI, Section 2, Articles 136–143) has defined the Common Heritage of Mankind Area and the global commons by applying five principles:

- The area under the ownership of no one
- Everyone controls its management
- Economic benefits shared by everyone
- Should be used only for peaceful activities
- Scientific research in these areas should be readily available to interested parties (Clancy 1998, 605–606).

The sovereignty over global commons is globally shared; hence, neither individuals nor countries can stay away from their responsibility to protect and conserve these spaces. However, it is not easy to compare global commons to one another because they carry different kinds of resources; and the responsible authorities have defined that their uses have effectively developed over different periods (Buck 2013, 11). As a result of the progression and transformation in the world, these domains have become accessible to the states for establishing their sovereignty over them. However, the legitimacy of such sovereignty has become limited because of the establishment of international institutions and the signing of international treaties. Because of such agreements and treaties, these regions have fallen under the jurisdiction of various specific international laws and have become a collective and shared responsibility of all the states.

At the global level, every nation ought to conserve these common areas. For conserving common resources, stakeholders like nation states and international institutions have formulated various plans and strategies. For instance, the United Nations and other related agencies have been playing a prominent role in the conception of the legal framework for the conservation of global commons.

The following are the significant treaties, which have been signed at the global level to protect the global commons:

Areas	Principles	Norms	Rules/procedures
Sea	The high seas should be open to all states, although states have interests beyond territorial waters.	The extension of the sovereignty of coastal states beyond its land territory and internal water; archipelagic states, its archipelagic waters and territorial sea.	• The Convention on the Law of the Sea, 1982. • International Tribunal for the Law of the Sea (ITLOS). Founded in 1996, Administrative Centre, Hamburg.

Areas	Principles	Norms	Rules/procedures
Air	The states have sovereignty over their air.	Air space should be open to all the states.	• Chicago convention—1947. • International Civil Aviation Organisation (ICAO) formulation—1944. Headquarters—Montreal.
Outer Space	Outer space belongs to all humankind.	Outer space, including the moon or any other celestial bodies, is equally sovereign to all nation-states. No states have complete sovereignty on outer space.	• The Outer Space Treaty—1967. • The United Nations Committee on the Peaceful Uses of Outer Spaces (COPUOS)—1959.
Antarctica	Antarctica region shall be used only for peaceful purposes.	To prohibit military activities in Antarctica and to scientifically preserve the territory as well as to ensure freedom to conduct a scientific investigation in the territory.	Antarctica Treaty System, signed in 1959, effective since 1961.

Source: Franzese (2014, 15).

The different treaties mentioned above specify that the signatories have negotiated the utilization of shared resources for the benefits of all. Such global level negotiations have resulted in the reduction of exploitation of natural resources and the recognition of these resources as common to all. The signatories agreed that the collective resources are not to be appropriated or managed against the interests of any nation.

CYBERSPACE AS A NEW GLOBAL DOMAIN

Apart from the four domains mentioned above, nowadays, cyberspace has made an entry into the discourse on global commons. Cyberspace is also known as the 'digital ecosystem' (Vogler 2012). The main difference of cyberspace, when compared to the other existing global commons, is that it is not a physical entity but a virtual entity. In 1984, a novelist, William Gibson coined the term 'cyberspace' and later it came into the usage of daily language (Cerf 2011). When cyberspace is considered as part of globally shared sovereignty, no state has complete sovereignty over cyberspace governance.

In 2005, the Strategy for Homeland Defence and Civil Support of the United States held that 'the global commons consist of international waters and airspace, space and cyberspace' (Joint Chiefs of Staff 2005). The DoD (Department of Defence) of the United States and NATO (North Atlantic Treaty Organization) equated cyberspace with a 'domain', similar to air, land and sea (Crowther 2017, 63). The United States Department of Defence defines cyberspace as 'a global domain within the information environment consisting of the interdependent network of information technology infrastructures, including the Internet, telecommunication network, computer systems and embedded processors and controllers' (Joint Chief of Staff 2018, 56). Even while we consider cyberspace as a category within global commons that shares many similarities with its other entities, it is also quite different from the others. Neither a sovereign state nor any single entity can own or control cyberspace, and it is open and accessible to all those who have requisite technological capabilities (NATO/OTAN 2011). The other global commons naturally exist and can be sustained without human action. However, in the case of cyberspace, it is fully human-made machinery. Hence the use, regulation, supervision and domination of this space are entirely vested in the hands of human beings.

In a broader view, cyberspace consists of two dimensions, namely, social and physical. Social space occurs thanks to the communication between users through enabled codes. The physical space infrastructure facilitates digital activity (Cavelty 2015). In the 1990s, the world's views regarding cyberspace domain have evolved as a result of the libertarian system. Although cyberspace is not a 'natural' phenomenon: social, political, and historical entities exert considerable influence on it (Guarino and Iasiello 2017, 4).

CYBER SPACE GOVERNANCE

Governance is a matter of controlling or regulating through legitimate means. However, many practical difficulties arise in governing global resources when compared to governing national resources. At the global level, the majority of the nations in the world are signatories to specific international covenants, treaties and laws among which some are legally binding, and some are not. Sometimes countries voluntarily follow the set of specific mandatory international rules. Apart from existing as legal entities, they are often considered as guidelines for countries to follow in managing global affairs. However, international institutional mechanisms are seldom capable of effective execution of laws.

The debate on cyber governance has bifurcated into several distinct views. On the one hand, it is viewed as an entity where information should flow freely, beyond the constraints of ordinary law, breaking the barriers of physical distance and geo-political boundaries. On the other hand, it has been argued that nation states should have the sovereign authority to impose restrictions and legislations to secure themselves from the threats emanating through online activities (Guarino and Iasiello 2017, 6). The argument of cyber sovereignty actively opposes any form of regulation imposed by the states.

However, in the 1990s, several arguments had emerged, highlighting the need to regulate the domain of cyberspace. Later, discussions surrounding cyberspace led to the formulation of two models of governance, namely, the creation of an international regime along the lines of the International Telecommunication Union (ITU), and a system of multi-stakeholder governance, similar to the European Union. Some points of view have also stressed on the need to go beyond national and international institutional mechanisms. Apart from these arguments, there is also a view that supports the inclusion of civil society institutions in the management of cyberspace as they are the active and significant participants in the cyber domain.

The various summits held on cyberspace governance are as follows:

Year	Organization/Summit	Major Highlights
2011	• Shanghai Cooperative Organization, held in Astana, Kazakhstan • In London, Global Conference on Cyberspace (GCCS)	• Put forward the International Code of Conduct for information security. • In the GCCS, presented the concept for the Convention on International Security, a high-level ministerial platform to discuss the key themes of cyberspace.
2012	• Budapest Conference	• Discussion on cybersecurity and norms of behaviour.
2013	• Seoul Conference on Cyberspace	• Developed a Framework for Commitment to Open and Secure Cyberspace.
2015	• Shanghai Cooperative Organization held in Ufa, Russia • Report of the UN Group of Governmental Experts (GGE) • Global Conference on Cyberspace (GCCS) in Hague • BRICS Summit, in Ufa	• The second version of the Code of Conduct signed. • References regarding novel cyber 'norms of behaviour' for the international community (CCDCOE). • Established, a multi-stakeholder forum and developed a Global Forum on Cyber Expertise. • Organized a Group of Experts of the BRICS countries on security, and for working out Rules of Global Cyberspace Governance.
2016	• NATO Summit in Warsaw	• Recognized cyberspace as a domain of operations and pledged to further develop NATO–EU cyber defence cooperation.

Year	Organization/Summit	Major Highlights
2017	• Global Conference on Cyber Space, New Delhi	• Aimed at an inclusive, sustainable, developmental, safe and secure cyberspace.
2018	• G7 Charlesvoix • UN • Cybersecurity Leadership Summit in Berlin • Global Commission on the Stability of Cyberspace • Paris Call for Trust and Democracy	• Made a commitment on defending democracy. • Set up a high-level panel on digital cooperation. • Discussed the digital transformation of companies. • Released the Singapore Norms package. • Made commitments to prevent malicious cyber activities and strengthen digital products, processes and services.
2019	• EU Cyber Summit, Dublin • Internet Governance Forum, Berlin	• Focused on the executive challenge in dealing with cyber risk. • Empowered young ambassadors.

Source: Kulikova (n.d., 84) and the internet (https://securityconference.org/en/news/full/msc-hosting-cyber-security-summit-2019-in-berlin/).

NATIONAL-LEVEL ATTEMPTS TO GOVERN CYBERSPACE

One of the prime security concerns of the nations in the contemporary global system is the threat emanating from the cyber domain. Every country is becoming increasingly vigilant in managing its digital and technological apparatus from global cyberthreats and cyberattacks. Such global cyber menace can endanger the entire functioning of a nation. The countries are tackling such imminent cybersecurity challenges mainly through the adoption of legislative and administrative measures. National-level governance mechanisms can bring cyberspace under the specific limitations of the states.

The specific laws and Acts that have been passed by major nations to manage cyberspace are given as follows:

China	• 2010: White paper released titled as 'The Internet in China'—an explicit mention of internet sovereignty over cyberspace • 2015: National Security Law—highlights security concerns beyond its territorial jurisdiction which covers outer space, polar beds and cyberspace • 2015: Anti-terror Law—legitimate power and authority to access encrypted data • 2016: Cybersecurity Law—on the Internet and information system • 2016: Overseas of the Non-Government Organisations and Management Law—to control the activities of the NGOs
Russia	• 1995: SORM-1 (System for Operative Investigative Activities)—a surveillance over mobile and landline to record calls • 1998: SORM-2—surveillance over the Internet traffic • 2014: SORM-3—overall surveillance media including Wi-Fi and social networks
USA	• 1999: Gramm–Leach–Bliley Act—financial institutions needed to describe how they manage and share their customers' private information • 2002: Federal Information Security Management Act (FISM)—to secure government operations, assets and information from any natural and human-made menaces • 2014: Cyber Security Information Sharing Act (CSIS)—law emphasizes on the Internet traffic information which has to be shared the US government and technology and manufacturing companies • 2014: Cyber Security Enhancement Act—it is a public–private partnership to support cybersecurity research and development, public awareness, preparedness and workforce development as well as to develop cybersecurity • 2015: Federal Exchange Data Breach Notification Act—'to notify individuals in the case that personal information of such individuals is known to have been acquired or accessed as a result of a breach of the security of any system maintained by the Exchange, and for other purposes'. (Congress.Gov)

	• 2015: National Cyber Security Protection Advancement Act—'it amends the Homeland Security Act of 2002 to allow the Department of Homeland Security's (DHS's) national cybersecurity and communications integration centre (NCCIC) to include tribal governments, information sharing and analysis centres, and private entities among its non-federal representatives'. (Congress.Gov)
India	• 2000: Information Technology Act—to deal with electronic commerce and cybercrime • 2004: Cyber Emergency Response Team (CERT)—a nodal agency to take on cybersecurity threats • 2004: National Technical Research Organization (NTRO)—a technical intelligence agency to develop offensive capability and has the responsibility to protect critical infrastructure institutions • 2008: Information Technology Act amended—including digital signatures, electronic transactions, cybersecurity and data protection • 2013: National Cyber Security Policy—it aims to create a secure cyberspace ecosystem and resilient cyberspace for business, government and citizens and also to protect public and private infrastructure • 2017: National Cyber Coordination Centre—it is an agency on e-surveillance and cybersecurity and functions as a coordinating agency for intelligence gathering activities and screening of communication metadata
France	• 1978: Law on Information and Liberty; protects citizens against cyber criminality • 2009: Creation of ANSSI, National Agency for the Security of Information Systems • 2014: Law against cyber harassment • 2015: Internet surveillance • 2019: PPC, Permanent posture of Cyber defence set-up • 2019: Draft bill against cyber hatred

The following are multiple technical techniques applied to manage cyberspace:

- Encryption: It is a method, which applies to data security. Data can be stored in a secret file. To encrypt data, there are specific technical tools that are applied. The first one is steganography, which is used

to hide a file in an innocent-looking manner. The second one is compression, which is used to keep information safely by reducing the size of files. The third one, chunking, is used to separate data into smaller parts. The last one is obfuscation, which is used to alter the character of the hex code to avoid data detection.
- Onion Routing (Tor): It is a useful tool to overcome the censorship and restrictions imposed by any controller. Tor functions by generating many anonymous connections using different routers.
- Plugging Transport: It is a tool to disguise Tor traffic, and it can transfer similar traffic from other standard services such as Skype or HTTPS. It can effectively pretend as 'good traffic'.
- Virtual Private Networks (VPNs) and Proxies: Any computer connected to VPNs can automatically prevent access to traffic. VPNs and proxies are used as a shield to encrypt all functions to and from a computer. Proxies are used as a mediator between client and server, removing direct communication between two parties.

The above-mentioned technological apparatuses are crucial elements in managing the security system and classified documents. Because of the advancement of science and technology, many nations are adopting innovative tools to safeguard their resources. Nations have been using safeguarding measures mainly to prevent the intrusion of others in their digital spaces. Upon examining the functions of these technological apparatuses, one can find that nations have been managing cyberspace by employing digital tools.

THE UNITED NATIONS ON CYBERSPACE GOVERNANCE

At the global level, the UN is the globally recognized institution for preserving the pacific order in the world. Currently, the world is facing severe security challenges from both physical and virtual realms. The UN is considered as one of the most responsible institutions in the world to ensure a secure world order. Nevertheless, there is an absence of a specific universal mechanism for cybersecurity. In 2004, the UN constituted a Group of Government Experts (GGE) in the field of information security. The prominent function of the GGE was to 'examine the existing and potential threats from cybersphere and possible cooperative measures to address them' (ORF 2014). The two significant successes of the UNGGE were the development of a framework on cybersecurity and the framing of international law on digital space (Digital Watch Observatory n.d.). There have been three GGEs functioning since its constitution, and its functions are very significant.

The report of the UNGGE 2013, submitted to the UN Secretary-General, stated that principles, which are part of international laws such as the UN Charter and the International Humanitarian Law, should apply to cyberspace too. It stressed the significance of Confidence Building Mechanisms (CBMs) to build trust among the nations, as well as to develop the capability for enhanced cooperation and effectiveness at the technical level (Kulikova n.d., 83).

The latest report of the UNGGE describes the three initial norms of a responsible state behaviour in cyberspace (Kulikova n.d., 86).

- The states should not conduct or wilfully promote any activities which are antithetical to the obligations under the international law and which purposely damage information and communication technologies (ICTs).
- The states should not conduct or wilfully promote any activities detrimental to the Counter Emergency Response Team (CERT) of another state.
- The states should not knowingly allow their territory for internationally harmful activities by using ICTs.

Moreover, the report also underlined that the confidence-building mechanisms and capacity-building objectives are necessary elements in the states' endeavours to establish long-term cyber stability architectures and to raise the global level of protection to cyberthreats (Kulikova n.d., 86).

The initiatives of the UN at the global level are explicitly related to ensuring a secure cyber environment for all the nations. Technologically, underdeveloped nations are highly vulnerable to cyberattacks; hence, the need for a secure and independent cyber environment is also a global demand.

CYBERSPACE AS A NEW GLOBAL COMMON

After analysing the multiple views on cyberspace, we have found that all are supportive of considering cyberspace as a new entity in the list of global commons. It shares many characteristics with other common pool resources. The existence of shared resources is indispensable for lives on the planet. Cyberspace is a common platform for users. The users are enjoying their freedom in storing and sharing of information. On a digital platform, data can be encrypted and decrypted according to the discretion of its users. Cyberspace is a unique field wherein unimpeded movement of information should occur. Being a virtual entity, cyberspace holds unusual independence and sovereignty compared to other collective physical entities. Cyberspace is connected with codes and wires, and to access it requires adequate technological expertise. However, in the present global scenario, those capabilities are vested only in the hands of some technologically advanced nations. Hence, such technologically advanced nations can easily access cyberspace and regulate its usage. Usually, this technological domination will restrict the access of other less technologically advanced nations. It will gradually move towards the establishment of supremacy over technologically undeveloped nations. Thus a mechanism has to be devised so that every entity has equitable sovereignty over it.

CONCLUSION

It is necessary to protect the free flow of information to all. Conservation of common pool resources is a shared responsibility of all stakeholders. Several arguments continue to emerge regarding the international governance of cyberspace as a common pool resource. Nation states are highly concerned about the security threats that arise from cyberspace, although it is the responsibility of states to protect the right to information and transparency in communication. The national-level cyberspace-governing mechanisms intend to bring their digital systems within the security structures. That might prompt the countries to proscribe independent access to information systems. Apart from this, at the global level, there is a rise of monopoly over the administration of cyberspace, especially from the technologically progressed nations. Cyberspace refers to a borderless digital environment, but physical infrastructures manage data and information mainly under the ownership of the private sector (Liaropoulos 2017, 28). The governability of cyberspace is increasingly a challenging one because of it being mostly under the dominance of the technologically innovative parties. However, specific international systems have been installed for conserving and protecting global collective entities by framing laws and signing treaties at the international level. When it comes to cyberspace, the international governing institutional mechanism is conspicuous by its absence. Each country is trying to occupy cyberspace as a private property. It is high time nations join hands for framing a viable cyber governance system at the global level to ensure seamless access to all the stakeholders to the digital space with a view to curtailing the domination of any single party over cyberspace.

REFERENCES

Bradshaw, S., L. DeNardis, F. O. Hampson, E. Jardine, and R. Mark. 2015, 21 July. 'The Emergence of Contention in Global Internet Governance'. Global Commission on Internet Governance Paper 17. Centre for International Governance Innovation. Available at: https://www.cigionline.org/publications/emergence-contention-global-internet-governance (accessed on 22 April 2020).

Buck, S. J. 2013. *The Global Commons, An Introduction*. Oxon: Earthscan.

Cavelty, M. D. 2015. 'Die materiellen Ursachen des Cyberkriegs: Cybersicherheitspolitik jenseits diskursiver Erklärungen' (The material causes of cyber war: Cyber security policy beyond discursive explanations, Journal of self-regulation and regulation). *Journal of Self-regulation and Regulation* 1: 167–184. Available at: https://www.academia.edu/16562343/Die_materiellen_Ursachen_des_Cyberkriegs_Cybersicherheitspolitik_jenseits_diskursiver_Erkl%C3%A4rungen_Journal_of_self-regulation_and_regulation_1_1_2015_pp._167–184 (accessed on 05 March 2020).

Clancy, E. A. 1998. 'The Tragedy of the Global Commons'. *Indiana Journal of Global Legal Studies* 5 (2): 601–619. Available at: https://www.jstor.org/stable/25691122?seq=1#metadata_info_tab_contents (accessed on 05 March 2020).

Congress.Gov. n.d.a 'H.R.555 - Federal Exchange Data Breach Notification Act of 2015'. Available at: https://www.congress.gov/bill/114th-congress/house-bill/555/titles (accessed on 22 April 2020).

———. n.d.b 'H.R.1731 - National Cybersecurity Protection Advancement Act of 2015'. Available at: https://www.congress.gov/bill/114th-congress/house-bill/1731 (accessed on 22 April 2020).

Crowther, G. A. 2017. 'The Cyber Domain'. *The Cyber Defense Review* 2 (3): 63–78. Available at: https://www.jstor.org/stable/26267386 (accessed on 5 March 2020).

Digital Watch Observatory. n.d. 'UN GGE and OEWG'. Available at: https://dig.watch/processes/un-gge (accessed on 5 March 2020).

Franzese, P. W. 2014, June. 'Sovereignty in Cyberspace, Can It Exist?'. *Air Force Law Review* 64: 1–42. Available at: https://www.law.upenn.edu/live/files/3473-franzese-p-sovereignty-in-cyberspace-can-it-exist (accessed on 5 March 2020).

Guarino, A., and E. Iasiello. 2017, 1 June. 'Imposing and Evading Cyber Borders: The Sovereignty Dilemma'. Tel Aviv: The Institute of National Security Studies. Available at: http://www.inss.org.il/publication/imposing-evading-cyber-borders-sovereignty-dilemma/ (accessed on 5 March 2020).

Joint Chiefs of Staff. 2005. 'Department of Defense Homeland Defense and Civil Support Joint Operating Concept'. Available at: http://www.jcs.mil/Portals/36/Documents/Doctrine/concepts/joc_hld.pdf?ver=2017-12-28-162017-823 (accessed on 5 March 2020).

———. 2018. 'DOD Dictionary of Military and Associated Terms'. Available at: http://www.jcs.mil/Portals/36/Documents/Doctrine/pubs/dictionary.pdf (accessed on 5 March 2020).

Kulikova, A. n.d. 'Working Out the Rules of Global Cyberspace Governance'. Available at: https://www.academia.edu/28553442/Working_out_the_Rules_of_Global_Cyberspace_Governance (accessed on 5 March 2020).

Liaropoulos, A. 2017. 'Cyberspace Governance and State Sovereignty'. In *Democracy and an Open-Economy World Order* edited by G. C. Bitros and N.C. Kyriazis, 25–36. Cham: Springer International Publishing. Available at: https://www.researchgate.net/publication/316040640_Cyberspace_Governance_and_State_SovereigntyU (accessed on 5 March 2020).

NATO/OTAN. 2011. 'Assured Access to the Global Commons, Findings and Recommendations'. Available at: http://www.act.nato.int/images/stories/events/2010/gc/aagc_recommendations.pdf (accessed on 5 March 2020).

NATO Unclassified. 2010. 'NATO and the Cyber Domain of the Global Commons'. Available at: https://www.act.nato.int/images/stories/events/2010/gc/cyberspace_frame_of_ref.pdf (accessed on 5 March 2020).

ORF (Observer Research Foundation). 2014, 1 February. 'The UN and Cyberspace Governance'. Available at: https://www.orfonline.org/article/the-un-and-cyberspace-governance/ (accessed on 05 March 2020).

Salmon, T. C., and M. F. Imber. 1998. *Issues in International Relations*. Oxon: Routledge.

Soroos, M. S. 1995. 'Managing the Atmosphere as a Global Commons'. Paper prepared for the Fifth Annual Common Property Conference of the International Association for the Study of Common Property, Bodø, Norway, 24–28 May. Bloomington, IN: Indiana University. Available at: http://dlc.dlib.indiana.edu/dlc/bitstream/handle/10535/1622/Managing_the_Atmosphere_as_a_Global_Commons.pdf?sequence=1U (accessed on 5 March 2020).

———. 1997. *Glossary of Environment Statistics*. 1997. New York: UN. Available at: https://unstats.un.org/unsd/publication/SeriesF/SeriesF_67E.pdf (accessed on 5 March 2020).

United Nations Convention on the Law of the Sea. 1982. 'Section 2: Principles Governing the Area'. Available at: https://www.un.org/Depts/los/convention_agreements/texts/unclos/part11-2.htm (accessed on 23 April 2020).

Vogler, J. 2012, 27 January. 'Global Commons Revisited'. Wiley Online Library. Available at: https://onlinelibrary.wiley.com/doi/full/10.1111/j.1758-5899.2011.00156.x (accessed on 5 March 2020).

World Conservation Strategy. 1980. 'Living Resource Conservation for Sustainable Development'. IUCN, UNEP, WWL. Available at: https://portals.iucn.org/library/sites/library/files/documents/WCS-004.pdf (accessed on 5 March 2020).

PART III

Environmental Hazards

Chapter 10

The Massive Problem of Microplastics in the Global Commons
An Overview

Kaushik Dowarah and
Suja P. Devipriya

INTRODUCTION

Today we cannot imagine a world without plastics. Due to its various properties, plastics dominate every sphere of human lives. Although the first synthetic plastic like Bakelite was invented in the early 20th century, its use was limited largely to the military up to World War II. Large-scale production began only in the 1950s (Geyer, Jambeck, and Law 2017). Plastic is inexpensive, lightweight, strong, durable, corrosion-resistant and have high thermal and electrical insulation properties. These factors enabled a wide range of applications and benefits, which ranged from medical use, technological advances, energy savings and numerous other social benefits. Naturally, this created a lot of enthusiasm in the early days of its mass production. But in those early days, the problems pertaining to waste management and debris could not be anticipated (Thompson et al. 2009).

Plastic began to be reported as a potential contaminant in the 1970s. Besides, there was no direct research in the field until the 1990s (Horton et al. 2016).

The quantum of plastic waste generated between the 1950s and the 1970s was relatively small, and therefore manageable. However, this waste more than tripled in two decades between the 1970s and the 1990s. Plastic waste produced in the first decade of the 2000s exceeded what was produced in the previous 40 years. Today we generate plastic waste of 300 million tonnes every year. Incidentally, 300 million tonnes is approximately the weight of the entire human population. More than 8.3 billion tonnes of plastic have been produced since the 1950s, about 60 per cent of which had ended up in the natural environment as waste and pollutants. An estimated 8 million tonnes of plastic end up in the oceans every year (UNEP 2018).

After production, plastic do not degrade naturally in the environment. Plastic that is now labelled 'biodegradable' will degrade only if subjected to a prolonged temperature of 50°C. Hence it is not sufficient as a solution for plastic waste management (Su et al. 2016). Plastic never entirely disappear. They merely fragment into ever-smaller particles over time through various processes. These processes could be mechanical forces acting on the larger pieces of plastic, thermo-oxidation, photolysis, thermo-degradation and/or other biological processes (Abidli et al. 2017). Hence, plastic produced decades ago is still present in tiny sizes somewhere in the environment, and these tiny pieces of plastic have now emerged as a potential hazard that we call 'microplastics'.

Microplastics are plastic particles that are smaller than the size of 5 mm. Although this size denomination of microplastic is disputed by some scholars, 5 mm is now generally accepted as the threshold for determining microplastic particles. As the fragmentation of larger plastic debris continues, the quantity of microplastics is only increasing with every passing day in the environment. The tiny size of microplastics makes it very difficult to manage, and they are transported very easily throughout the environment. This gives microplastics the potential to dominate any given system.

This chapter reviews some of the existing studies on microplastics with the aim of highlighting the different aspects of the problem, and the potential dangers it can create.

SOURCES AND FACTORS CONTRIBUTING TO THE ABUNDANCE AND DISTRIBUTION OF MICROPLASTICS AMONG DIFFERENT ECOSYSTEMS

Domestic and Industrial Sewage

Domestic sewage and industrial wastes are a major source of microplastics. Plastic forms part of almost every household item that we now use. Synthetic garments, carpets and non-woven fabrics are a major source of plastic microfibres. It is estimated that in every washing done by a washing machine, 6 million microfibres per 5 kg of wash is discharged (Zhao 2018). A single wash of polyester garment can release up to 2 gm of microfibres. The synthetic fleece gives off 1,900 fibres per wash (Clark, Morritt, and McGoran 2017). Rayon is used widely in clothing, furnishing, female hygiene products and sanitary napkins. It disintegrates rapidly and hence exists abundantly (Lusher, McHugh, and Thompson, 2012). Micro-beads used in toothpastes, cosmetics (for exfoliation), paints, coatings and industrial pellets, form another major source of microplastics (Watts et al. 2016). Industrial use of micro-pellets air blasting, or as feedstock for the production of plastics, is another source of microplastics (Wang et al. 2017). In Hong Kong, about 342.2 billion pieces of microbeads are discharged along with treated or untreated sewage (Tsang et al. 2017). These tiny microplastics can make it through the filtering apparatus of wastewater treatment plants and hence are very difficult to remove (Laglbauer et al. 2014). Microplastics prevalence has a positive correlation with population density and the status of urban or suburban developments within a watershed (Zhang et al. 2015; Wang et al. 2017).

Fishing and Recreational Activities

Fishing and recreational activities associated with water bodies is another major source of microplastics, especially microfibres. Fishing gears, made up of highly resistant polymers (nylon, polyamide, polyester and polyethylene terephthalate), contribute largely to the litter deposited at the seafloor (Alomer et al. 2017). Around 640,000 tonnes of fishing gears end up discarded in the marine environment every year. Lost ropes, fishing nets, recreational sailing gears, etc., are major sources of microfibres in the ocean, and it is estimated that they contribute 3,968 tonnes of microfibres per month (Bessa et al. 2018). Additionally, a lot of plastic is used in mussel and oyster farming, which also contribute to the stock of microplastic fragments in the sea (Abidli et al. 2017). Proximity to Salmon farms also showed higher microplastic detection in the surroundings (Blumenrödera 2017).

Maritime Activities

Recreational boats and vessels visiting a harbour leave behind significant amounts of microplastics. The major source is from the abrasive plastic particles used in the cleaning of vessels by air-blast and equipment utilized in harbour activities (Tamminga, Hengstmann, and Fischer 2018).

Biofouling

Most synthetic plastic materials have a density lower than that of the saline water of the sea. They get aligned in the water column as per their densities. However, they do not persist in this location for long. A lot of plastic litter ends up in the ocean floor as well. The sinking of plastics is brought about by the rapid formation of microfilm and biologically enhanced aggregation on the surface of the microplastics, which leads them to the bottom sediments gradually, where they accumulate at low rates of degradation (Castañeda 2014; Wang 2017). An increased surface to volume ratio increases the occurrence of biofouling. As the average size of plastic decreases with increasing distance from the shore, lesser amounts of microplastics are detected offshore due to sinking (Obbard 2018).

Hydrographic Conditions

The accumulation of microplastics in a particular ecosystem also depends upon various hydrographic factors such as its location, wave action, currents, etc. Semi-enclosed water bodies have a higher propensity to act as a sink for microplastics, as they have limited exchange of water with water basins. Examples can be cited here of the Mediterranean Sea, the Gulf of Mexico, Arctic sea, Baltic Sea, Black Sea and Fjords, where high quantities of plastic debris have reportedly been detected (Mauro, Kupchik, and Benfield 2017). Canyon features may turn shelf-break of a continent into major microplastics hotspots (Naji 2017).

It has been found that at high tides, the concentration of microplastics is higher than at low tides at places with a high population in the vicinity. Moreover, during an episode of high tide, mangroves are capable of trapping incoming microplastics in their complex root systems and soil (Naji et al. 2017). Damming of rivers could also serve as a potential hotspot for the accumulation of microplastics (Di and Wang 2018; Zhang et al. 2015).

Compared to lakes, rivers are less prone to microplastics accumulation as hydrodynamics in a river is much stronger which facilitates evacuation (Wang 2017). The general morphological characteristics of a lake basin is often very irregular as we can see the existence of morphological features such as bays, island and lateral arms, coupled with the force of the wind. This creates complex hydrological movements, which determines the spatial distribution of microplastics (Sighicelli 2018).

Tidal currents and riverine inflow facilitate complex circulation of waters. This often causes the re-suspension of some microplastics that otherwise get deposited at the bottom. The velocities of the water flow, its depth, the prevalence of storms or floods, etc., also determine the spatial and temporal distribution of microplastics (Wang 2017).

Atmospheric Factors

Large amounts of microplastics are transported as a result of atmospheric fallout. This explains the presence of microplastics even in the extremely remote places on Earth. Perennial windy weather facilitates atmospheric transport of microplastics (Zhang et al. 2016). It has been reported that atmospheric fallout in Paris is 28–280 particles per m^2 per day (Obbard 2018).

Long Range Transport

Microplastics have been detected in the remote regions of the poles, where there is near zero population. This presence has been explained by wind-driven surface oceanic currents and by geostrophic circulation resulting in the long-range transport of microplastics particles. Microplastics are trapped efficiently in sea ice and can be carried to different places as they drift. Positive buoyancy and chemical stability of microplastics make them perfect for long-range transport (Obbard 2018). Microplastics in sediments are more stable because they are transported slowly, relative to those that are suspended in water (Su et al. 2016).

MICROPLASTICS IN FRESHWATER SYSTEMS

Most freshwater ecosystems across the planet report the presence of microplastics. It has been detected in significant amounts even in the remote lakes of the Tibetan plateau and in the Arctic and Antarctic waters. This demonstrates the ubiquitous nature of microplastics and its ability to transport itself through various mediums into all kinds of ecosystems. Many major rivers of the world pass through the vicinity of major cities or population centres. These are also hotspots for population growth and rapid industrialization. Such factors as population density and industrialization result in severe microplastics pollution in these rivers. These rivers also end up carrying huge loads of microplastics from the interior landmass into the oceanic systems.

Compared to rivers, lakes are more stable, allowing a longer resident time for microplastics in these ecosystems. Damming of rivers serves as a potential spot for microplastics accumulation. Since oceans form the global sump of all riverine systems, fed by these riverine systems, microplastics pollution is observed to be more severe in the oceans. Microplastics have significantly been detected in substantial amounts in the sediments and waters of freshwater bodies that have been included in this review (Table 10.1).

The shape of the microplastics helps determine their probable sources. Fibres are likely to be released from fishing-gears, clothes,

Table 10.1 Prevalence of Microplastics in Sediments and Waters of Some Freshwater Bodies

Location	Sediment	Water	Shape (%)	Reference
Shanghai	802 ± 594 particles/kg	—	Sphere: 88.98 Fibre: 7.55 Fragment: 3.47	Peng (2018)
Yangtze River	—	$8,512 \times 10^3$/km^2 (Main stream) $6,040.75 \times 10^3$/km^2 (Estuarine region)	—	Zhang (2015)
Thames River	349.50 ± 303.00 particles/kg	—	Fibres: 47.4 Fragments: 49.3 Films: 3.3	Horton (2016)
Lake Winnipeg	—	400,500 particles/km^2	—	Anderson (2017)
Lake Chiusi Lake Bolsena	2,117 ± 695/m^2 1,922 ± 662/m^2	1.51/m^3 1.11/m^3	Fibres: 70.61 Fragments: 29.39 Fibres: 66.81 Fragment: 33.12	Fischer (2016)
Tibetan Plateau	285.5 ± 616.5/m^2	—	—	Zhang (2016)

(Continued)

Table 10.1 (Continued)

Location	Sediment	Water	Shape (%)	Reference
Three Gorges Reservoir	25–300 particles/kg	1,597–12,611 particles/m^3	—	Di (2018)
Antua River, Portugal	225.25 ± 109.52 particles/kg	396.75 ± 291.01 particles/m^3	—	Rodrigues (2018)
Hanjiang, Yangtze	—	5,292.50 ± 4,782.05 particles/m^3	—	Wang (2017)
Taihu Lake	11–234.61 particles/kg	0.01 × 10^6 – 6.8 × 10^6 particles/km^2	Fibres: 66	Su (2016)
St Lawrence River	13,832 (±13677) particles/m^2	—	—	Castaneda (2014)
Subalpine Lakes (Maggiore, Iseo, and Garda)	—	396,000, 40,000, 25,000 particles/km^2 respectively	—	Singhicelli (2018)
Rhine River	—	892,777 particles/km^2	Spherules: 58.4 Fragments: 37.5 Others: 1.1	Mani (2015)

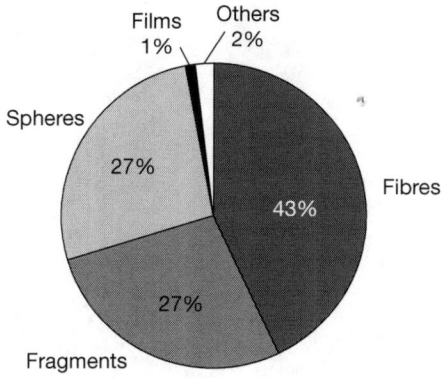

Figure 10.1 *Proportions of Different Shapes of Microplastics Averaged from the Studies Referred to in Table 10.1*

carpets, etc. Microbeads and pellets originate from cosmetics, cleansers, industrial pellets, etc. Fragments are generally broken off from larger plastic materials used in various walks of human life. The average proportions of different shapes in the studied samples of microplastics, available from six locations (Shanghai, Thames River, Lake Chiusi, Lake Bolsena, Lake Taihu and Rhine River) are shown in Figure 10.1. Most of the particles are microfibres, a fact which indicates that synthetic clothes and fishing gears are a dominant source of microplastics in the rivers and lakes.

Microplastics in the Marine Environment

Recent global estimates have determined the concentration of plastics that are found to be floating in the oceans as $51.2 \times 1,012$ particles with an estimated mass of 236 thousand metric tons. The Mediterranean is estimated to contain over half of these particles (i.e., $28.2 \times 1,012$ particles; Compa et al. 2018).

Studies in the Mediterranean basin estimate the occurrence of 890,000 plastic objects per km^2. A major portion of these floating plastics is composed of small fragments whose sizes range from 0.33 to 1.0 mm (small microplastics) to 1.01–4.75 mm (large microplastics) (Nadal, Alomar and Deudero 2016). Table 10.2 shows the concentration of

Table 10.2 Prevalence of Microplastics as Detected in the Waters and Sediments of Some of the Marine Environments from across the World

Location	Sediment	Water	Shape (%)	Reference
Arctic Sea	—	0.34 ± 0.31 particles/m^3 (16 cm depth) 2.68 ± 2.95 particles/m^3 (6 m depth)	Fibres: 95 Fragments: 4.9 Film: 0.1	Lusher (2015)
Ross Sea	—	670.32 particles/m^2	Fibres: 42 Films 35 Fragments: 22.2	Munari (2017)
Louisiana coast	—	9.1 ± 2.0 particles/m^3	—	Mauro (2017)
Solvenia shoreline	Infralittoral zone: 155.6 particles/kg Shoreline: 133.3 particles/kg	—	—	Laglbauer (2014)
South Funen Archipelago	—	12,897 ± 3,922 particles/km^2	Fragments: 31.46 Fibres: 68.54	Tamminga (2018)
Sacpa Flow, Scotland	730–2300 particles/kg	—	—	Blumenroder (2017)
Irish continental shelf	7.67 ± 2.09 particles/m^2	—	Fibres: 85 Fragments: 15	Martin (2017)

Location	Concentration (per kg / per 100m²)	Concentration (per m³ / m² / L / km²)	Composition (%)	Reference
Persian gulf, Iran	61 ± 49 particles/kg	—	Fibre: 88 Films: 11.2 Fragments: 0.8	Naji (2017)
Bizerte Lagoon, Tunisia	7,960 ± 6,840 particles/kg	—	—	Abidli (2017)
Arctic Central Basin	—	0–7.5 particles/m³ (underway, 8.5 m) 0–375 particles/m³ (8–4,369 m)	Fibres: 94 Fragments: 6	Kanhai (2018)
Bhai Sea, North Yellow Sea, South Yellow Sea	171.8 ± 55.4 particles/kg 123.6 ± 71.6 particles/kg 72 ± 27.2 particles/kg	—	Fibres 93.88 Fragments: 2.55 Pellet: 2.04 Film: 1.53	Zhao (2018)
Hong Kong Marine Environment	49–297 particles/kg 61–27,098 particles/100m²	—	Pellet: 60 Fragments: 33.15 Fibres: 3.35 Line: 3.55	Tsang (2017)
Galician/Cantabrian Coast	—	0.011–0.285/m² 0.035–0.086/m²	—	Bellas (2016)
French Belgian Dutch coastline	6 ± 5.7 particles/kg	0.4 ± 0.3 particles/L	—	Cauwenberghe (2015)
Rapa Nui, Easter Island	—	64,907.5 ± 18,296.5/km²	—	Ory (2017)

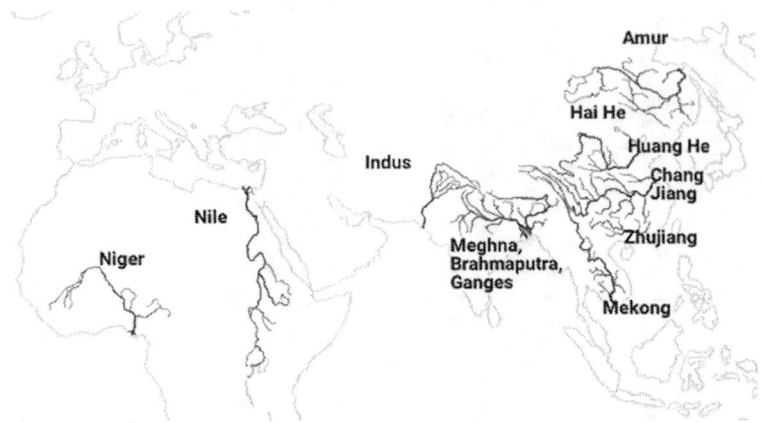

Figure 10.2 *Ten Major Rivers Carrying 90% of the Plastics Ending Up in Oceans*
Source: UNEP (2018).

microplastic particles in the waters and sediments of different marine locations across the world.

The majority of the microplastic particles detected in the marine sediments and waters are fibres (Figure 10.3). This observation establishes the dominant contribution of fishing activities, maritime actives, and domestic sewage (laundering) towards the microplastics load in these environments. The main point source of plastics in the oceans are the rivers. Figure 10.2 shows the 10 major rivers that carry 90 per cent of the plastic wastes ending up in the ocean (UNEP 2018).

MICROPLASTICS IN BIOTA

The huge problem of microplastics in the biota begins with those living organisms that reside in contaminated environments and thus get exposed to them. Living biota takes up microplastics from the environment in various ways. Microplastics are observed mostly in the gills and intestines of marine fishes. These indicate that both reparation and ingestion are major pathways of microplastics uptake (Yin et al. 2018). Adherence to a contaminated surrounding is another way of microplastics uptake (Qu et al. 2018).

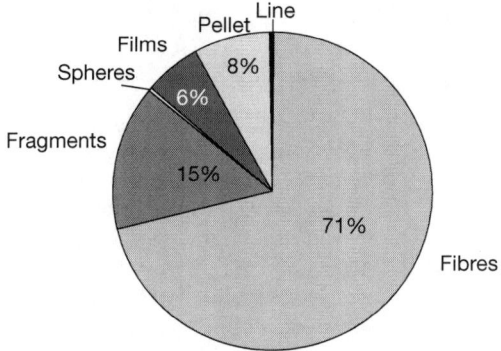

Figure 10.3 *Proportion of Microplastics of Different Shapes as Averaged from the Studies Referred to in Table 10.2*

When the colours of the prey and the plastic particles are similar, those particles are likely to give a false impression that they are the prey. This increases the possibility of their ingestion instead of the prey (or along with the prey). Thus, the colour of the particle also plays a significant part in determining whether it enters the biota or not. Studies have established that black is the most abundantly ingested colour, followed by blue (Figure 10.5).

Particle selection by organisms dwelling in the pelagic region depends almost entirely on the mouth biometry and hardly on the nutritional quality. Decapods (e.g., shrimps) have smooth external skeletons, which are colourless and transparent, resembling certain plastic particles, and hence, the latter may be mistaken for potential prey. Fishes intake fibres that resemble the colour of their planktonic preys (Nadal, Alomar, and Deudero 2016). *G.laevifrons* feed on red algae, and they are found to take up red particles resembling their food (Mizraji et al. 2017).

Microplastics have now been found in a wide variety of organisms ranging from algae to high fishes (Table 10.3). As reported recently by a few studies considered in this review, microplastic fibres are the most abundantly ingested particles by aquatic organisms (Figure 10.4). Hence it can be speculated that fishing nets, equipment and synthetic clothing contribute hugely to the problem of microplastics.

Table 10.3 A summary of the Studied Impacts of Microplastics on Different Species

Fishes	• Intestinal blockage, physical damage, histopathological alterations, change in behavior, change in lipid metabolism, respiratory stress, reduced food intake, and impairment of ion regulation. • Reduced foraging time, slower swimming speed, and shoaling behaviour. • Overexpression of neurological genes.
Crabs	• Decrease in the energy available tor growth. Increased Ca^{2+} ions, proteins, and haemocyanin concentration in the haemolymph. Transient intervention in gas exchange and ion regulation
Oysters	• Respiratory stress, impairment in fatty acid metabolism, and changes in hemocyte size and oxidative activity. Fecundity and reduction in sperm velocity. Biodeposition capacity is reduced and hence the creation of biogenic reefs.
Crustaceans	• Decrease in energy acquisition and reduction in growth. • Mortality because of starvation. Also, metabolic depression and reduced egg production and hence population decline.
Mussels	• Respiratory stress and pseudo-faeces production and decrease in filtering activity indicating reduced energy acquisition and starvation.
Marine worms	• Reduced feeding capacity. Dilution of organic content in the sediments and since marine worms are deposit feeders, they are starved of nutrients.
Algae	• Reduced chlorophyll content and photosynthetic efficiency. Also, reduction in uptake of nutrition, right, CO_2, and O_2. • Inhibition of algal growth and hence reduced primary productivity.

Table 10.4 Microplastics Detected in Different Species and Their Composition in Terms of Shape and Colour

Species	Ingestion of Microplastics	% of Sample with Microplastics	Shape (%)	Colour (%)	Reference
Amberstripe scads Decapterus muroadsi	2.5 ± 0.4 particles/individual	80	Fragments 92 Thread 6 Film 2	Blue 40 Transparent 26 White 26 Black 4 Grey 2 Green 2	Ory (2017)
Mussels Mytilus edulis, Perna viridian	0.77–8.22 particles/individual	—	—	—	Qu (2018)
Bogue Boops boops	3.75 ± 0.25 particles/individual	57.8	—	—	Nadal (2016)
Sardine Sardina pilchardus, European anchovy Engraulis encrasicolus	0.2 ± 0.31 particles/individual	100	Fibres 83	Blue 46 Transparent 21 Pink 4 Black 12 White 8 Red 8	Compa (2018)

(Continued)

Table 10.4 (Continued)

Species	Ingestion of Microplastics	% of Sample with Microplastics	Shape (%)	Colour (%)	Reference
Dogfish *Scyliorhinus canicula*, Red mullets *Mullus barbatus*, Hakes *Merluccius merluccius*	1.56 ± 0.5 particles/individual	—	Fibres 71 Spheres 24 Films 3.2 Fragments 1.6	Black 51 Red 13 Grey 12.7 Others 23.3	Bellas (2016)
Atlantic Mackerel *Scomber scomnrus*	0.58 ± 1.05 particles/individual	32	Fibres 72 Fragments 28	Black 22 Red 28 Blue 28 Orange 11 Green 11	Nelms (2018)
Captive Grey Seals *Halichoerus grypus*	0.87 ± 1.09 particles/individual	48	Fragment 69 Fibres 31	Black 27 Transparent 23 Red 23 Blue 15 Orange 12	Nelms (2018)
Atlantic mackerel *Scomber scomnrus*	0.46 ± 0.78 particles/individual	31	—	—	Nelms (2018)
Mussel *Mytilus galloprovincialis*	6.3 particles/individual	—	—	—	Renzi (2018)

Species	Abundance	Shape	Colour	Reference
Surmullet *Mullus surmuletus*	0.42 ± 0.04 particles/individual	27.30	—	—	Alomer (2017)
Mussel *Mytilus edulis*	0.2 ± 0.3 particles/g muscle	100	—	—	Cauwenberghe (2015)
Marine Worm *Arenicola marina*	1.2 ± 2.8 particles/g muscle	—	—	—	Cauwenberghe (2015)
Indian Mackerel *Rastrilliger kanagurta*, Honeycomb grouper *Epinephalus merra*	—	30	Fibres 80 Fragments 20	Transparent 20 Black 10 Red 4	Kumar (2018)
European flounder *Platichthys floss*	0.54 ± 80 particles/individual	75	—	Black 62.67 Red 14 Blue 7.67 Transparent 15.67	McGoran (2017)
European Smelt *Osmerus eperlanus*	0.2 ± 0.42 particles/individual	20	—	Black 100	McGoran (2017)
Seabass *Dicentrarchus labrax*	0.38 ± 0.61 particles/individual	13	Fibre 96 Fragment 4	Blue 47 Transparent 30 Black 11 Others 11	Bessa (2018)
Seabream *Diplodus vulgaris*	3.14 ± 3.25 particles/individual	73	—	—	Bessa (2018)

(Continued)

Table 10.4 (Continued)

Species	Ingestion of Microplastics	% of Sample with Microplastics	Shape (%)	Colour (%)	Reference
European flounder *Platichthys floss*	0.18 ± 0.55 particles/individual	23	—	—	Bessa (2018)
10 fish species	1.90 ± 0.10 particles/individual	36.5	Fibres 68.3 Fragments 16.1 Beads 11.5 Films 4.1	—	Lusher (2012)
69 fish species	1.06 ± 0.3 particles/individual	9	Fibres 90 Films 6 Fragments 4	—	Vendel (2017)
Bartail flathead *Platycephalus indicus*	1.85 ± 0.46 particles/g muscle	—	—	—	Akhbarizadeh (2018)
Pickhandle barracuda *Sphyraena jello*	0.57 ± 0.17 particles/g muscle	—	—	—	Akhbarizadeh (2018)
Shrimp scad *Alepes djedaba*	0.80 ± 0.12 particles/g muscle	—	—	—	Akhbarizadeh (2018)
Orange-spotted grouper *Epinephelus coioides*	0.78 ± 0.22 particles/g muscle	—	—	—	Akhbarizadeh (2018)

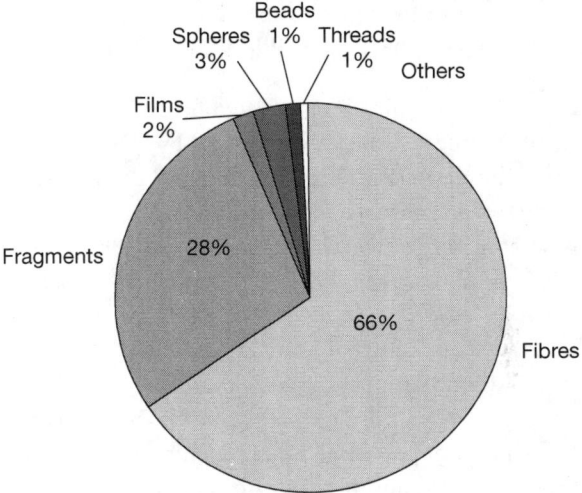

Figure 10.4 *Proportions of Microplastics of Different Shapes Detected in Different Species (Table 10.3)*

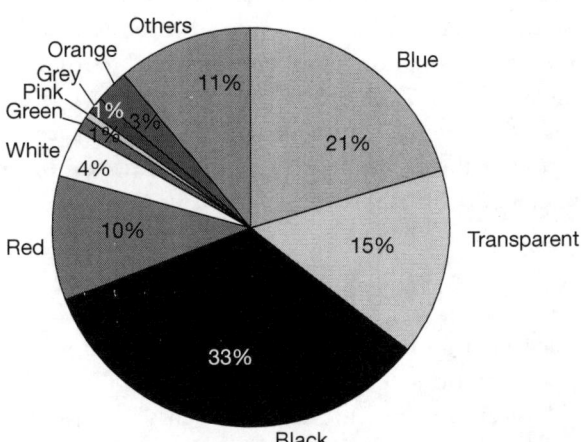

Figure 10.5 *Proportions of Particles Ingested by Species on the Basis of Colour (Table 10.3)*

IMPACTS OF MICROPLASTICS ON BIOTA AND POSSIBILITIES OF TROPHIC TRANSFER

Microplastics can harm animals in two significant ways, namely physical and chemical. Physical damages are caused by the shape, colour and dimension of the particles. These could be in the nature of internal abrasions, intestinal blockage, reduction in the energy and fertility of organisms because of the lowering of feeding and energy assimilation in the body. Chemical damage can be caused either by the chemical contaminants that get adsorbed on the surface of the particles and the additives added industrially to make products attractive, or by the chemical composition of the microplastics particle itself. Chemical damage can cause physiological alterations in the organisms. Microplastics potentiate the toxic effects of chemical contaminants (Rainieria et al. 2018). The chemistry of the monomers that constitute a plastic fragment and the additives (added industrially) leads to carcinogenesis and disruption of the endocrine system in organisms (Nadal, Alomar, and Deudero 2016). In a study conducted by Alomer et al. (2017), polychlorinated biphenyl (PCB) concentration was found to be 106 times higher on microplastic pellets than the concentration in the water column in which the particles existed. The additives are loosely bound to the surface of the particles and not chemically. Hence, they easily leach to the cells of the organisms and can cause adverse biological problems such as endocrine disruption, estrogen effects and testosterone reduction (Alomer et al. 2017). A part of the microplastics that enter fishes through ingestion are likely to be excreted through faeces which are likely to settle at the benthic zone, posing threats to the organisms there (Yin et al. 2018).

Microplastics in Fishes

Microplastics entering fishes by ingestion is reported to cause histopathological alterations, changes in lipid metabolism, blockage of intestine, physical damages and changes in behaviour (Jovanovi 2017). It also causes respiratory stress, reduced food intake and causes impairment of ion regulation (Lin 2018). The increase in microplastics ingestion caused a reduction in weight for *G.laevifrons* (Mizraji et al. 2017).

Fishes exposed to microplastics showed a reduced foraging time, slower swimming speed and altered their shoaling behaviour. Reduction in swimming speed could reduce predation and also create vulnerability to be preyed upon. Behavioural change is caused by a change in the water content of the brain as microplastics (which have a strong affinity towards lipids) get trapped in organs such as brains that are rich in lipids (Yin et al. 2018).

Microplastic ingestion by fishes can cause an overexpression of some genes pertaining to the neurological system (Rainieria et al. 2018). Contaminants sorped in the microplastic particles produce lesions and vacuolisation in the liver and also induces stress in the liver (Alomer et al. 2017; Rainieria et al. 2018; Yin et al. 2018). In juvenile African Catfish (*Claria gariepinus*), Low Density Polyethylene (LD-PE) caused damage of tissues in the liver, and there was an induction of genes that concerns the reproductive process (Rainieria et al. 2018). Microplastics alter the morphology of the intestines inducing a change in the digestive process and nutrient absorption, which in turn, impairs growth (Rainieria et al. 2018; Lin 2018). The amount of microplastics getting accumulated in a fish's gastrointestinal (GI) tract in one lifetime seems to be high, and it is likely to get higher in the future (Jovanovi 2017). In Japanese medaka (*Oryzias latipes*), alterations in the distributions of cholesterol between muscle and liver were noticed. Microplastics also produced changes in the metabolism and various alterations at the tissue and cellular level. It has been observed that microplastics enhance the toxicity of PAH, PCBs and PBDEs, as compared to the toxicity of the microplastics or the contaminants individually (Rainieria et al. 2018). Detection of microplastics in fishes, like *Boops boops,* which feed on a large variety of organisms such as seaweeds, sponges and small crustaceans, could indicate a trophic transfer of microplastics. Also, since *Boops boops* are prey to higher fishes like swordfish, there remains no doubt that they could initiate transfer among food webs (Nadal, Alomar, and Deudero 2016).

Microplastics in Crabs

A study conducted by Watts et al. (2016), the crab species *Carcinus maenas,* showed that there was a decrease in the energy available for growth due to the consumption of plastic-contaminated food. Microplastics significantly increased the Ca^{2+} ions and haemocyanin concentration in the haemolymph. Protein concentration was seen to increase as well, although not significantly. Microplastic contaminations did produce some adverse effects in crabs by intervening in gas exchange and ion regulation, but these were transient effects, and resilience was seen in maintaining osmoregulation and respiratory function. Crabs also showed a reduction in growth and food consumption because of microplastics ingestion (Compa et al. 2018). Shore crabs feed on mussels and they take up microplastics through mussels that are contaminated with microplastics and this shows the potential of microplastics to be transferred through predation (Watts et al. 2016).

Microplastics in Oysters

Microplastic doses elevate the respiration rates in oysters and hence bring about respiratory stress. Oysters exposed to microplastics also reportedly impacted fecundity (Sussarellu et al. 2016; Welden and Cowie 2016). There was a reduction of 23 per cent in sperm velocity, indicating a possible reduction in their ability to fertilize oocytes. In one case of exposed oysters, food intake increased in order to compensate for energy caused by adversities posed by microplastics in energy assimilation. Fatty acid metabolism of oysters is impaired, and changes in haemocyte size and oxidative activity occur because of microplastics contamination (Sussarellu et al. 2016).

Oysters serve as a mediator in the creation of biogenic reefs that are hotspots of diversity of biotic communities. In a laboratory experiment conducted by Green (2016) on European Flat Oysters, *Ostrea odulis*, it was observed that there were 1.6 times more organisms of different species present in the uncontaminated mesocosms as compared to the one dosed with microplastics. This indicates that microplastics can impact biodeposition by oysters, which in turn could swipe away certain key grazers (periwinkles, amphipods and isopods) and this reduction in the herbivory of an ecosystem could have a cascading impact on the productivity of the ecosystem (Green 2016).

Microplastics in Crustaceans

In a laboratory experiment by Blarer and Burkhardt-Holm (2016) on the freshwater Amphipod *Gammarus fossarum*, the amphipods failed to discriminate their food and microplastic particles. Ingestion of microplastics reduced their assimilation capacity significantly as they were present in the digestive tract. A significant reduction in growth was observed in the amphipod *Hyalella Aztec*, most probably because of reduced food intake. A decrease in energy acquisition could mean lesser growth, low survival rates, fecundities, and a longer period for development (Blarer and Burkhardt-Holm 2016; Welden and Cowie 2016). The presence of plastic in the diet was found to weaken the langoustine, *Nephros norvegicus*. An increase in mortality was also observed, probably caused by starvation resulting from reduced nutrient availability and false satiation caused by plastic ingestion. Starvation also causes metabolic depression and reduced egg production; Hence, a population decline can take place (Welden and Cowie 2016).

Microplastics in Mussels

There is a strong correlation between the concentration of microplastics in water and that found in the mussels that reside in it. A wide range of marine species preys on mussels. Human beings also consume mussels. Their contamination may lead to adverse impacts on the entire food web (Renzi, Guerranti, and Blašković 2018). In the blue mussel *Mytilus Edulis*, tiny microplastic particles passed through the midgut glands or epithelial cells present in the digestive tract. This indicates a concern of biomagnification along the food chain as they are preyed upon by shore crabs, shrimps or crucian carps (Blarer and Burkhardt-Holm 2016). Exposed mussels showed elevated respiration and hence respiratory stress to maintain physiological homeostasis. *M. Edulis* also showed pseudo-feces production, and also there was a decrease in their filtering ability indicating reduced acquisition of available energy and, in turn, starvation (Cauwenberghe et al. 2015).

Microplastics in Marine Worms

The marine worm *Arenicola marina* showed reduced feeding capacity because of microplastic contamination (Compa et al. 2018). The presence of microplastics in sediments dilutes the organic matter content in them and this adversely affects the deposit-feeding lugworms *Arenicola marina* by reducing their weight and assimilation efficiency (Blarer and Burkhardt-Holm 2016). Lugworms also have a non-selective feeding strategy, which means they will feed anything that comes their way, and this makes them vulnerable to microplastics ingestion (Cauwenberghe et al. 2015).

Microplastics in Algae

Microplastics inhibit the growth of microalgae. They also impair algal photosynthesis by bringing down chlorophyll content and photosynthetic efficiency of the microalgae. They block the caveoles present on algal cells, thereby impacting energy transfer and the exchange of molecules between the cells and their environment, which, in turn, reduces their uptake of nutrition, light, CO_2 and O_2. Intervention in the growth of the algae will cause a reduction in primary productivity, and this will entail an imbalance in the entire ecosystem (Zhang et al. 2017).

VULNERABILITY OF HUMAN BEINGS TO MICROPLASTICS CONTAMINATION

The human consumer market is constantly growing with time. The consumption of seafood has increased in the past decades, owing to their positive health benefits. Seafood is rich in proteins, vitamins, omega–3 poly-unsaturated fatty acids and minerals, all of which are considered beneficial to our health.

The presence of contaminants such as microplastics in seafood could induce carcinogenic as well as mutagenic and teratogenic effects, and this could nullify the health benefits they hold (Akhbarizadeh, Moore, and Keshavarzi 2018). As per the reports of FAO, 1,207,764 tonnes of *S. pilchardus* and 271,488 tonnes of *E. encrasicolus* were caught in 2014 (Compa et al. 2018). Global capture in 2013 for *Boops* was 39,411 tonnes (Nadal, Alomar, and Deudero 2016). These enormous quantities of seafood consumed annually by humans—if contaminated by microplastics—can pose a very serious threat to human health and well-being. Today, in view of the contamination of marine species, the meal size (for seafood) considered safe for adults is only 300 gm/week, and that of children is 50 gm/week (Akhbarizadeh, Moore, and Keshavarzi 2018).

Microplastics can also cause pathogenic spread and sea salt contamination. Tiny anthropogenic debris causes physical damage, which leads to cellular necrosis, inflammation, and laceration of the GI tract (Putnam et al. 2018). The cooking of tissues has been found to reduce the amount of microplastics in them, as a relevant level of microplastics was detected in the cooking water (Renzi, Guerranti, and Blašković 2018). When digestive enzymes and acids act on LD-PE, ethylene monomers can be released. This can result in the formation of ethylene oxide and ethylene glycol, which are toxic for humans (Alomer et al. 2017). The nutritional composition of fishes is altered due to microplastics contamination. Reduced nutritional quality and/or reduced growth of fishes also adversely impact their economic value, and hence results in a loss for human beings (Lin 2018).

CONCLUSION

The convenience that plastics bring to our lives is undeniable. However, the concerns regarding the adverse impact of plastic waste are much more significant. Methods of management of that waste (or the lack of it) may, in time, overturn any or all of the benefits we see in plastics today. The larger pieces of plastic that we dispose of in the environment may not cause as much damage as what can potentially be caused by what becomes of that plastic once we have left it in the environment unattended. Continuous fragmentation of unattended plastic into microplastics is now the biggest concern humanity faces today. The adverse effect of microplastics on flora, fauna, the environment and finally on human health and wellbeing can be devastating.

This threat is not in the realm of probability anymore. We are, in fact, already witnessing its destructive effects. Even if the impact is not overtly obvious to the human experience, its adversity is being scientifically documented and empirically established. The time to act is now. It can begin with eliminating (or at least reducing) the source of the problem, namely, as the slogan goes 'Use Less Plastic' (and may be try to get to a position of eliminating its use altogether). The concern of microplastics in the global commons can surely be tackled, but it requires will, cooperation, coordination, resources, motivation, dedication and knowledge. Large areas of knowledge regarding the treatment of microplastics remain vacant. The need for research to fulfil this knowledge gap is now, so that effective strategies can be formulated to manage and control this tiny menace.

REFERENCES

Abidli, S., H. Toumi, Y. Lahbib, and N. T. E. Menif. 2017. 'The First Evaluation of Microplastics in Sediments from the Complex Lagoon—Channel of Bizerte (Northern Tunisia)'. *Water Air Soil Pollution* 228 (7): 262. doi: 10.1007/s11270-017-3439-9.

Akhbarizadeh, R., F. Moore, and B. Keshavarzi. 2018. 'Investigating a Probable Relationship between Microplastics and Potentially Toxic Elements in Fish Muscles from Northeast of Persian Gulf'. *Environmental Pollution* 232: 154–163. doi: 10.1016/j.envpol.2017.09.028.

Alomer, C., A. Suredab, X. Capó, B. Guijarroa, S. Tejada, and S. Deudero. 2017. 'Microplastic Ingestion by Mullus Surmuletus Linnaeus, 1758 Fish and Its Potential for Causing Oxidative Stress'. *Environmental Research* 159: 135–142. doi: 10.1016/j.envres.2017.07.043.

Anderson, P. J., S. Warrack, V. Langen, J. K. Challis, M. L. Hanson, and, M. D. Rennie. 2017. 'Microplastic Contamination in Lake Winnipeg, Canada'. *Environmental Pollution* 225: 223–231. doi: 10.1016/j.envpol.2017.02.072.

Bellas, J., J. Martínez-Armental, A. Martínez-Cámara, V. Besada, and C. Martínez-Gómez. 2016. 'Ingestion of Microplastics by Demersal Fish from the Spanish Atlantic and Mediterranean Coasts'. *Marine Pollution Bulletin* 109 (1): 55–60. doi: 10.1016/j.marpolbul.2016.06.026.

Bessa, F., P. Barríaa, J. M. Netoa, J. P. G. L. Frias, V. Oteroc, P. Sobrald, and J. C. Marques. 2018. 'Occurrence of Microplastics in Commercial Fish from a Natural Estuarine Environment'. *Marine Pollution Bulletin* 128: 575–584. doi: 10.1016/j.marpolbul.2018.01.044.

Blarer, P., and P. Burkhardt-Holm. 2016. 'Microplastics Affect Aassimilation Efficiency in the Freshwater Amphipod *Gammarus fossarum*'. *Environmental Science Pollution Research* 23 (23): 23522–23532. doi: 10.1007/s11356-016-7584-2.

Blumenrödera, J., P. Secheta, J. E. Kakkonenb, and M. G. J. Hartl. 2017. 'Microplastic Contamination of Intertidal Sediments of Scapa Flow, Orkney: A first Assessment'. *Marine Pollution Bulletin* 124 (1): 112–120. doi: 10.1016/j.marpolbul.2017.07.009.

Castañeda, R. A., S. Avlijas, M. A. Simard, and A. Ricciardi. 2014. 'Microplastic Pollution in St. Lawrence River Sediments'. *Journal canadien des sciences halieutiques et aquatiques* 71 (12): 1767–1771. doi: 10.1139/cjfas-2014-0281.

Cauwenberghe, L. V., M. Claessens, M. B. Vandegehuchte, and C. R. Jansse. 2015. 'Microplastics Are Taken Up by Mussels (*Mytilus Edulis*) and Lugworms (*Arenicola Marina*) Living in Natural Habitats'. *Environmental Pollution* 199: 10–17. doi: 10.1016/j.envpol.2015.01.008.

Compa, M., A. Ventero, M. Iglesias, and S. Deudero. 2018. 'Ingestion of Microplastics and Natural Fibres in Sardina Pilchardus (Walbaum, 1792) and Engraulis Encrasicolus (Linnaeus, 1758) along the Spanish Mediterranean Coast'. *Marine Pollution Bulletin* 128: 89–96. doi: 10.1016/j.marpolbul.2018.01.009.

Di, M., and J. Wang. 2018. 'Microplastics in Surface Waters and Sediments of the Three Gorges Reservoir, China'. *Science of the Total Environment* 616–617: 1620–1627. doi: 10.1016/j.scitotenv.2017.10.150.

Fischer, E. K., L. Paglialonga, E. Czech, and M. Tamminga. 2016. 'Microplastic Pollution in Lakes and Lake Shoreline Sediments—A Case Study on Lake Bolsena and Lake Chiusi (central Italy). *Environmental Pollution* 213: 648–657. doi: 10.1016/j.envpol.2016.03.012.

Geyer, R., J. R. Jambeck, and K. L. Law. 2017. 'Production, Use, and Fate of All Plastics Ever Made'. *Science advances* 3 (7): e1700782. doi: 10.1126/sciadv.1700782.

Green, D. S. 2016. 'Effects of Microplastics on European Flat Oysters, *Ostrea Edulis* and their Associated Benthic Communities. *Environmental Pollution* 216: 95–103. doi: 10.1016/j.envpol.2016.05.043.

Horton, A. A., C. Svendsen, R. J. Williams, D. J. Spurgeon, and E. Lahive. 2016. 'Large Microplastic Particles in Sediments of Tributaries of the River Thames, UK – Abundance, Sources and Methods for Effective Quantification'. *Marine Pollution Bulletin* 114 (1): 218–226. doi: 10.1016/j.marpolbul.2016.09.004.

Jovanović, B. 2017. 'Ingestion of Microplastics by Fish and Its Potential Consequences from a Physical Perspective. *Integrated Environmental Assessment and Management* 13 (3): 510–515. doi: 10.1002/ieam.1913.

Kanhai, L. D. K., K. Gårdfeldtc, O. Lyashevskaa, M. Hasellöv, R. C. Thompson, and Ian O'Connor. 2018. 'Microplastics in Sub-surface Waters of the Arctic Central Basin'. *Marine Pollution Bulletin* 130: 8–18. doi: 10.1016/j.marpolbul.2018.03.011.

Kumar, V. E., G. Ravikumar, and K. I. Jeyasanta. 2018. 'Occurrence of Microplastics in Fishes from Two Landing Sites in Tuticorin, South East Coast of India'. *Marine Pollution Bulletin* 135: 889–894. doi: 10.1016/j.marpolbul.2018.08.023.

Laglbauer, B. J. L., R. M. Franco-Santos, M. Andreu-Cazenave, L. Brunelli, M. Papadatou, A. Palatinus, M. Grego, and T. Deprez. 2014. 'Macrodebris and Microplastics from Beaches in Slovenia'. *Marine Pollution Bulletin* 89: 356–366. doi: 10.1016/j.marpolbul.2014.09.036.

Lin, L., Zuo, L. Z., Peng, J. P., Cai, L. Q., Fok, L., Yan, Y., ... and Xu, X. R. 2018. 'Occurrence and distribution of microplastics in an urban river: A case study in the Pearl River along Guangzhou City, China'. *Science of the Total Environment*, 644, 375–381.

Lusher, A. L., M. McHugh, and R. C. Thompson. 2012. 'Occurrence of Microplastics in the Gastrointestinal Tract of Pelagic and Demersal Fish from the English Channel'. *Marine Pollution Bulletin* 67 (1–2): 94–99. doi: 10.1016/j.marpolbul.2012.11.028.

Lusher, A. L., V. Tirelli, Ian O'Connor, and R. Officer. 2015. 'Microplastics in Arctic Polar Waters: The First Reported Values of Particles in Surface and Sub-surface Samples. *Scientific Reports* 5: 14947. doi: 10.1038/srep14947.

Mani, T., A. Hauk, U. Walter, and P. Burkhardt-Holm. 2015. 'Microplastics Profile along the Rhine River'. *Scientific Reports* 5: 17988. doi: 10.1038/srep17988.

Martin, J., A. Lusher, R. C. Thompson, and A. Morley. 2017. 'The Deposition and Accumulation of Microplastics in Marine Sediments and Bottom Water from the Irish Continental Shelf'. *Scientific Reports* 7: 10,772. doi: 10.1038/s41598-017-11079-2.

Mauro, R. D., M. J. Kupchik, and M. C. Benfield. 2017. 'Abundant Plankton-sized Microplastic Particles in Shelf Waters of the Northern Gulf of Mexico'. *Environmental Pollution* 230: 798–809. doi: 10.1016/j.envpol.2017.07.030.

McGoran, A. R., P. F. Clark, and D. Morritt. 2017. 'Presence of Microplastic in the Digestive Tracts of European Flounder, *Platichthys Flesus*, and European Smelt, *Osmerus Eperlanus*, from the River Thames'. *Environmental Pollution* 220: 744–751. doi: 10.1016/j.envpol.2016.09.078.

Mizraji, R., C. Ahrendt, D. Pérez-Venegas, J. Vargas, J. Pulgar, M. Aldana, F. P. Ojeda, C. Duarte, and C. Galbán-Malagón. 2017. 'Is the Feeding Type Related with the Content of Microplastics in Intertidal Fish Gut?' *Marine Pollution Bulletin* 116 (1–2): 498–500. doi: 10.1016/j.marpolbul.2017.01.008.

Munaria, C., V. Infantinia, M. Scoponib, E. Rastellib, C. Corinaldesie, and M. Mistria. 2017. 'Microplastics in the Sediments of Terra Nova Bay (Ross Sea, Antarctica)'. *Marine Pollution Bulletin* 122: 161–165. doi: 10.1016/j.marpolbul.2017.06.039.

Nadal, M. A., C. Alomar, and S. Deudero. 2016. 'High Levels of Microplastic Ingestion by the Semipelagic Fish Bogue *Boops Boops* (L.) around the

Balearic Islands. *Environmental Pollution* 214: 517–523. doi: 10.1016/j.envpol.2016.04.054.

Naji, A., Z. Esmaili, S. A. Mason, and A. D. Vethaak. 2017. 'The Occurrence of Microplastic Contamination in Littoral Sediments of the Persian Gulf, Iran. *Environmental Science and Pollution Research* 24 (25): 20459–20468. doi: 10.1007/s11356-017-9587-z.

Nelms, S. E., T. S. Galloway, B. J. Godley, D. S. Jarvis, and P. K. Lindeque. 2018. 'Investigating Microplastic Trophic Transfer in Marine Top Predators'. *Environmental Pollution* 238: 999–1007. doi: 10.1016/j.envpol.2018.02.016.

Obbard, R. W. 2018. 'Microplastics in Polar Regions: The Role of Long Range Transport'. *Current Opinion in Environmental Science & Health* 1: 24–29. doi: 10.1016/j.coesh.2017.10.004.

Ory, N. C., P. Sobral, J. L. Ferreira, and M. Thiel. 2017. 'Amberstripe Scad *Decapterus Muroadsi* (Carangidae) Fish Ingest Blue Microplastics Resembling their Copepod Prey along the Coast of Rapa Nui (Easter Island) in the South Pacific Subtropical Gyre'. *Science of the Total Environment* 586: 430–437. doi: 10.1016/j.scitotenv.2017.01.175.

Peng, G., P. Xu, B. Zhu, M. Bai, and D. Li. 2018. 'Microplastics in Freshwater River Sediments in Shanghai, China: A Case Study of Risk Assessment in Mega-cities'. *Environmental Pollution* 234: 448–456. doi: 10.1016/j.envpol.2017.11.034.

Putnam, A., C. Hammer, H. VanBrocklin, B. Buksa, and A. Clune. 2017. 'Microplastic Biomagnification in Invertebrates, Fish, and Cormorants in Lake Champlain'. *Lake Champlain Sea Grant*. doi: 10.13140/RG.2.2.31969.10089.

Qu, X., L. Su, H. Li, M. Liang, and H. Shi. 2018. 'Assessing the Relationship between the Abundance and Properties of Microplastics in Water and in Mussels'. *Science of the Total Environment* 621: 679–686. doi: 10.1016/j.scitotenv.2017.11.284.

Rainieria, S., N. Conlledoa, B. K. Larsenb, K. Granbyc, and A. Barranco. 2018. 'Combined Effects of Microplastics and Chemical Contaminants on the Organ Toxicity of Zebrafish (*Danio Rerio*)'. *Environmental Research* 162: 135–143. doi: 10.1016/j.envres.2017.12.019.

Renzi, M., C. Guerranti, and A. Blašković. 2018. 'Microplastic Contents from Maricultured and Natural Mussels'. *Marine Pollution Bulletin* 131: 248–251. doi: 10.1016/j.marpolbul.2018.04.035.

Rodrigues, M. O., N. Abrantes, F. J. M. Gonçalves, H. Nogueira, J. C. Marques, and A. M. M. Gonçalves. 2018. 'Spatial and Temporal Distribution of Microplastics in Water and Sediments of a Freshwater System (Antuã River, Portugal)'. *Science of the Total Environment* 633: 1549–1559. doi: 10.1016/j.scitotenv.2018.03.233.

Sighicelli, M., L. Pietrelli, F. Lecce, V. Iannilli, M. Falconieri, L. Coscia, S. D. Vito, S. Nuglio, and G. Zampetti. 2018. 'Microplastic Pollution in the Surface Waters of Italian Subalpine Lakes'. *Environmental Pollution* 236: 645–651. doi: 10.1016/j.envpol.2018.02.008.

Su, L., Y. Xue, L. Li, D. Yang, P. Kolandhasamy, D. Li, and H. Shi. 2016. 'Microplastics in Taihu Lake, China'. *Environmental Pollution* 216: 711–719. doi: 10.1016/j.envpol.2016.06.036.
Sussarellu, R., M. Suquet, Y. Thomas, C. Lambert, C. Fabioux, M. E. J. Pernet, N. L. Goïc, V. Quillien, C. Mingant, Y. Epelboin, C. Corporeau, J. Guyomarch, J. Robbens, I. Paul-Pont, P. Soudant, and A. Huvet. 2016. 'Oyster Reproduction is Affected by Exposure to Polystyrene Microplastics'. *Proceedings of the National Academy of Sciences of the United States of America* 113: 2430–2435. doi: 10.1073/pnas.1519019113.
Tamminga, M., E. Hengstmann, and E. K. Fischer. 2018. 'Microplastic Analysis in the South Funen Archipelago, Baltic Sea, Implementing Manta Trawling and Bulk Sampling'. *Marine Pollution Bulletin* 128: 601–608. doi: 10.1016/j.marpolbul.2018.01.066.
Thompson, R. C., C. J. Moore, F. S. Saal, and S. H. Swan. 2009. 'Plastics, the Environment and Human Health: Current Consensus and Future Trends'. *Philosophical Transactions of the Royal Society B* 364: 2153–2166.
Tsang, Y. Y., C. W. Mak, C. Liebich, S. W. Lam, E. T.-P. Sze, and K. M. Chan. 2017. 'Microplastic Pollution in the Marine Waters and Sediments of Hong Kong'. *Marine Pollution Bulletin* 115: 20–28. doi: 10.1016/j.marpolbul.2016.11.003.
UNEP. 2018. *Single-Use Plastics: A Roadmap for Sustainability*. Available at: https://www.reloopplatform.org/wp-content/uploads/2018/06/UNEP-report-on-single-use-plastic.pdf (accessed on 23 April 2020).
Vendel, A. L., F. Bessa, V. E. N. Alves, A. L. A. Amorim, J. Patrício, and A. R. T. Palma. 2017. 'Widespread Microplastic Ingestion by Fish Assemblages in Tropical Estuaries Subjected to Anthropogenic Pressures'. *Marine Pollution Bulletin* 117 (1–2): 448–455. doi: 10.1016/j.marpolbul.2017.01.081.
Wang, W., A. W. Ndungu, Z. Li, and J. Wang. 2017. 'Microplastics Pollution in Inland Freshwaters of China: A Case Study in Urban Surface Waters of Wuhan, China'. *Science of the Total Environment* 575: 1369–1374. doi: 10.1016/j.scitotenv.2016.09.213.
Watts, A. J .R., M. A. Urbina, R. M. Goodhead, J. Moger, C. Lewis, and T. S. Galloway. 2016. 'Effect of Microplastic on the Gills of the Shore Crab *Carcinus Maenas*'. *Evironment Science & Technology* 50 (10): 5364–5369. doi: 10.1021/acs.est.6b01187.2016.
Welden N. A. C., and Cowie, P. R. 2016. 'Long-term Microplastic Retention Causes Reduced Body Condition in the Langoustine, *Nephrops Norvegicus*'. *Environmental Pollution* 218: 895–900. doi: 10.1016/j.envpol.2016.08.020.
Yin, L., B. Chen, B. Xia, X. Shi, and K. Qu. 2018. 'Polystyrene Microplastics Alter the Behavior, Energy Reserve and Nutritional Composition of Marine Jacopever (*Sebastes Schlegelii*)'. *Journal of Hazardous Materials* 360: 96–105. doi: 10.1016/j.jhazmat.2018.07.110.
Zhang, C., X. Chen, J. Wang, and L. Tan. 2017. 'Toxic Effects of Microplastic on Marine Microalgae *Skeletonema Costatum*: Interactions between Microplastic

and Algae'. *Environmental Pollution* 220 (B): 1282–1288. doi: 10.1016/j. envpol.2016.11.005.

Zhang, K., J. Su, X. Xiong, X. Wu, C. Wu, and J. Liu. 2016. 'Microplastic Pollution of Lakeshore Sediments from Remote Lakes in Tibet Plateau, China'. *Environmental Pollution* 219: 450–455. doi: 10.1016/j.envpol.2016.05.048.

Zhang, K., W. Gong, J. Lv, X. Xiong, and C. Wu. 2015. 'Accumulation of Floating Microplastics behind the Three Gorges Dam'. *Environmental Pollution* 204: 117–123. doi: 10.1016/j.envpol.2015.04.023.

Zhao, J., W. Ran, J. Teng, Y. Liu, H. Liu, X. Yin, R. Cao, and Q. Wang. 2018. 'Microplastic Pollution in Sediments from the Bohai Sea and the Yellow Sea, China'. *Science of the Total Environment* 640–641: 637–645. doi: 10.1016/j. scitotenv.2018.05.346.

Chapter 11

The Indian Ocean Garbage
Rethinking the Narrative on
South Asian Waters

Anusha Sooriyan, Namita Sharma and
Mohanan Bhaskaran Pillai

INTRODUCTION

For ages, people have looked upon oceans as an inexhaustible opportunity and resource provider. Ample quantities of food, fisheries, biomedical organisms and minerals are found in the seas. Routes for transport facilities such as trade and shipping are dependent on waters. Seas are the regulators of the earth's climate. The ocean is an all-in-one treasured source for the humans, and they have taken it for granted. Activities such as careless exploitation of and convenient dumping in the ocean have done damage to marine species, human lives, security and their environment.

Marine litter is pervasive in world oceans and is contributing to the ever-increasing environmental problems faced by planet Earth. The complexity of the issue has been worsened by the nature of the garbage and their constant movement towards the ocean. These marine pollutants are of different kinds, processed or unprocessed, disposed, and discarded in the seas intentionally or unintentionally. Over the years, the abandoned waste forms a large garbage patch or marine debris, which is more hazardous in the longer run.

The Pacific Ocean carries the largest garbage patch that was found in the 1990s by Charles Moore. Four other similar patches have been discovered later in the Mediterranean, the Atlantic, the North Sea, and the Indian Ocean regions. South Asian nations house one-fifth of the world's population among the coastal nations in the Indian Ocean region. These nations have mismanaged plastic waste and contributed heavily to the Indian Ocean garbage patch (Sarker, Rehman, and Giessen 2018). India stands at the 12th position with 0.60 million tonnes (and China tops the list with 8.82 million tonnes) per year of mismanaged plastic waste. There are 11 other Asian and Southeast Asian countries on the list, including Sri Lanka, Bangladesh, Pakistan and Burma (UNEP-SAS 2007). It is only in recent years that the South Asian nations have been keenly looking at marine garbage and other litter deposits with unease. Regional groupings such as the South Asian Seas Action Plan (SASP) and the South Asia Cooperative Environment Programme (SACEP) exchange views on integrated coastal zones and issues related to marine health. This integration is a positive step in encouraging the member states to take appropriate action to fix the problem.

This chapter comprises four sections. The first section deals with the statistics and data of the waste generated, its types, sources and its impact on the marine health of South Asian territorial seas. The second section studies the existing umbrella of national and international laws on marine environment protection that the South Asian coastal nations follow. It also points out the gaps existing in this legal community. The third section extensively ponders on the idea of shared responsibility in the region. It questions the collective and individual interests of the South Asian nations in the protection of the Indian Ocean environment. The last section argues that among the South Asian nations, India, with its longest coastline and huge coastal population, has the obligation to pay attention to its environmental activities and ocean health.

UNDERSTANDING THE VULNERABILITY

South Asia is a vast region that has common access to the Indian Ocean. Landlocked countries in South Asia, such as Nepal, Bhutan and Afghanistan, do not benefit from the ocean waters, compared to the coastal states. Hence, it is appropriate to say that wastes generated in the sea by these nations are comparatively less than the coastal states, namely India, Bangladesh, Pakistan, Maldives and Sri Lanka.

Indeed a country's coastline and population help determine which country contributes the most to the litter accumulated in waters. India has a coastline spanning 7,516 km, which is the longest in South Asia. India's neighbour in the east, that is, Bangladesh has the smallest coastline of 580 km. These coastal states highly depend on the sea for their occupation and livelihood. The people living on the shores and various other factors are the agents causing pollution in the waters.

The Garbage Generated by the Coastal States of South Asia

The formation of marine debris is largely due to plastic and the mismanaged plastic waste which enters into the sea. Researchers have quantified the amount of plastic litter that ends up in the ocean, and the data has been alarming. The table below throws light on the figures of plastic waste and mismanaged litter contributed by the coastal nations of South Asia, which are among the top 20 countries producing marine litter. Production of plastic litter by the nations mentioned below has worsened the overall health index of the oceans.

Despite having a smaller coastline than India, countries such as Pakistan and Bangladesh, pollute the ocean tremendously with plastic litter. Approximately 80 per cent and above is the scale of untreated plastic that is let into the oceans. Sri Lanka is certainly the largest marine debris generator and occupies the fifth rank in the list of top 20 countries producing marine litter (UNEP-SAS 2007). This would mean that the plastic waste management system in these major South Asian countries is defective.

Plastic Dump from Land (2010)	Bangladesh	India	Pakistan	Sri Lanka
Plastics in oceans	8%	3%	13%	7%
Mismanaged plastic	89%	87%	88%	84%
Marine debris per year (MMT/year)	0.12–0.31	0.09–0.24	0.07–0.19	0.26–0.64
Rank (Among 20 countries)	10	12	15	5

Source: https://science.sciencemag.org/content/347/6223/768/tab-figures-data

Note: MMT—million metric tonnes.

Source of the Ocean Garbage

Pollutants of ocean waters vary according to the land, region, demography and size of the population. These cannot be easily traced as the disparity among the South Asian coastal states remains large. Human activity has managed to negatively affect the global marine ecosystem and South Asia in particular. Also, over the years, researchers and scientists have identified elements causing a decline in the marine environment (UNEP-SAS 2007). According to the United Nations Environment Programme (UNEP) report, the main sources of coastal and marine pollution are untreated sewage, chemicals releasing from industries and factories, solid waste, oil slicks, chemicals used for agriculture (such as fertilizers and pesticides) and ship wreckages.

In the year 2018, the World Wide Fund for Nature, Pakistan conducted an inquiry on the sea view of Karachi. The study revealed that the continuous releasing of untreated sewage in the Arabian Sea through Karachi's sea view threatened marine life and habitat. Due to a tonne of garbage dumped into the sea, Pakistan incurred a loss of 40 per cent of marine life. Similar cases have been noted in the scenic islands of Maldives, where the idea of sewage treatment is almost alien to most of the offices, hotels and resorts. Chemicals from clinical labs, industrial waste, and domestic sewage are poured directly into the sea. They affect not only the quality of the ocean water but also the marine ecosystem.

Bangladesh has been a hub for the low-cost clothing industry and also a major exporter of textiles to Europe. These textiles have been continually releasing chemicals, colours and toxic stench into the canals that flow down to the sea. The foul odour and colour of the water streams and canal describe the environmental disaster the state is facing (Yardley 2013).

Cases of oil spills in India have risen in number and frequency. The Ennore oil spill in 2017 (Bay of Bengal) and the Mumbai oil spill in 2010 (Arabian Sea) reported severe damage to the coastal population, marine mammals, beaches and marshlands. Oil spill directly affects the seawater ecosystem. Apart from frequent oil spills, ship-breaking activities in Pakistan's Gidani yard, and the Indian yard at Alang-Sosiya, Gujarat generate solid and hazardous waste such as paint chips, ceramic tiles, fibreglass, oil sludge and plastic. Ships in India and Bangladesh are dismantled on the beach rather than on dry docks, which adds to the toxicity of the soil, water and air.

The Impact on Marine Life in South Asian Waters

Mangroves in the Indian part of the delta of Sundarbans, in the coasts of Bangladesh, Sri Lanka and Pakistan are widely spread. These plantations are part of the larger marine life and are rich in biodiversity. The Sundarbans (the largest mangrove forest which is common to both Bangladesh and India) are under the radar of threat. Power plants are being constructed on the shores of these wetlands. Effluents from coal transportation as well as from power plants will endanger the ecology of the delta belt (Juneja 2015).

Further, South Asia is home to approximately 250 species of coral species and over 1,200 reef-associated fish species. The strip of coral reef (i.e., 3.14% of global reef area) in the Maldives is turning dead due to bleaching, plastic trash and chemicals discharged into the sea (Sarker, Rehman, and Giessen 2018).

Data of 2007 indicate the mysterious death of dolphins and fishes due to strangling in floating trash nets in Gujarat and Tamil Nadu (Sarker, Rehman, and Giessen 2018). The fishermen lose their fishing nets and other tools in the ocean. This causes the materials to float on the ocean surface. Countries like Sri Lanka and Pakistan have reported similar crises. Loss of marine animals is hurting the marine biodiversity of South Asian waters.

Impact on the Coastal Population

The inflow of tourism in South Asia and South East Asia has been surpassing prior numbers since 2005. This is expected to increase by 7+ per cent in the coming years, according to the UN World Tourism Organization (UNWTO) reports. This would mean the clearing of the mangroves and the vital marine ecosystem in order to pave the way for coastal infrastructure, increased transportation and emission of pollution, more litter on the beaches, and rise in the garbage dumped into the sea. The tourism industry in South Asia, which looks blooming on the surface, could be nearing its doom due to unplanned development.

In Sri Lanka, the major stakeholders, who are affected by the issue of marine debris, are pedestrians, tourist resorts and establishments, fishermen and city authorities (Sureshkumar 2007). The lack of manpower and adequate funds to maintain clean beaches are the major problems faced by local authorities. Coastal shores and beaches, which were major tourist destinations earlier, are now being avoided by tourists. It affects the local livelihood and economy.

LEGAL DIMENSIONS
International Recognition

Due to the ambiguous nature of International maritime borders, oceans and the freedom of navigation has been a subject of continuous discussion. International laws on the protection of maritime boundaries of states have been in place since the early 20th century. However, with the development of modern law, especially in the later half of the

20th century, growing concerns regarding the condition of oceans or ocean health have given rise to a number of international conventions and legal formations. The problems of marine environment including pollution, loss of biodiversity, protection of endangered species and marine mammals have been increasingly addressed by modern international laws. The oceans are no longer seen as dumping grounds with infinite capacity to accommodate man-made hazardous wastes. The United Nations Convention on the Law of the Sea initiated in 1982 is the strongest and most comprehensive framework on laws concerning international waters (Al Arif and Karim 2015). It is a full-fledged treaty which includes both generic and specific obligations of the states to prevent, reduce and control pollution. Articles 192–237 (Part XII) of the United Nations Convention on the Law of the Sea (UNCLOS) are devoted to the protection and preservation of the marine environment. Article 194 of the UNCLOS targets all forms of marine pollution and Article 192 makes it the business of the governments, flag States and coastal or port States to protect and preserve the marine environment. The UNCLOS being a framework convention, all other global conventions covering specific areas, such as the International Maritime Organization (IMO) Convention and the UNEP Convention, are generally interpreted in terms of this 1982 convention.

The UNEP is another important global environmental authority within the United Nations that sets the global environmental agenda, serves as an advocate for the global environment and looks into the implementation of environmental projects. Although the management of chemical waste is one of the broad subjects that the UNEP focuses on, lately, it has also addressed issues concerning marine health.

The International Convention Relating to Intervention on the High Seas in Cases of Oil Pollution Casualties is another multilateral treaty signed in 1969. This treaty encourages and empowers the coastal nations to take measures in cases of oil spills, which come with devastating consequences. It also empowers the coastal nations to take necessary actions beyond their maritime territorial boundaries. In the year 1973, an extension was added to the treaty, which broadens its concerns from oil spills to other sources of marine pollution. Bangladesh, India, Pakistan and Sri Lanka are members of this convention among other South Asian nations.

Ship wreckages and their remains that settle on the ocean floor have become an increasing threat to ocean health. In order to counter the pollution and waste created by the collision of both small and large ships, the Convention for the Prevention of Pollution from Ships (1973 MARPOL Convention) was established in the year 1973 (Al Arif and Karim 2015) The aim of this convention is to prevent maritime environmental pollution caused by the release of oil and other harmful substances into the ocean. Under this convention, states are obligated to obey its provisions with regard to ships flying their flags and also other ships that are under their jurisdiction. Bangladesh, India, Maldives, Pakistan and Sri Lanka are signatories to this convention.

Programmes and Laws in the South Asian Region

Apart from international laws and conventions, regional institutes play a significant role in ocean governance and ensure better participation among the member countries in the prevention of marine pollution and with regard to the cleaning up of the oceans (Al Arif and Karim 2015). In the South Asian Region of the Indian Ocean, almost all the countries are members of UNCLOS. However, at the regional level, there are no significant conventions or legal frameworks. The South Asian Association for Regional Cooperation (SAARC), along with other areas for cooperation, has identified the environment as an important factor on which the South Asian states need to work together. The South Asian Seas Environment Programme (SASEP), which operates under the United Nations Development Programme, is one body that works towards marine pollution prevention in South Asia. Programmes like this work under regional conventions and action plans. One of those action plans was the Action Plan for the Protection and Management of the Marine and Coastal Environment of the South Asian Seas Region, established in 1995. South Asia Co-operative Environment Programme (SACEP 2007), Development of Regional Action Plan on Marine Litter in the South Asian Region, Coastal and Marine Risk Mitigation Plan for South Asia, etc. are few initiatives that deal extensively with the issue of marine litter in the region. Protection, prevention and reduction of marine pollution in the South Asian region are the principal objectives of this action plan. The hurdles occurring during the implementation of the action plans, especially in South Asia, arise from the internal land-based conflicts of interests among the countries. Within the paradigm of national security, the South Asian nations are yet to realize the significance of maritime security and the marine environment in particular.

Established in 1997, the Indian Ocean Rim Association (IORA) is an intergovernmental organization with growing importance in the Indian Ocean region (IORA 2015). The focus area of this 22-member organization includes disaster risk management, fisheries management, blue economy and maritime safety and security, among others. Among the South Asian nations, Bangladesh, Sri Lanka and India are the only nations that are parties to IORA. Owing to the fact that not all countries of the region are a part of this organization, tackling common maritime issues like ocean garbage and marine pollution proves difficult. Apart from this, the blue economy under the IORA puts more emphasis on the economic utilization of marine resources while marine health and its preservation are not its priority areas. Only 10 per cent of the member states are developed economies that adopt a spirit of cooperation.

Scope of National Laws

India

With a total coastline of 7,517 km, India is one of the major beneficiaries of the Indian Ocean in the south Asian region in the context of tourism, trade and other maritime activities. Although India is a committed member of the UNCLOS and other UN initiatives on marine environmental protection, it does not have any comprehensive law on the preservation of ocean or the reduction of maritime pollution. Article 48A of the Indian Constitution focuses on the protection of forests and wildlife. It does not specifically mention marine pollution and its prevention. The Coast Guard Act, established in 1950 under the Ministry of Defence, levies huge penalties in case of pollution of port waters (Al Arif and Karim 2015). The Water (Prevention and Control of Pollution) Act of 1974 addresses the need to protect the oceans from pollutants emerging from the land, a jurisdiction up to 5 km in the sea. The Environment Protection Act (EPA) prescribes the levels of discharging the effluents through various activities listed in the Coastal Regulation Zone. Apart from these Acts, India has been an ardent signatory of International maritime frameworks like UNCLOS and MARPOL conventions.

Sri Lanka

With laws framed and dedicated to controlling marine pollution, Sri Lanka has the most comprehensive legal framework on the prevention of marine pollution. The Marine Pollution Prevention Act, 2008 of Sri Lanka is the highest legislation that gives effect to all the International conventions of which Sri Lanka is a member (Al Arif and Karim 2015) The act is entitled 'An Act to provide for the prevention, reduction, and control of pollution of Sri Lankan Waters; to give effect to international conventions for the prevention of the pollution of Sea or for the matters connected with or incidental thereto'. This act, which is divided into eight parts, serves as a national framework for working towards marine pollution and, at the same time, ensures that the national obligations towards international conventions like UNCLOS are fulfilled (Al Arif and Karim 2015). While India and Bangladesh were projected to be very prosperous nations in the context of ship-breaking industry, the government of Sri Lanka released a draft on ship-breaking policy, with the intention of stopping all kinds of ship-breaking activities in the year 2009.

Bangladesh

Bangladesh has a considerable number of laws in place to combat environmental problems. The Constitution of Bangladesh specifically included article 18A, which deals with the improvement and protection of the environment and biodiversity. The first enactment by the Bangladeshi government (Sarker, Rehman, and Giessen 2018) that aimed to determine maritime boundaries and focused on marine pollution was The Territorial Water and Maritime Zones Act 1974. This act enables the government to take measures on preventing and protecting the environment in the territorial region as well as in the high seas. The Coast Guard Force of Bangladesh (under the Coast Guard

Act of 1994) detects activities causing pollution in the maritime zone and takes measures of prevention.

Maldives

Being an island nation, the protection of maritime environmental health is of utmost importance to the nation. There is no specific national maritime law in the Maldives to contain marine pollution. However, there is a general law called Environmental Protection and Preservation Act. This act enacted in 1993 focuses on overall environmental protection and includes the prevention of marine pollution. Like in Bangladesh, a Coast Guard Force of Maldives has been established to monitor any activities leading to marine pollution. Implementation of the MARPOL convention with specific laws in the Maldives has not yet seen the light of day.

Pakistan

Pakistan Environment Protection Act 1977 is a general act on environmental protection in Pakistan. There is no specific act or convention at the national level to counter the causes and effects of marine pollution in Pakistan. The Marine Security Agency Act of Pakistan 1994 is mainly responsible for protecting the country's maritime security interests. However, it also assists other departments in taking the required measures in the area of marine health and pollution. Besides, Section 554 of the Pakistan Merchant Shipping Ordinance 2001 is responsible for the management of waste that enters the ocean and for levying penalty in cases of sewage discharge into the ocean.

CONSENSUS AND RESPONSIBILITY IN THE SOUTH ASIAN REGION

The origin of marine garbage can be both land- and sea-based. It is hard to point out the exact origin of a particular marine waste, and this is why no particular country or state can be held responsible for marine pollution. From an environmental point of view, the problem of marine pollution and the cleaning up of the ocean garbage are transnational in nature. With the development of modern international laws, there has been a growing sense of responsibility and accountability among countries regarding the deteriorating condition of the oceans. This sense of responsibility has also been witnessed among the South Asian nations regarding the huge garbage dump in the Indian Ocean. However, what matters most is the implementation process and the amount of work that is being done. The Indian Ocean is one of the most polluted oceans in the world, and as such, it needs urgent environmental attention. The Indian coastal population generates around 0.8 kg of solid waste and garbage per capita per day. This quantity is higher than any other nation in the Indian Ocean region and is largely due to its longest coastline. Under the SAARC Environment Action Plan, the SAARC leaders, in a number of their meetings and summits, have raised concern on the deteriorating environmental condition. However, the focus was primarily on climate change and the containment of greenhouse gases. Maritime pollution, as a significant threat to the environment, has not yet been paid the required attention. Landlocked countries like Nepal and Bhutan quite naturally impute the garbage problem in the Indian Ocean to the sole responsibility of the coastal states like India and Sri Lanka.

The global community as a whole needs to understand that international waters are a resource that belongs to all, and that working on its prevention, irrespective of the geographical location, is everyone's duty. However, it must be acknowledged that individual states have been taking small measures according to their capacity, which will help in the long run. The global action on the use of plastics and the positive attitude of the South Asian countries towards this crackdown reflect their concern for environmental protection. The sense of responsibility towards nature and its protection from human-made threats should not be a concern only for government agencies. People, at their level, are also required to own up to their actions because responsible citizens make responsible nations. Also, NGOs have, in recent times, come to play a significant role in the conservation of the environment. In the case of marine pollution, there have been beach clean-up drives and other practical and real-time missions to combat pollution. Responsible governments are required to help or fund such activities. These measures are taken by organizations or institutions within a nation. However, when it comes to larger regional missions and projects, countries seem not to want to cooperate on certain levels because of their conflicting bilateral relations.

Marine beach littering is one of the main sources of pollution in coastal nations (Marlin 2011–2013). Monitoring littering behaviour of the common masses through programmes in collaboration with local agencies could go a long way, as it is cost–effective as well. The problem of marine pollution is such that there are no measures to identify or pinpoint the state that litters the most. In such a situation, all the nations of the world are required to share the responsibility for our shared nature.

Our attitudes and behaviour towards waste management, consumption and production patterns, recycling and littering are very much influenced by the modern lifestyle. A reckless attitude towards the environment and especially mass ignorance towards littering, have had serious consequences on the marine environment. Awareness is important. To solve the problem, there needs to be a clear understanding of the magnitude of the issue. Once the intensity of the problem is identified, responsible decisions and actions can follow. This is also the case with people and institutions. In order to control the activities leading to massive marine pollution, a self-realization at the individual level is necessary.

INDIA'S ACTION PLAN IN THE SAARC REGION

India's coastline supports millions of coastal human population, which is dependent on the rich and abundant marine resources. Nearly 250 million people live within a radius of 50km from the coastline of India. Hence, marine and coastal ecosystems of India play a vital role in India's overall growth.

Fishing is one common occupation of the people living in the coastal area (Ray 2008). Given the number of total coastal population, their economic dependence on the ocean, with its intricacies is immense. As mentioned earlier, their direct impact on the Indian marine environment has resulted in:

1. Habitat destruction
2. Excessive harvesting of coastal and marine resources
3. Pollution from industrial waste, aquaculture, upstream activities along the rivers

The textile industry, distilleries, paper and pulp industries, dye factories, pharmaceutical industry and the chemical manufacturing industry are major sources of industrial water pollution in India. The Central Pollution Control Board has stipulated certain standards for the quantity of emission of effluents in water bodies; the compliance of these industries in this regard remains very poor (UNDP and ASCI 2009).

India's Laws on Ocean Protection	Scope
The Coast Guard Act, 1950	Heavy penalties for the pollution of port waters in 1993, Coast Guard under Ministry of Defence made directly responsible for combating marine pollution. (UNEP India–ASCI 2009)
The Merchant Shipping Act, 1958	Prevention of pollution from ships and offshore platforms in the Exclusive Economic Zone. Majorly for disasters like oil spills, ship breaking activities and collision. (UNEP India–ASCI 2009)
The Water (Prevention and Control of Pollution) Act, 1974	Controlling pollution arising from land-based sources with a jurisdiction of up to 5 km in the sea.
The Maritime Zones of India Act, 1976	Government to take measures for protection of the marine animals, coral reef and mangroves.
Coast Guard formulated National Oil Spill Disaster Contingency Plan, 1996	Actions to be taken on oil spills and such disaster (revised in 2015).
National Marine Litter Policy, 2018	Action Plan to check plastic waste flowing into oceans.

The Federal government of India considers marine pollution to be an issue of governance concurrently by both state and central governments. But till date, there has been no law which enforces marine pollution or makes it a binding responsibility for the government or the states. The table above shows a list of policies and laws that have been implemented and revised from time to time. Laws have been framed and a certain amount of checks and balance has been put in place. These laws are, however, adapted to suit one's own convenience.

At the global level, India is a signatory to several environmental protection conventions. Right from the International Convention for the Prevention of Pollution from Ships (MARPOL Convention 73/78), Basel convention to the Regional Seas Programme setting the ground on a regional scale in South Asia, India's fight against marine litter has been high-spirited. India was among the first countries to sign the Action Plan for the Protection and Management of the Marine and Coastal Environment of the South Asian Seas Region (1995) Sri Lanka, Bangladesh, Pakistan and the Maldives have also shown great interest in collaborating within the framework of this programme. The plan aims to survey and assess present social and economic activities, review local/municipal legislation to see whether it is in line with international agreements for the prevention and control of marine pollution. (UNDP and ASCI 2009) Similarly, the Regional Oil and Chemical Marine Pollution Contingency Plan for South Asia (2000) has also been a key factor of integration for the South Asian coastal states.

Ocean clean-up drives and campaigns by NGO's and other environmental organizations along the coastlines of Mumbai, Chennai, Orissa, Goa etc, are on the rise. Not only do these organizations conduct campaigns and drives on the Indian coast, but they also help and fund such activities in the neighbouring coastal nations. These campaigns are perceived as leisure and recreational activities. Such a perception encourages more and more people to join and defend the right cause.

A campaign recently conducted by the Indian Coast Guard on the International Coastal Cleanup Day (ICC–2018) was highly successful in India. The following table shows the amount of garbage collected by different Indian coastal states as part of the ICC programme:

Sl. No	State/UT	No of Participants	Debris Collected (kgs)
1.	Gujarat	2,621	11,437
2.	Daman	457	625
3.	Maharashtra	4,697	16,900
4.	Goa	1,300	1,940
5.	Karnataka	1,296	3,475
6.	Kerala	850	4,800
7.	L & M Islands	1,034	3,000
8.	Puducherry	366	1,000
9.	Tamil Nadu	2,538	9,190
10.	Andhra Pradesh	2,450	8,340
11.	Odisha	422	153
12.	West Bengal	1,175	2,670
13.	A & N Islands	2,820	7,690
	Total	22,026	71,220

Source: indiancoastguard.gov.in

Existing measures of education and awareness campaigns (UNEP-SAS 2007) such as the Swachh Bharat initiatives like Swachh Sagar Abhiyan conducted on a monthly basis by the centre and state governments, as well as the National Maritime Foundation, can make a significant contribution to improving ocean health. The amount of garbage that continues to appear on the beaches, and in the oceans, indicates that many people and communities living in the coastal areas have not yet changed their behaviour. The management of debris entering and exiting the water bodies in itself can help reduce ocean garbage.

The tourism industry and tourists need special sessions on anti-littering mechanisms. Only then will the consciousness arise. Penalty for those who litter should not just remain on paper but has to be enforced. Plastic packaging companies, and those associated with boating activities, need to be regulated for providing an experience of eco-tourism to travellers. Indeed keeping the marine environment clean, safe, and sound will attract more investments into the country.

CONCLUSION

The Indian Ocean in the South Asian region is in an alarmingly critical condition with continuous and unmonitored solid waste dumping. The sources of these pollutants vary in an undeniably significant manner. Such a state of affairs makes it difficult to identify the origin of these pollutants. Global organizations as well as individual nations have attempted to respond to the vulnerability of the Indian Ocean in the South Asian region. However, mere discussions and conventions do not suffice. The lack of implementation of action plans at both the global and regional levels is evident. This is mainly due to conflicts between national and international laws. Besides, there is altogether different contestation between the developed and the underdeveloped countries regarding their responsibility in maritime protection.

The measures currently taken by different state agencies have been ad hoc or superficial in nature. The Environment Protection Agencies in developing countries mostly take measures that seem to be directed towards the symptoms and not the causes. The different deadlines that are set up to reach a level of achievement appear to be never-ending. Moreover, when there is a change of government, projects initiated by the previous government usually get diluted or are seldom continued.

The lack of effective management of marine litter in the region arises due to a number of reasons like technological and managerial gaps, lack of effective mechanisms to control the land-based sources of debris, and very little cooperation at the regional and national levels among the nations of the region (UNEP n.d.). Networking between grass-root administrations with regional forums should be made easier and accessible for better communication.

In order to bring about a pollution-free marine ecosystem, the major stakeholders such as non–governmental organizations, community-based organizations, fishermen societies, etc., are required to come together. Also, cooperative programmes with a nexus between developed states and private partners on marine protection will bring about beneficial results. There is also a requirement of facilities for recycling of solid wastes in the affected coastal areas.

Above all, a marine protection committee, with a comprehensive marine litter assessment and management programme, should be formed with all the countries of the SAS as members. This committee can set up different branches, each with a set of objectives, and work towards spreading awareness about the realities of marine pollution, the little steps that people can take at their level, etc. An annual marine environment assessment by the SAARC association can generate yearly reports on the progress made and the future outlook. Exclusive policy-think tanks on marine-life protection and marine environment security in South Asia should be established and conduct meetings/summits on a regular basis for suggesting the necessary actions to be undertaken.

The blue economy is an interesting area which the region needs to look at closely. The European Union (EU), the Indian Ocean Rim Association (IORA), the African Union (AU), and many more regional groupings have incorporated the blue economy into their priority framework. (Banchariya 2018) The blue economy can not only foster maritime economic development but also help deal with issues like marine environment protection. It will be useful to raise funds and use them for ocean clean-ups, garbage collecting technology, and many more campaigns to safeguard waters from getting contaminated. Bangladesh and India are the countries in South Asia that are exploring the 'blue' way but have not tried hard to drive the economy towards marine biodiversity protection. Last but not least, when the world community sits and discusses the environment on a broad level, marine pollution, and the increasing threats to the maritime environment should be given importance and obligatory attention.

REFERENCES

Al Arif, A., and Karim, Md E. 2015. 'Marine Pollution and the South Asian Coastal States: A Legal Appraisal'. Available at: https://ssrn.com/abstract=2590009 (accessed on 22 April 2020).
Banchariya, S. 2018. 'Unexplored Blue Economy in India'. *Times of India*, 6 August. Available at: https://timesofindia.indiatimes.com/home/education/news/

unexplored-blue-economy-in-india/articleshow/65292887.cms (accessed on 22 April 2020).
IORA (Indian Ocean Rim Association). 2015. 'Blue Economy'. Available at: http://www.iora.int/en/priorities-focus-areas/blue-economy (accessed on 22 April 2020).
Juneja, S. 2015. 'Sundarbans at Risk'. *DownToEarth,* 07 June. Available at: https://www.downtoearth.org.in/coverage/sundarbans-at-risk-36862 (accessed on 22 April 2020).
Marlin. 2011–2013. *Final Report of Baltic Marine Litter Project Marlin.* European Union. Available at: https://www.cbss.org/wp-content/uploads/2012/08/marlin-baltic-marine-litter-report.pdf (accessed on 22 April 2020).
Ocean Conservancy. 2015. *Stemming the Tide: Land-based Strategies for a Plastic-free Ocean.* Ocean conservancy and McKinsey Center for Business and Environment. Available at: https://oceanconservancy.org/wp-content/uploads/2017/04/full-report-stemming-the.pdf (accessed on 22 April 2020).
Ray, A. 2008. 'Waste Management in Developing Asia: Can Trade and Cooperation Help?' *The Journal of Environment* 17 (1): 3–25. Available at: https://journals.sagepub.com/doi/10.1177/1070496507310742 (accessed on 22 April 2020).
SACEP (South Asia Cooperative Environment Programme. 2007. *Marine Litter in the South Asian Seas Region.* Colombo: United Nations Environment Programme. Available at: https://www.unenvironment.org/resources/report/marine-litter-south-asian-seas-region (accessed on 22 April 2020).
Sarker, P. K., Md Saifur Rehman, and Lukas Giessen 2018. 'Regional Governance by the South Asia Cooperative Environment Program(SACEP)? Institutional Design and Customizable Regime Policy Offering Flexible Political Options'. *Land Use Policy* 77: 454–470. doi:10.1016/j.landusepol.2018.05.009.
Sureshkumar, N. 2007. *Evaluation and Assessment of Marine Debris/Litter: National Report of Sri Lanka.*
UNDP and ASCI. 2009. *Analysis of Existing Environmental Instruments in India.* New Delhi: UNDP and ASCI. Available at: https://www.undp.org/content/dam/india/docs/analysis_of_existing_environmental_instruments_in_india.pdf (accessed on 22 April 2020).
UNEP. n.d. 'Why does UN Environment Matter?'. Available at United Nations Environment Programme: https://www.unenvironment.org/about-un-environment/why-does-un-environment-matter (accessed on 22 April 2020).
UNEP (United Nations Environment Programme)–South Asian Seas. n.d. Available at: https://www.unenvironment.org/explore-topics/oceans-seas/what-we-do/working-regional-seas/regional-seas-programmes/south-asian (accessed on 22 April 2020).
Yardley, J. 2013. 'Bangladesh Pollution, Told in Colors and Smells'. *The New York Times,* 14 July. Available at: https://www.nytimes.com/2013/07/15/world/asia/bangladesh-pollution-told-in-colors-and-smells.html (accessed on 22 April 2020).

Chapter 12

Expanding Indian Nuclear Industry and Environmental Hazards
A Special Reference to the Establishment and Development of Nuclear Reactors in the Post-2005 Era

K. R. Sreelekha

The two major landmark episodes in post-1990 India's history were the New Economic Policy adopted by India in 1991 and the Indo-US Nuclear Deal of 2005. These two episodes still have an influencing impact on every sphere of India's life. The landmark Indo-US Nuclear Deal was signed by the President of the United States and the Prime Minister of India in 2005. The final ratification of the deal by the US Congress in 2008 opened a new sphere of activity for India with regard to nuclear trade and nuclear cooperation, and also added a new dimension to international non-proliferation. The deal lifted a three-decade US moratorium on nuclear trade with India; it provided US assistance to India's civilian nuclear energy programme and expanded US-India cooperation in energy and satellite technology (Bajoria and Pan 2010). The landmark Indo-US Nuclear Deal is considered as a concrete materialization of post-liberalized India's strategic ambitions. A prosperous economy is needed to perpetuate this ambitious plan. But India's energy sector failed to support the ever-growing demands of its economy and to feed the demands from its household sector. The policy analyst observes that the Indo-US Nuclear Deal is an accurate result of the intersection between ambitious India's political-economic aspirations and the reprioritization of India's foreign policy objectives.

Indian leaders and strategists believed that a nuclear deal would materialize India's strategic objectives. As believed and expected, the deal put an end to the three-decade-old US moratorium on nuclear trade with India, and the benefits of the deal are as follows:

1. Foreign firms are allowed to build nuclear reactors in India.
2. India can receive imported fuel for its nuclear reactors.
3. Transfer of technology from abroad to enrich or reprocess the fuel.
4. India's capacity to expand and install indigenous nuclear reactors.

ENERGY SITUATION IN INDIA

A significant section of Indian society does not have proper access to electricity, and those who have access face a shortage of it. A simultaneous increase in the population and growing demands from the economy made the Indian situation quite vulnerable with regard to energy consumption. Here comes nuclear energy as a source of cheap as well as clean energy. The signing of the Indo-US Nuclear Deal is considered by India as a green signal in its future endeavours to nuclear aspiration. But nuclear power constitutes only 2.77 per cent of India's energy mix (Energy Statistic Report 2016). The thermal sector constitutes 54 per cent, hydroelectricity constitutes 21 per cent, gas 10 per cent and renewable energy 10 per cent. However, India's decision makers have chosen the nuclear option which is contributing only 3 per cent to the energy mix, and largely abandoned renewable energy source, which has a 10 per cent share in India's total energy mix. India's decision makers preferred to explore the nuclear option as a viable one for future development, keeping apart the possibility of a sustainable economy based on the renewable economy. This is the point of intersection between the political economy of domestic policy preferences and the prioritization of foreign policy practices. The Indo-US Nuclear Deal was a proper mix of both these principles. As a result, India witnessed an increasing trend in favour of establishing new nuclear reactors and reviving the existing ones. The Government of India's Department of Atomic Energy (DAE) endorses nuclear power as a cost-effective, cheap and clean energy resource (DAE website) and claims that embracing the nuclear option would help India deliver its global commitments and be a viable option for addressing climate change. This posture obviously reveals the fact that the policy-makers are sure about India's priorities and commitments.

INDIA'S NUCLEAR INDUSTRY

The trend in favour of nuclear reactors is declining globally after the Fukushima disaster, but for India, the nuclear reactors continue to be an interesting option. Ever since the initiative of the Indo-US Nuclear Deal, there has been an upswing in favour of nuclear energy, and the revival of nuclear reactors installed was the trend in India. R. K. Sinha, the former Chairman of the Atomic Energy Commission and former Secretary of the DAE, stated that 'as the number of nuclear reactors rose, the need for uranium hit the domestic reactors, adversely affecting their performance. [...] By 2006–2007, the performance of Indian reactors had reduced to 50–55 per cent due to a shortage of nuclear fuel' (*The Economic Times* 2018). To give an example, the fifth unit of the Rajasthan Atomic Power Station (RAPS-5) at Rawatbhata achieved a record of continuous operation for 765 days at its full capacity of 220 MWe on 6 September 2014 (Subramanian 2014). The plant was indigenously built by the Nuclear Power Corporation of India Limited (NPCIL). The revival of the plant shows the technical accuracy achieved by the NPCIL and uninterrupted nuclear fuel supply facilitated by India's commitment to the Nuclear Deal and membership in the Nuclear Suppliers Group (NSG). Hence, it can be argued that a general trend prevails in favour of expanding the nuclear industry in post-2005 India.

WHY THIS UPSWING?

Post-liberalized India's attempt to emerge as a leading power in the Asian continent is one of the reasons for this upswing in favour of being a nuclear power.

Politico-economic Aspirations

India's aspiration to become a lead state in the continent persuaded it to feed the increasing demand from its economy. In order to meet the increasing demand arising out of its expanding economic production and industrial development, India had to find a cheap energy resource. India's search ended with the nuclear option, as the decision-makers thought that the adoption of the nuclear energy would materialize many other objectives as well. Citing energy crisis is just a camouflage to embrace a nuclear policy, which has a multidimensional impact on India, both internally and externally.

Strategic Security Ambitions

The very signing of the Indo-US Nuclear Deal itself elevated India's status both regionally and in the Asian continent as a lead state. Consequently, membership in the NSG has accelerated India's aspirations to have strategic cooperation with the NSG member states. The DAE, Government of India, made a reply to the floor of the Indian Parliament that 'pursuant to the Civil Nuclear Cooperation, around 7810 MT of Natural Uranium and about 100 MT of Enriched Uranium has been imported from France, Russia, Kazakhstan and Canada since the year 2009 till today' (Department of Atomic Energy 2017). Concomitant with the Indo-US Nuclear Deal, initiated in the year 2005, the NSG membership in 2008, which lifted the nuclear trade sanctions imposed on India in 1974, ultimately facilitated India's nuclear trade and technology transfer with NSG members for civilian purposes. This engagement with the NSG provided leverage for India in the realm of strategic security. Globally, other states started giving weight to India as they had done with China in the recent past.

The Paris Treaty

To address the climate change, countries adopted Paris agreement at the COP21 in Paris on 12 December 2015 ... in the agreement all the countries agreed to work to limit global temperature rise to well below 2 degree Celsius. The pace of change is quickening as more people are turning to renewable energy and a range of other measures that will reduce emissions and increase adaptation efforts. (UN n.d.)

India started signalling its commitment to The Paris Treaty and ratified the agreement in October 2016. The Treaty called for the cutting down of greenhouse gas emissions to combat global warming. India (7% share in the global total) is listed as the fourth largest carbon-emitting state by the 2016 Report on Trends in Global CO_2 Emissions (PBL 2016). As a result of India's commitment to this agreement, India has to ensure that at least 40 per cent of its electricity will be generated from non-fossil sources by 2030. India hopes that declaring solidarity with the agreement by embracing a nuclear option would please the global states and can build partnerships. Such a step will further India's future aspirations at varying levels, like political, economic as well as strategic security. It is also interesting to note that India's bilateral and multilateral engagement in the recent past have witnessed a manifold increase in the post-2005 era, which shows that these Indian initiatives were intended to actively strengthen India's ties with global states.

The upswing in favour of the nuclear reactors as a solution to the increasing demands of India's economy looks, therefore, quite natural. But the cost of clinging to such a decision is erroneous as India's future has to pay for it, and one of the major areas, which is going to be affected by this policy option, is India's environment.

ENVIRONMENTAL IMPACT

Research and studies related to the impact of the nuclear reactors upon the environment and the public are usually carried out and conducted by governmental agencies like Atomic Energy Regulatory Board (AERB) and other agencies under the DAE. Regular studies conducted by these agencies state that there are no obvious environmental hazards and challenges to human security because of the very presence of a nuclear reactor in a particular place/region, until and unless there occurs an accident in a nuclear reactor. A response to an unstarred question raised in the Lok Sabha in 2016 states that Environmental Survey Laboratories (ESLs) are installed in all atomic power plant/radioactive waste management sites and that these ESLs carry out pre-operational survey around the plant site up to a distance of 30 km radius to establish the pre-operational baseline radioactivity levels around the site. ESLs are equipped with highly sensitive instruments to analyse extremely low levels of radioactivity in the environmental samples. They ensure that there is no unacceptable build-up of radioactivity in the surrounding environment. Nevertheless, it is also a fact that the general public and the environment are regularly exposed to radioactivity, at least at a minute level, leading to complications in the future. Then the question that remains to be asked is: where do the major challenges come from?

NUCLEAR REACTORS AND THE INDIRECT CHAIN OF HAZARDS

The study pinpoints to the fact that there exists an indirect chain of hazards involved in the whole process, which means that the nature of threat is largely indirect ranging from (a) the mining of raw nuclear fuels such as uranium and thorium, (b) the transportation of raw material from one place to another, (c) poor precautionary measures provided to the labourers and indigenous people who are exposed to the mining and processing of raw radioactive materials and (d) high risk of radiation and health hazards while participating in the nuclear fuel processing industry.

UCIL TO FEED THE NUCLEAR REACTORS

Reports and studies state that experience from India's mining fields is such that life and environment had depleted beyond imagination. One of such incidents is reported from the Jadugoda village of Jharkhand and East Singhbhum, where the state-owned Uranium Corporation of India Ltd (UCIL) has been engaged in mining for the last five decades. The way in which the company extracts, transports and processes uranium ore in a negligent manner has alarmed the life of the region.

UCIL, the public sector giant, was established in 1967, and its current capacity is 1,000 tonnes of uranium ore per day. Jadugoda mines' uranium ore supply accounts for 25 per cent of raw material that fuels 5,000 MWe of nuclear power generation in the country (PTI 2014). A number of studies have been done on the Jadugoda region and the impact of radiation on the population such as 'Radiation and Tribal Health in Jadugoda: The Contention Between Science and Sufferings' by C. J. Sonowal and Sunilkumar Jojo, 'The Impact of Uranium Mine on Health of Tribal People: A Study of Jadugoda Region' by Neha Kumari. These studies are very specific and share concerns about increasing levels of mining uranium to feed nuclear reactors all over India. The studies also nail down the UCIL's gross negligence to ensure minimum health security, food security and environmental security of the population of the region. On the floor of the Indian Parliament Lok Sabha, the prime minister, in his reply to an unstarred question, has stated that Atomic Minerals Directorate for Exploration and Research has established the presence of 171,672 tonnes of uranium, as of 30 June 2011 in new regions of Andhra Pradesh, Chhattisgarh, Himachal Pradesh, Jharkhand, Karnataka, Maharashtra, Meghalaya, Rajasthan, Uttar Pradesh and Uttarakhand (Department of Atomic Energy 2011). As a reply to the question over the possibility of revenues generated from the said reserves, it was stated on the floor of the Parliament that no direct revenues would be generated from the uranium reserves. However, the reserves will enable the functioning of nuclear power reactors and the generation of electricity (Department of Atomic Energy 2011).

The role of the UCIL in feeding the ever-increasing demands of India's nuclear reactors and India's continuous funding of such exploration projects is apparent. However, this has been done by compromising human security as well as the environmental security of the people living in the region.

HUMAN-MADE RADIATIONS

Human-made radiations include mining, milling and processing of nuclear raw materials while preparing them as nuclear fuel. At the initial stage of installing, a nuclear facility also disseminates a noticeable rate of radiation and CO_2. Another major threat is the disposal of nuclear waste. If not disposed of properly, it is harmful and can endanger the water, soil and air quality of the region. In December 2015, the National Human Rights Commission, India has taken *suo motu* cognizance of a media report from a study amidst government apathy. The report says that radioactive and toxic waste has leaked from India's oldest and most important uranium mine at Jadugoda, East Singhbhum district, Jharkhand, affecting people, livestock, rivers, forest and agricultural produce in the area (National Human Rights Commission 2015). The National Human Rights Commission issued a notice to the Secretary, DAE, Government of India, the Chairman, UCIL and the Chief Secretary, Government of Jharkhand in a report that states that adequate measures have not been taken to prevent toxic leaks from the site by India's nuclear establishment. The labourers, who were engaged in the transportation of raw materials from the mining fields to the processing plant, were highly exposed to these radioactive materials, which posed threats to their life and survival. The poor and illiterate masses were the primary victims of such acts.

WATER, AIR AND SOIL CONTAMINATION

During the process of power generation, nuclear reactors use a large quantity of water, and this contaminated water is not properly treated in many cases. A study conducted by Professor Dipak Ghosh, Physicist, Faculty of Science at Jadavpur University, Kolkata, found that the contamination of water in the Subarnarekha River (Jadugoda region) had reached higher levels with radioactive particles. The Kudankulam Nuclear Power Plant is situated in the southern part of Tamil Nadu. Idinthakarai is another village quite close to another nuclear power plant. The main occupation of the people of this village is fishing on the shores and in the deep sea. In Kudankulam, around 80 per cent of the employable workforce is jobless, while in Idinthakarai, 60 per cent are involved in fishing (Moorty 2000). What worried the fishing community most is that there is a security ring over a distance of 500 m from the beach, preventing them from fishing there (Subramanian 2011). In the Gogi region of the Karnataka state, the villagers started complaining of various illnesses, which they attributed to the contamination of water due to mining. A study was conducted to determine the uranium concentration in groundwater samples in the Gogi region, which aimed at generating baseline information on uranium radioactivity in groundwater samples around the proposed uranium mining area (Reddy et. al. 2014). A DAE-funded study found that water from Gogi village was unfit for human consumption due to high radioactivity. Its findings were not communicated to the local people or the people, and no follow-up action has been taken so far (Padmanabhan and Makolil 2015).

According to the United States Nuclear Regulatory Commission, an operating nuclear power plant produces a very small amount of radioactive gases and liquids as well as a small amount of radiation. It states that if one lives within 50 miles of a nuclear power plant, one would be exposed to an average radiation dose of about 0.01 millirem per year (Padmanabhan and Makolil 2015). As regards the radiological protection of the public, the AERB takes care of the following measures for the protection of the public while nuclear power plants is in operation: it ensures that the sources contributing to the generation of radioactive solid, liquid and gaseous wastes and their release in the environment are examined with respect to the minimization of the waste at the source and design level. The AERB prescribes that the effective dose to which a member of the public (whole body) is exposed is 1 man-millisievert (mSv)/year. But this is the kind of radiation that a member of the public is forced to receive when he or she is close to a nuclear reactor. The report also did not deny the fact that nuclear reactors are not free from atmospheric emissions. Therefore, the whole claim of nuclear energy being a cheap and clean option can be thwarted by citing these malicious impacts. Though it is claimed as a clean and cheap energy option, it is an acclaimed fact that nuclear reactors emit low levels of radiation into the environment. Differing opinions exist among scientists over the effects of such constant radiation, varying from serious health issues to transformations in human beings' DNA. These low levels of radiation cause damage to the flora and fauna as well.

We have experiences from Jadugoda, and the southern coastal regions of Tamil Nadu and Kerala, which show how the exploration process endangered the life in that region. The water and atmospheric contaminations have a consequent impact over the soil and the agricultural production of the area. One can logically conclude that though a nuclear plant feeds the energy security of a region, it destroys the food security of that region at the same time.

EMISSION OF CARBON DIOXIDE

Nuclear power has been called as a clean energy option as it does not emit CO_2. Though the operating nuclear power plants do not emit CO_2, the whole process behind establishing a nuclear plant disseminates lots of CO_2 into the atmosphere. The mining of uranium releases a high amount of CO_2 into the environment, and high levels of CO_2 are emitted in activities related to running and building of a nuclear plant.

NUCLEAR WASTE

Waste from nuclear power plants is a huge concern for humanity as it can remain active for hundreds of years. In India, as of now, the waste from the power plants has been stored at the nuclear plant itself, but it has to be buried in some other place for safety purposes. In case of an accident, radioactive waste could leak; this possibility is high for those nuclear power plants that are on the coastal zones and those at the seismic-sensitive areas. The efforts of the scientists to solve this problem resulted in an initiative to build deep geological repositories. There are unconfirmed news reports in the media that a nuclear disposal site is underway at Gogi, Karnataka, and there are speculations that the Indian-based Neutrino Observatory at the Idukki and Theni districts of Kerala and Tamil Nadu states, can be possible destinations, but secrecy prevails over these matters. Only the DAE knows the truth. A veil of secrecy covers the whole idea and the plans of DAE are not known.

THORIUM AS A VIABLE ALTERNATIVE

Recent surveys on nuclear fuel resources have increasingly concentrated on thorium as a viable alternative to uranium. This is because even though thorium itself is not fissile, through neutron capture and subsequent β-decay reactions, Th-232 can be transmuted to U-233 (Ewing, Krall, and Englert 2012). During 1970–2004, India produced a total of 2,399 publications in the field of thorium. The maximum number of publications came out in 2000. The average number of publications per year was 68.54. There were only nine publications in 1970; post-1970, there was a consistent growth in the number of publications. Such an increase shows that Indian nuclear scientists are highly interested in the field. DAE institutions topped the research on thorium (Kademani et al. 2006). Various institutions contributing to thorium research can be categorized under two sectors: (a) institutions under the DAE and (b) non-DAE institutions, of which DAE is the largest contributor of literature. Indian establishments intensified dedication in carrying out mining, exploration, and development of thorium as a viable option to feed next-generation nuclear reactors in India. Thorium is three times abundant in Earth's crust than uranium, and this deposit contains other mineral resources of value.

THE ENVIRONMENTAL COST OF THORIUM MINING

India possesses a substantial level of thorium deposits along its southern coasts of Tamil Nadu and Kerala. This phenomenon has intensified the vulnerability of India's southern coastal regions for illegal mining, legal mining as well as illegal extraction and export of monazite sands. A few private companies have won the bid to purchase the lease licenses to mine and export them. Since these minerals were classified as 'atomic minerals' under the Atomic Energy Act of 1962, Tamil Nadu has breached the law violating fundamental principles of environmental as well as coastal security. A news report reads that Tamil Nadu has been the biggest victim of illegal sand mining in the country. According to the report recently submitted by senior lawyer and rights activist V. Suresh, appointed as amicus curiae by the Madras High Court, in the case relating to illegalities in the mining of beach sand minerals in Thoothukudi, Thirunelveli and Kanyakumari, out of 1.5 crore tonnes of raw sand mined between 2000 and 2017, 57 per cent had been mined illegally (Chaitanya and Ramakrishnan 2017). The beach sands of India, especially of the southern coastal zones in Tamil Nadu, Odisha, Kerala and Andhra Pradesh, are rich in minerals. A study conducted by the Institute of Ocean Management of Anna University revealed that Tamil Nadu has the highest concentration of Monazite, an atomic mineral, and contains 8–10 per cent thorium, which is a nuclear fuel (Chaitanya and Ramakrishnan 2017). An amendment to the Coastal Regulation Zones 1991 was made by the Union Ministry of Environment (Notification 2011), which stated that allowing mining in ecologically sensitive coastal zones actually threatened the already fragile coastal zones of India and would also invite disasters like saltwater intrusion, qualitative as well as quantitative degradation of groundwater level and so on.

Rare-earth mining is one of the major challenges faced by southern coastal regions of India. Rare-earth refers to a group of 17 elements, which are classified based on their atomic weight. This means most of the rare earth occurs in nature in combination with other elements. Naturally occurring radioactive minerals often possess a significant level of occupational as well as environmental radiation during mining, milling and chemical process of extraction of rare earth elements and compounds (Pillai 2007). Depending on the monazite concentration in the raw sand, radiation exposures of the order of 0.13–1.00 mSv per tonne are involved in the mining and separation of monazite (Pillai 2007). The coastal line of Kollam districts in Kerala has a decade-long story of their fight against the mining of beach sands. Since the 1960s, the mining process has been happening in places like Chavara and Alappad, which have a heavy concentration of mineral-rich beach sands. Villages along these coastal lines almost disappeared, and many environmental hazards started appearing.

Two public sector companies, Indian Rare Earth, which comes under the union government, and state-owned Kerala Minerals and Metals Limited, have engaged in the mining of rare earth since the 1960s. Both companies continue to engage in the mining process despite peoples' protests. Mining in this area has displaced many villages. Pollution of water bodies, scarcity of drinking water, depletion of fish stock and erosion of the land are the issues faced by this region due to mining. Apart from these crises, the region and the people are exposed to environmental radiation as a result of processing these atomic minerals. The environmental activists from the regions state that monazite and ilmenite are the main extracts from this mining, and full processing of these minerals does not happen in India. We export rutile mineral. Therefore, the main profit is for foreign companies; technically, our country does not benefit much (John 2018). Peoples' agitation is still going on in these southern coastal regions of Tamil Nadu and Kerala in their attempt to retain their villages and environment.

Nuclear reactors, as such, do not pose a direct threat until and unless an accident occurs. However, there are indirect challenges involved in nuclear energy production. The whole process of feeding a nuclear reactor generates long-term environmental hazards. The environmental cost of pursuing a nuclear energy policy thus comes at the expense of our environmental protection. It reveals the fact that tremendous damage has already been inflicted and still is continuing. India's villages and its rural population are victims of such decisions as India's villages, forests and coastal regions are being exploited heavily to feed urban India's strategic needs, resulting in rural India perishing in the chaos to fulfil urban India's dream. Such disregard creates a wide disparity between the urban and rural India. This is not the idea behind sustainable development. Being one of the largest democracies in the world, India has to adopt more sustainable notions of development based on clean and green energy like renewable energy sources. Nuclear energy is not clean as it depletes our environment. It is not green but red as it can endanger the entire humanity.

REFERENCES

Bajoria, J., and E. Pan. 2010, 5 November. *The U.S.–India Nuclear Deal*. New York: Council on Foreign Relations. Available at: www.cfr.org/backgrounder/us-india-nuclear-deal (accessed on 11 March 2020).

Chaitanya, S. V. K, and S. Ramakrishnan. 2017. 'Greed for Atomic Minerals to Leave Tamil Nadu in Peril'. *New Indian Express*, 13 October.

Costal Regulation Zone Notification. 2011. Ministry of Environment and Forests (Department of Environment, Forests and Wildlife), Available at: http://www.environmentwb.gov.in/pdf/CRZ-Notification-2011.pdf, (accessed on 15 May 2020).

Department of Atomic Energy. n.d. Government of India. Available at: http://www.dae.nic.in/?q=node/926 (accessed on September 30, 2019)

———. 2011. *Unstarred Question No. 3601, To Be Answered on 24 August 2011. Lok Sabha on Uranium Reserves.* Available at: http://www.dae.nic.in/writereaddata/3601_lsus240811.pdf (accessed on 30 September 2019).

———. 2017. *Rajya Sabha, Starred Question No. 368.* Available at: http://dae.nic.in/writereaddata/parl/budget2017/rssq368.pdf(accessed on 30 September 2019).

Energy Statistics. 2016. 'Central statistics Office, Ministry of Statistics and Programme Implementation'. Government of India, P-10. Available at: http://www.mospi.gov.in/sites/default/files/publication_reports/Energy_statistics_2016.pdf (accessed on 15 May 2020).

Ewing, R. C., L. Krall, and M. Englert. 2012 'Is Nuclear Fission a Sustainable Source of Energy?' *MRS Bulletin* 37: 417–424.

Frontline. 2014. 'India's Nuclear Power'. 3 October. Available at: https://www.frontline.in/other/data-card/indias-nuclear-power/article6407818.ece (accessed on 22 April 2020).

John, H. 2018, 22 October. *Villages Vanish in This Coastal District of Kerala as They Succumb to Sand Mining.* Available at: https://india.mongabay.com/2018/10/22/villages-vanish-in-this-coastal-district-of-kerala-as-they-succumb-to-sand-mining/

Kademani, B. S., V. Kumar, A. Sagar, A. Kumar, L. Mohan, and S. Ganesh. 2006. 'Scientometric Dimensions of Thorium Research in India'. *DESIDOC Bulletin of Information Technology* 26 (3): 9–25.

Moorty, D. N. 2000. 'Living with Nuclear Power'. *The Indian Express*, 16 February.

National Human Rights Commission. 2015, 16 December. *NHRC Notices to Centre and Government of Jharkhand over Reported Apathy Towards Checking the Radioactive and Toxic Waste Leaking from a Mine in Jaduguda.* Available at: http://nhrc.nic.in/press-release/nhrc-notices-centre-and-government-jharkhand-over-reported-apathy-towards-checking (accessed on 11 March 2020).

Padmanabhan, V. T., and J. Makolil. 2015, 22 February. 'India's Underground Radioactive Waste Disposal Site at Gogi in Karnataka? Part I: Final Disposal of High Level Radioactive Waste—Global Practices and Indian experiments'. Cochin: Society Of science, Environment and ethics. Available at: https://www.researchgate.net/profile/padmanabhan_vt/publication/272621683_india%27s_underground_radioactive_waste_disposal_site_at_gogi_in_karnataka/links/54ea37410cf25ba91c82a3bd/indias-underground-radioactive-waste-disposal-site-at-gogi-in-karnataka.pdf (accessed on 11 March 2020).

PBL. 2016. 'Netherlands Environmental Assessment Agency'. *Trends in Global Co_2 Emissions, 2016 Report.* Available at: http://edgar.jrc.ec.europa.eu/news_docs/jrc-2016-trends-in-global-co2-emissions-2016-report-103425.pdf (accessed on 11 March 2020).

Pillai, P. M. B. 2007. 'Naturally Occurring Radioactive Material (NORM V)'. Proceeding of an International Symposium, Seville, Spain, 19–22 March 2007. Vienna: IAEA.

PTI. 2014. 'Uranium Corporation of India Hopes to Get Renewal of Jadugoda Mine Lease Soon'. *The Economic Times*, 6 October. Available at: https://economictimes.indiatimes.com/news/politics-and-nation/uranium-corporation-of-india-hopes-to-get-renewal-of-jaduguda-mine-lease-soon/articleshow/44506905.cms (accessed on 22 April 2020).

Reddy, P. J., S. P. D. Bhade, S. Anilkumar, R. V. Kolekar, R. Singh, K. S. Pradeepkumar, S. Rajesh, and V. Pulhani. 2014. 'Measurement of Uranium Concentration in Ground Water in Gogi Region, Karnataka Using Liquid Scintillation Spectrometry'. In *National Symposium on Environment: Climate Change and Its Impact*, edited by G. G. Pandit, I. V. Saradhi, S. K. Sahu, and D. N. Sharma. Kottayam: Mahatma Gandhi University. Available at: https://inis.iaea.org/search/search.aspx?orig_q=RN:46034709 (accessed on 22 April 2020).

Subramanian, T. S. 2011. 'Power and Protest'. Frontline(Print Edition) October 21, 2011,https://frontline.thehindu.com/science-and-technology/article30177242.ece (accessed September 30, 2019).

Subramanian, T. S. 2014. RAPS Unit-5 sets a Record, The Hindu, September 7, 2014, https://www.thehindu.com/news/national/raps-unit5-sets-a-record/article6386663.ece (accessed September 30, 2019).

The Economic Times. 2018. 'Indo-US Nuclear Deal Helped Fuel Domestic Power Plants, Gave India Access to Critical Tech: Experts.' *The Economic Times*, 11 October. Available at: https://economictimes.indiatimes.com/industry/energy/power/indo-us-nuke-deal-helped-fuel-domestic-power-plants-gave-india-access-to-critical-tech-experts/articleshow/66161128.cms (accessed on 22 April 2020).

UN. n.d. 'Climate Action'. Available at: https://www.un.org/sustainable development/climate-action/

United States Nuclear Regulatory Commission. n.d. *Frequently Asked Questions (FAQ) about Radiation Protection*. Available at: https://www.nrc.gov/about-nrc/radiation/related-info/faq.html#5 (accessed on 11 March 2020).

PART IV

Poverty, Alienation and Social Exclusion

Chapter 13

Civil Society
Positing the Role of NGOs in
Depoliticizing Political Action

Arsha V. Sathyan

INTRODUCTION

In achieving the goals of sustainable development, non-governmental organizations (NGOs) and civil society are looked upon as essential stakeholders in governance at the regional, national and global levels. This chapter is based on an action research[1] on Mahatma Gandhi National Rural Employment Guarantee Act (MGNREGA)[2] conducted in a rural village called Dudhera in Bamhani Panchayat of Samnapur block under the Dindori District of Madhya Pradesh.

The MGNREGA is a law enacted in 2005 and implemented in 2006. The primary aim of this Act is to provide at least 100

---

[1] This chapter is an extract from an MPhil thesis submitted to the Centre for Development Practice, Ambedkar University Delhi by Arsha V. Sathyan.
[2] The NREGA (National Rural Employment Guarantee Act), renamed as the MGNREGA in 2009. In this study, references to the NREGA made by the authors have been retained as such. Elsewhere, the Act has been referred to as the MGNREGA.

days of guaranteed wage employment in a financial year to rural households whose adult members volunteer to do unskilled manual work. Within the framework of this Act, a rural adult member can demand work from the State, which then is liable to provide work within 15 days. If the State is unable to do so, the worker has the right to demand an unemployment allowance from the State. The Act ensures 'employment guarantee' through a series of legal entitlements, amounting to justiciable rights, the denial of which can be contested through official proceedings, including proceedings in a court of law. This provision guarantees the livelihood security of the rural poor while at the same time upholding the significance of the right to work.

The empirical study conducted in Dudhera found that the implementation in the village has continually violated the rights of the workers guaranteed in the Act. As part of the action research, workers of Dudhera coming under MGNREGA filed an RTI (Right to Information), which enquired about their unpaid and delayed money, and managed to catch the attention of the officials, who had continuously siphoned off their money. The workers finally received the held-up payments that were forced to be released by the authorities. Following this, people acquired confidence and felt empowered to demand work under MGNREGA for the first time since its inception in 2006. After demanding work, they did not receive work on time. Therefore, they applied for the unemployment allowance. The claim for unemployment allowance turned out to be a bitter pill for the Panchayat. After the claim for unemployment allowance was made, there was an unexpected intervention by PRADAN, an NGO in the field, which tried to discourage the villagers from claiming unemployment allowance. However, the villagers decided to proceed with the claim for unemployment allowance.

With these facts in the background, this chapter tries to engage with the issue of how, while passing progressive laws like MGNREGA, the state is trying to restrain citizenship and how, quite ironically, even the NGOs seem to be indulging in something similar by attempting to dissuade people from politically articulating themselves.

THE ROLE OF NGOS IN DEPOLITICIZING POLITICAL ACTION

The word 'NGO' is being applied popularly to a wide range of civil society organizations that operate at various levels and are involved in local, regional, national and international issues (Kamat 2003). An operational document of the World Bank defined NGOs as 'private organizations that pursue activities to relieve suffering, promote the interests of the poor, protect the environment, provide basic social services or undertake community development' (Malena 1995, 7). In India, 'NGOs can be defined as organizations that are generally formed by professionals or quasi professionals from the middle or lower-middle class, either to serve or work with the poor, or to channel financial support to community-based or grassroots organizations' (Sen 1999).

Many voluntary initiatives were prevalent in India from even before independence. Many of these collectively fall under the category of 'civil society.' Despite attempts to classify NGOs in India based on their composition, origin, funding size, ideological orientation, terms like NGO, CBO (community based organizations), GSO (grassroots support organization), MSO (membership support organizations) and CSO (civil society organization) are used without further clarification even by donor agencies, government officials and scholars (Chhotray 2013).

In a liberal democratic understanding, civil society is a culmination of private interests and individual desires that are stabilized by the free market. Agents of civil society, that is, NGOs deal with the public welfare of a marginalized section of the society. Their work thus touches on rights, health, women empowerment, livelihood security and so on. This role of NGOs strengthens the capacities of civil societies, and by doing so makes the civil society an 'honest broker' of people's interest (Kamat 2004).

The culmination of public and private interests by civil societies is problematic and has to be analysed with a special focus on the actual practice of NGOs on the field.

In this particular site of action research, the non-governmental, outside actor was PRADAN. Despite the fact that PRADAN is involved in a series of activities like introducing more efficient ways of agricultural techniques, methods of water harvesting, providing services like poultry to improve livelihoods, and women empowerment initiations like SHGs and gender training for the benefit of the impoverished the people of Dudhera, it seems curious why they were worried about the fact that ordinary women and men are capable of initiating political initiatives and challenging the hegemonic structures of state power. Most of the NGOs approach communities as a closed-circuit entity whose problems are generated from within and, therefore, must be solved from inside. This is essentially 'apolitical and managerial approach to community development draws upon the liberal notion of empowerment wherein the poor are encouraged to be entrepreneurial and find solutions to their livelihood needs.' (Kamat 2003)

The NGO PRADAN's indifference towards the political initiatives of the local community sustains the reduction of human beings to mere subjects of the state or consumers of the services and does not empower them as citizens. Also, its services are not able to make the community self-reliant or enable. Instead, it recreates situations where continual intervention by this sector is needed in order to perpetuate their existence and usefulness. It makes the community dependent on them. As Chandhoke remarks,

> Skilled professionals not only save the state from being accountable, they are not accountable to the people themselves. And they create and foster structures of dependency upon bodies that deliver services, rather than encourage the growth of political awareness. But if people are galvanised to demand services rather than mobilised against abuses of power, they may lose political rights altogether. NGO's can therefore render otherwise self-confident citizens dependent and helpless as well as neutralize challenges to the political order. Instead of self-confident citizens who are aware of their rights and who demand fulfillment of their basic entitlements, we may well find that people have been constituted as consumers of delivery services. We may well discover that civil society has lost its potential for democracy because it has been de-politicized. (Chandhoke 2003)

NGOs holding the vision of professionalization of community most often use a functionalist problem-solving approach towards issues like poverty and inequality and adopt a paternalistic attitude towards the poor instead of focusing on larger economic and social processes like structural adjustment and international debt policies even though they directly impact the poor (Kamat 2015).

It is well known that the NGOs play an intermediate role between the state and its citizens. Most of the NGOs revolve around the service delivery of the various policies of the state. This narrow focus on state policies is precisely what is problematic. The state, when it is implementing a policy is not merely providing a service to the consumers, rather it is fulfilling the claims of the citizens. The NGOs reductively approach the state policy without taking into account the politics involved in it. The functioning of the NGOs is such that they mediate the access of citizens to the policies. They assume the role of agents of delivery. It is important to note at this point that the NGOs themselves are dependent on various funding agencies for their functioning. It is to be noted that most NGO activity is limited to doing some interventionary work in 'rural areas', which is approached as a finite time-bound project upon whose completion the NGO compiles a report, indicating the completion of the undertaken objective of the project, which is then submitted to the funding agency. This initiates a cycle of proposal and completion reports of projects that the NGO seeks for further funding. Hence, it is vital to locate the politics of the funding agency itself.

By acting as a simple service-delivering agent of the funding agency, the NGOs translate the strong political possibility of catering to citizens' claims into the logic of consumption. When the citizen transmutes into a consumer of the supplier-state, the nature, scope and implication of the polity get altered. In other words, rights get diluted into mere services, to access which people have to be 'good' consumers. And by becoming passive (powerless) beneficiaries (facilitated by the NGOs), people forfeit even their limited ability to demand accountability from the state. For instance, the human rights discourse, as practiced by the NGOs, has done disservice at a larger structural level. As Chandhoke (2003) argues, for NGOs 'rights have not emerged from the struggles of the people, but from the baskets of funding agencies'. This nature of the functioning of the NGOs needs to be problematized because it is precisely this process that hinders the possibility of politicization and political mobilization of the community, based on the consciousness of being a citizen who has an active claim upon the state as a matter of right.

This is the reason why the NGOs are assessed as an apolitical face of the civil society, which are also capable of depoliticizing the movemental arena. According to Amita Baviskar (2010), the dynamics of the social movements have changed since the 1990s when the social movements in India started associating themselves with the global networks and NGO alliances. They institutionalized the movements through various levels of support like funding, networking, publicity, advocacy and documentation. Jayal (2001) argues that the NGOs are able to transform the political agenda of social movements when they are tied up with oppositional social movements. For instance, ARCH-Vahini, a voluntary agency based in Gujarat, was active in the initial stage of Narmada Bachao Andolan. Later they disagreed with the leadership of the struggle on the strategy of the movement and turned dismissive of it. Such dissmissiveness and convenienist strategizing on the part of the NGO sprout from their peripheral engagement with the field and due to upholding an 'NGO mindset' (Jenkins 2010). In the opinion of Anupama Roy (2010), the emergence of NGO-facilitated activism in a liberalized economic context displaces the 'political space of women's issue from the public/political domain into a depoliticized and domesticated domain of negotiations and welfare.'

NGO activity in rural areas is conducted with the aim of 'empowering' the rural community when it comes to microcredit programmes. Kamat (2015) explains that in a neo-liberal economic context, microcredit programmes are in tune with the global capital system. These micro-credit programmes force the community, especially women, to compete among themselves in a restricted and fluctuating market environment. They sustain a contradictory situation in, which on the one hand, the government fails to provide employment, and on the other hand, there exists an abstract promise of livelihood security from the NGOs. The neoliberal notion of empowerment, which incorporates the idea of the individual capacity to access the marketplace, has reduced the value of public welfare. It also limits the identity of a 'citizen' merely to that of a 'client'. This conveniently ignores the issues of public goods and services or the issue of distribution in this notion of empowerment and participation.

The above discussion makes it amply clear that despite the role of the NGO in adding vibrancy to democracy, there also exist profound limitations to NGOs. Most often, NGOs tend to be preoccupied with a short-term agenda due to which intersectional structures of power are not addressed. The intervention of the NGO thus ceases to be holistic. 'NGOs to ignore issues of class, caste, gender and environmental justice in their own work, but even more dangerously, they will effectively marginalize and de-legitimize those people's movements for whom these issues form the core of their struggles' (Kamat 2003).

At a juncture where the community in Dudhera had submitted their application demanding unemployment allowance, a PRADAN employee suggested that it would be better to demand work since it was the rainy season, and they could face health issues. Such a response reveals that PRADAN employees had become self-styled spokespersons for the community. As we analyse the activities of NGOs in general, it becomes clear that these voluntary agencies dictate what kind of development should happen in the third world, what kind of education people should receive, what kind of democracy should be institutionalized, what rights they should demand and possess, and what they should do to be empowered (Chandhoke 2003). This is where the difference of PRADAN's argument suggesting the community to make another demand for work and the villagers' argument to stick with the application for unemployment allowance gains significance. In Dudhera village, the MGNREGA was being implemented for years by violating all the entitlements of workers—their entitlements to work on demand, minimum wages, payments within 15 days, basic work facilities. It was in such a situation that the community came together and filed an RTI first to seek information about their unpaid wages. Further, it was for the first time that they decided to demand work. Even after the stipulated 15 days, they did not receive work. Around 20 people got work after 25–30 days for 3–6 days. It was at this time they decided that they would apply for unemployment allowance. The community itself took the initiative and applied for unemployment allowance to seek accountability from the state. However, there was no response from the authorities.

In this situation, PRADAN's suggestion that they demand work again would recreate the same demand–supply system. Instead, what was necessary was to mobilize people against the system, which had always been irresponsible towards them. By supporting the claim for unemployment allowance, it was possible for the community to negotiate, mediate, challenge the official hegemony of the authority and question the state, which has always considered the community as powerless both in material terms and in their culture, and make the authority accountable and responsible for its actions.

BEYOND NGOS: THE CIVIL SOCIETY

The arguments above do not constitute an attempt to discharge civil society. They are intended to drive home the point that civil society can be seen as a site for political engagement. Thus, it has the potential for democratic transformation. As Chandhoke (2003) points out,

> The sphere has historically been associated with norms of democracy, accessibility, participation, publicity and accountability. The institutions of civil society are associational, representative and deliberative forums, social movements and a free press. The inhabitant of this sphere is the rights-bearing and legally-defined citizen. And the protection of the members of civil society is found in the language of rights.

In Chandhoke's view, the agendas of civil society should be designed in such a way as to (a) locate the struggles of masses; (b) emphasize the legitimate rights of people in a democracy to make demands on the state; (c) insist on state accountability; and (d) stress the importance of an autonomous site where people could engage in democratic projects for their own sake (Chandhoke 2007). In this context, the civil society is also invited to dwell upon the politics of protest as much as it does upon the politics of power (Chandhoke 2001) in which every citizen has the democratic right to intervene in issues that are crucial to public life and shape them, and he or she has the political competence to do so. To challenge this is to deny the basic right of citizens to participate in the making of a public and political discourse that affects them individually and collectively.

There are numerous instances of resistance against the state under the label of civil society. India has witnessed many such initiatives at various points where the civil society provided the inevitable strength for democracy. The early 1970s witnessed a number of social movements challenging the agenda of the state, such as the anti-caste movement, the farmers' movement and the women's movement. In the 1980s, the civil liberties movement and the environmental movement were the two most powerful movements of contemporary India (Chandhoke 2007).

There are also other actors of the civil society that need to be specially mentioned because of their strong and effective political action initiatives—Mazdoor Kisan Shakti Sangathan (MKSS), National Campaign for People's Right to Information (NCPRI), Right to Work and Right to Food Campaigns. This kind of political action believes that the state is potentially a protector of the deprived sections of the society, even if it has many flaws. Thus, a deep engagement with the state, its policies, and its functioning would make the state more accountable and transparent. Through this process, it aims to force the state to ensure the rights of the citizen and design ways in which these rights could be realized on the ground in their true form.

MKSS, started as a grassroot movement in the rural areas of Rajasthan in the 1990s on the right to information and the rights of rural workers to basic entitlements with the aim of rooting out corruption and bringing accountability (Bhatia and Dreze 1998). Sangathan's actions are based on 'generic citizen-centric accountability framework like a grievance redress law, and social audits' (Mathew 2015). The MKSS' radical engagement as a people's movement gained momentum with the ascendance of the United Progressive Alliance (UPA) government in 2004. This sets the scene for the subsequent enactment of historic pieces of the legislation such as the Right to Information Act 2005, National Rural Employment Guarantee Act (NREGA) 2005 and Forest Rights Act 2006. It is widely acknowledged that inputs from civil society organizations such as MKSS, NCPRI, and many others played a major role in the enactment of these laws. Similarly, under

UPA-II, the Right to Education Act 2009 (RTE Act) and the National Food Security Act (NFSA) 2013 have benefited from significant civil society inputs (Shah 2014). Indeed, many of the rights-based legislations were preceded by intense collective action through civil society engagements.

However, the change in nature of the civil society was marked during the 1990s when many civil society organizations, dominated by professionalized NGOs, started campaigning for the efficient delivery of the social goods in which the state was no longer seen as the object of political contestation, but as a provider of social goods. Also, the donor agencies of the NGOs were ready to partner with the state in service-delivery, which turned the citizen into the consumer of agendas and policies. When civil society organizations do not question the accountability of the state, fight for their rights, or do not raise issues that are uncomfortable for the government, and when they become partners of the government, the constituency of the civil society is depoliticized (Chandhoke 2012).

There exists a complex scenario of civil society where, on the one hand, civil society organizations began to partner with the state in service delivery, and on the other hand, they set to engage in the politics of advocacy, such as the right to food campaign, right to work or the right to health (Chandhoke 2012). Recounting her experience with Samaj Pragati Sahyog (SPS), a local NGO, Chhahotray (2013) states that there are NGOs whose stance as 'working state' would also create a platform for resistance and subordinate politics.

Further, the fact is that NGOs cannot be expected to act as symbolic civil society actors to achieve objectives like democratization and higher state of accountability as it is essentially unsuitable for understanding the intricacies of the interrelationships between the state and civil society (Khilnani 2001). They can mobilize and lobby people for economic and social rights, but the realization of these rights ultimately lies in the structures of the government (Chandhoke 2009).

Therefore, we can suggest with some certainty that the autonomy of the civil society is constrained. Within the frontiers of what is politically permissible, actors in the civil society can exercise constant vigilance against the arbitrary exercise of power, check and monitor violations of human rights, demand accountability, combat unjust policies and demand that the state delivers what it promises. They can do all this as long as they respect the frontiers laid down by the state, frontiers that may exclude rather than include, disempower rather than empower (Chandhoke 2001).

REFERENCES

Baviskar, A. 2010. 'Social Movements'. In *The Oxford Companion to Politics in India*, edited by N. G. Jayal and P. B. Mehta, 386. New Delhi: Oxford University Press.
Bhatia, B., and J. Dreze. 1998. *Campaign in Rural India: Freedom of Information Is Key to Anti-corruption Campaign*. Berlin: Transparency International.
Chandhoke, N. 2001. 'The "Civil" and the "Political" in Civil Society'. *Democratization* 8 (2): 1–24.
———. 2003. *The Conceits of Civil Society*. New Delhi: Oxford University Press.
———. 2007. 'Civil Society'. *Development in Practice* 17 (4–5): 607–614.
———. 2009. 'Putting Civil Society in Its Place'. *Economic & Political Weekly* 44 (7): 12–16.
———. 2012, 9 June. 'Whatever Has Happened to Civil Society?' *Economic & Political Weekly* 47 (23): 39–45.
Chhotray, V. 2013. 'How Samaj Pragati Sahyog Works the State and Why It Succeeds'. In *Water Governance and Civil Society Responses in South Asia*, edited by N. C. Narayanan, S. Parasuraman, and R. Ariyabandu, 90–12. New Delhi: Routledge. Available at: http://citeseerx.ist.psu.edu/viewdoc/download?doi=10.1.1.549.4446&rep=rep1&type=pdf (accessed on 12 March 2020).
Jayal, N. G. 2001. 'India'. In *Governance and Civil Society in a Global Age*, edited by T. Yamamoto, 116. Tokyo: Japan Center for International Exchange.
Jenkins, R. 2010. 'Non-governmental Organizations'. In *The Oxford Companion to Politics in India*, edited by N. G. Jayal and P. B. Mehta, 438. New Delhi: Oxford University Press.
Kamat, S. 2003. 'The NGO Phenomenon and Political Culture in the Third World'. *Development* 46 (1): 88–93.
———. 2004. 'The Privatization of Public Interest: Theorizing NGO Discourse in a Neoliberal Era'. *Review of International Political Economy* 11 (1): 155–176.
———. 2015. 'NGOs and the New Democracy: The False Saviours of International Development'. *Harvard International Review* 25 (1): 65–69.
Khilnani, S. 2001. 'The Development of Civil Society'. In *Civil Society: History and Possibilities*, edited by S. Kaviraj, and S. Khilnani, 11–32. Cambridge: Cambridge University Press.

Malena, C. 1995. 'Working with NGOs: A Practical Guide to Operational Collaboration Between the World Bank and Nongovernmental Organizations'. Working Paper No. 15013. Washington, DC: The World Bank. Available at: http://documents.worldbank.org/curated/en/1995/03/697561/working-ngos-practical-guide-operational-collaboration-between-world-bank-nongovernmental-organizations (accessed on 23 April 2020).

Mathew, B. 2015. '"Only Half the Battle Is Won": Aruna Roy and Nikhil Dey Speak about the MKSS Experience and Their Campaign for Citizen-centric Accountability'. *The Hindu*, 15 May. Available at: https://www.thehindu.com/features/magazine/only-half-the-battle-is-won/article7264573.ece (accessed on 23 April 2020).

Roy, A. 2010. 'The Women's Movement'. In *The Oxford Companion to Politics in India*, edited by N. G. Jayal and P. B. Mehta, 419. New Delhi: Oxford University Press.

Sen, S. 1999. 'Some Aspects of State–NGO Relationships in India in the Post-Independence Era'. *Development and Change* 30 (2): 327–355.

Shah, M. 2014. 'Civil Society and Indian Democracy: Possibilities of Social Transformation'. *Economic and Political Weekly*, 37–42.

Chapter 14

Sustainable Management Practices of the Traditional Society in Contested Landscapes

Devjit Nandi and Debashis Sarkar

INTRODUCTION

Historically, the tribal provinces of Central India were ruled by tribal kings and other feudal lords. There were state forests and private forests in the Central Province and Berar region, and at times, many restrictions were imposed by the local rulers, resulting in a strained relationship between the rulers and the tribals (Bailey 1960). In many princely states, the coronation of the rulers needed to be ratified by the Adivasis through rituals and ceremonies (Kumar 2014).

Shifting cultivation was one of the major land use practices in Central India. Shifting cultivation was part of a mixed-use agroforestry landscape that included domesticated forests and grasslands (Sivaramakrishnan 1999). Shifting cultivation was practiced even during the Pre-British and the British Eras. Shifting cultivation was the main pattern of the land and forest use for most of the primitive tribal groups (PTGs) in most of the country during colonial rule. It existed in almost all the forest areas in different forms, and was known by different names, such as *podu*, *bagada* in Odisha, *bewar* and *dhya* in Central Provinces

(Baker 1991), which was looked upon as a significant threat to forest resources by the British planners.

Shifting cultivation, also called as *bewar* locally, which is a different form of agriculture which was practiced in the lowlands and by the primitive tribes, had not been understood properly by the planners as another kind of land-use systems. Thus, the planners always tried to eradicate shifting cultivation. Mainstream agriculture has mainly revolved around cultivated land, while the shifting agriculture practiced by the primitive tribes embraces the commons (mainly forests and grasslands). This indeed is a holistic and sustainable agro-ecosystem. On the other hand, mainstream agriculture is highly dependent on external inputs.

Did Protected Areas Regenerate Forests or Marginalize the Forest People?

In protected areas, there have been various restrictions imposed on the local people and also a large-scale relocation from the forest. The Wild Life (Protection) Act (WLPA 1972) further curtailed the rights of the people, particularly of the primitive tribes living in their ancestral lands. Their right to livelihood inside the forest has been curtailed. Their right to use the forest is simply a concession made rather than a privilege preserved (Lasgorceix 2009). These forest-dependent communities have been termed as 'encroachers' in their own land, which they have been cultivating for ages. During the globalization era of the 1990s, when there was a shift in India's economy from regulated to the open market, the forest became a valuable commodity. All this further led to an unprecedented rate of eviction of the tribals from Protected Areas (Asher 2007).

There is a cumulative impact of these strategies of management and control on the relationship between human beings and the forest. A large tract of reservation of forest due to national parks meant an effective loss of control of the people over the habitat of the forest-based community. Due to the government's policy of revenue earnings, the forest remained open to tourism, rather than to local villagers, hastening further destruction of the forest. Agricultural practices by the local community on forest land in Protected Areas was discouraged as it was perceived as unscientific, leading to the destruction of the forest. Agriculture can be seen to be playing an important complementary role in enriching biodiversity and wildlife management. Agriculture, grazing, forestry and other human-managed ecosystems cover at least two-thirds of the terrestrial surface of the planet, whereas Protected Areas cover only about 6 per cent, the remaining percentage is wilderness, urban lands and so on (McNeely and Norgard, 1992).

ABOUT THIS STUDY

This article attempts to analyse whether Sustainable Development Goals (SDGs) have any concern for the poor. Ecological concerns are on the SDG agenda. They run the risk of being hijacked by the ecological and developmental interests of the rich and focus on economic growth at the cost of the poor's livelihood. The Keynesian theory, which states that 'the centralized state is best placed to provide public goods like the public sector, government departments, etc.,' stands no longer for welfare and public goods. Provisions are being made in treaties to make the commons a part of global governance.

SDG Goal number 15 is particularly oriented towards managing the forests sustainably, restoring the degraded lands and successfully combating desertification, reducing degraded natural habitats and ending biodiversity loss. This chapter analyses this goal in context of the Forest Rights Act (FRA) and its implementation in Chhattisgarh. The Forest Rights Act 2006 is a historic decision by the government of India to provide a sustainable livelihood, protecting the cultural and traditional value of the indigenous communities, and is also an essential component of SDG, where the government is bound to make efforts that will help ensure the livelihoods of many who are directly dependent on forests and other ecosystems. Biodiversity will thrive, and the benefits of these natural resources will be enjoyed by generations to come.

This study is based on data collected from primary sources, and from direct observation and engagement with the local communities inhabiting the area falling within the limits of the Achanakmar Tiger Reserve. It was not possible to collect documents from the authorities on the number of Forest Rights claims submitted and the exact number of the individual forest rights distributed. However, it has been observed from other studies that in Chhattisgarh the number of community forest rights claims is conspicuous (Nandi 2015). One of the major concerns of the FRA process has been the distribution of titles of Individual Forest Fights, which has been carried out in an arbitrary manner. Forest Rights Committees (FRC) have been constituted at the Panchayat level, which is against the Act.

Objectives of the Study

- To highlight the challenges of integration of resource conservation and SDG in India. Such difficulties are part of a fundamental problem concerning the participation in resource management of the indigenous communities living inside the forests within the proximity of the Protected Areas and the forest department promoting monoculture.
- To examine the unfolding of the traditional forest-related knowledge of the Baiga primitive communities regarding climate vagaries
- To provide guidelines to the Government on the initiatives of the communities.

Research Questions

In order to achieve the above objectives, the following questions need to be answered.

1. To what extent do the local people participate in the process of Conservation?
2. What is the empowerment and vision of the local communities in terms of education, skill development, nutrition and food security?
3. What is the level of cooperation between the communities and the government in fulfilling the objectives of biodiversity conservation?
4. What kind of policy and strategies are the Baiga communities pursuing with regard to Sustainable development Goals and with regard to land and forest claims?

Methodology

Our study was carried out in the villages of Achanakmar Wildlife Sanctuary in Kota and Pendra Block of the Bilaspur district and the Lormi Block of the Mungeli Districts of Chhattisgarh in Central India. The study was conducted by taking into account the status of Government's commitment to SDG no. 15 in both the core and the buffer areas. The forest areas of Achanakmar Sanctuary include the following communities: Baiga, Gond, Oraon and other forest dwellers. From the population living in these villages, the Baiga community was sampled as a part of the case study representing all other communities that have filed land and forest claims. This community is the only primitive community that is forest dependent, and which is in the lower rungs of the society. This community is at the heart of the Sustainable development due to their land and community forest claims. Due to the practice of shifting cultivation, this community has never been a resource accumulator and has been a victim of the government forest policies, forced eviction, loss of resource and depletion of forest. Our inquiry adopts a case study approach and empirically examines the effects of government programmes and the resource management and governance practice initiatives of the local community. The study aims to evaluate the attainment of SDG and analyse the empowerment of the community.

FOREST RIGHTS ACT

With the passing of the FRA 2006, one of the major legislative texts in Indian history, the forest communities are given a prime role in forest management. The act aims at maintaining ecological balance with a view to providing sustainable livelihood options to forest-dwelling indigenous people. The major objective of this act has been to strike a balance between the potentially conflicting interests of the forest-dwelling communities and the protection of forests and wildlife resources. The primitive tribes of Central India have claimed their territorial rights to restore their ecosystem and support their lives as a means to achieve SDG for all by 2030.

The FRA deals with diverse individual and community forest rights as well as the right to community tenures over the 'habitat' of

'Particularly Vulnerable Tribal Groups' (PVTGs) and pre-agricultural communities, which have been neglected since independence. The preamble of the act is to undo the 'historical injustice' done to indigenous communities. It aims to empower the communities with the 'responsibilities and authority for sustainable use, conservation of biodiversity and maintenance of ecological balance' (MoLJ 2007). The historical injustice done to the tribals needs to be understood in a liberal manner and looked upon as an obliteration of pre-existing rights rather than as state appropriation. However, the FRA did not emerge in an 'unproblematic and consensual' way (Bose 2010). Different stakeholder groups struggled for their interests over a long period of time. The history of this contestation dates back to the colonial era when the rights of the people were systematically usurped (Agarwal 2009).

Key Benefits of the Act

The FRA provides forest rights to those who primarily reside in the forest or forestland, or those who depend on forest or forestland for livelihoods (bona fide livelihood needs). As for other forest dwellers (OTFD), they have to be residents of the area of their claim for 75 years. The law recognizes three types of rights: (a) land rights; (b) right to use and collect and (c) right to protect and conserve.

The Act contains rights to
- forest land for habitation and self-cultivation
- minor forest produce
- fish and other products of water bodies
- grazing
- seasonal resource access of nomadic or pastoralist communities
- protect, regenerate, conserve and manage community forest resources
- intellectual property and traditional knowledge relating to biodiversity
- traditional and customary rights such as right of way, collection of soil for household purposes and access to religious sites

Community Rights

The provision of the right to protect, conserve, regenerate and manage community forest resources under Section 3(1-i) of the FRA has created a scope for the legal recognition of these traditional community conservation initiatives in forest land (including wetlands and mangroves). There are basically two types of rights envisaged under Community Rights, which are broadly termed as Community Rights (CR) and Community Resource Rights (CRR). Section 3(1) provides for various community rights of access and use of CRR, usufruct rights or collection rights including Non-Timber Forest Products (NTFPs) such as *tendu* leaves, herbs and medicinal plants that are traditionally collected (Section 3(1)(c)). The right to protect and conserve means that the Forest-Dependent People will have a right to protect and conserve under Section 3(1). Whereas section 3(2) provides for the diversion of forest land for developmental facilities like schools, hospitals, Anganwadi, irrigation, roads and so on. A separate guideline has been issued by the Ministry of Tribal Affairs on 18 May 2009 on the procedure for the diversion of forest land for developmental facilities provided under Section 3(2).

Rights of PVTGs and Nomadic Tribes

The tribal and forest-dependent communities have faced maximum alienation from their customary forested habitats at least for 150 years with the initiation of permanent settlement by the British followed by unabated alienation after independence. The act has major provisions under the rights termed as 'territorial rights', for the Primitive tribes' traditional areas of use by nomadic or pastoralist communities that move with their herds, as opposed to practicing settled agriculture under Section 3(1)(e).

Similarly, Section 5 gives the community a general power to protect wildlife, forests and so on. This is vital for thousands of village communities who are protecting their forests and wildlife against threats from forest mafias, industries and land grabbers, most of whom operate in connivance with the Forest Department.

The Contribution of Forest Rights to Conservation

The FRA secures individual and common tenures over forest lands and forests. The Act recognizes territorial rights of PTGs, rights of pre-agricultural communities and rights over community conservation initiatives. Since the beginning of implementation in 2008, forest communities have used the provisions under the Act to claim a wide variety of forest rights. Besides, the Act provides rights for the conversion of forest villages into revenue villages, rights of communities displaced due to state development interventions, and rights for the creation of development facilities in the forest villages such as schools, health centres, roads, electricity and irrigation. The provision of such a diversity of rights to traditional resource access, use and interactions reflects the strong conservation ethic of the diverse communities the Act intends to protect.

INITIATIVES BY INDIGENOUS COMMUNITIES IN EXERCISING THEIR RIGHTS

Control of and access to forest resources by the indigenous communities usually involves a structure of their existing privileges and rights and regulations, varying from common resources to exclusive individual rights over land and resources. The definition of rights varied according to the existing ecosystem. It varied from one area to another, one community to another and also over different time. Unlike the rational legal system, flexibility, mobility and adaptability are the main characteristic of customary systems (Michon 1999). The forest policies in India were always burdened with several ambiguities. During the colonial period it has been more revenue earning and a major economic instrument in national development, while post 1992 after the Rio de Janeiro Earth Summit, there has been major thrust on utilization of forest land and, protection of forest resources for present and future. The Forests Administration was assigned the double task of generating profit for the nation and allowing the indigenous communities to collect minor forest produce who would do the conservation task for the government in lieu of these concessions. The state utilization of forests is characterized by compartmentalization and not in totality. Management of forests has always been for regenerating revenue from forest rather than sustainability of resources, be it mining of timber resources or through ecotourism in the name of wildlife conservation. The chronic un-sustainability of the state sponsored harvesting of resources has been another cause of conflict between the nation and the customary system of forest management. The Forest Rights Act is the first law of its kind, which if would have been properly implemented would have fulfilled both the objectives of the government of resource conservation as well as revenue generation. The historical forest rights legislation has the basic provision of formation of committees, which could accommodate the needs of local dependent community and developing the commons. The major lacuna in implementation of Forest Rights Act has been the weakness of the state in law enforcement, due to political influence, pressure of forest department, lack of political will to devolve power to tribal's and unwillingness to confront the mining and infrastructure companies, who have utmost disrespect for the laws concerning common citizens. The implementation of Forest Rights Act (FRA), which has been targeted majorly for the Indigenous communities, is the reflection of the political commitment of the government towards the devolution process. The impact of devolution of FRA should have been visible by the status of economic improvement and initiatives taken by government for enabling the conservation and regeneration of forests. An important indicator of enabling condition for implementation of FRA is the convergence of village management plan with the forest working plan. FRA has the provision for the management and conservation of forests through the gram sabha's after the Community forest claims have been made under section 4(1) (e) of the Forest rights act. The political unwillingness to strengthen the local institutions and not handing over the management practice to the gram sabha legally, rather were involved in dilution of the act to deprive the indigenous community even after accepting the historical injustice meted to the forest dwelling communities. Navrachna played a very important role in the forest areas with the community in promoting and supporting the conservation and management of forests resources. Navrachna encouraged the gram sabha to identify their resources and their management units, develop their plans, build local institutions and take initiatives for conservation and regeneration. The claims for community territorial rights were aimed to empower the tribal communities to exercise their forests rights by addressing their access to and control over forests. The core of forest rights mobilization has been to regain their lost autonomy developing people's capacity to control and develop their own resources. From the perspective of tribal community, a relationship with nature must be some form of political sovereignty, to control and govern land and resources; a form of community control which maintains the particular set of social relations and also the distinct cultural relations as well as political autonomy (Cornell,1988). The tribal people's effort to reclaim control over ancestral land and a stake a resource management role are guided by the following concerns: First, the area of their existence is central to their indigeneity, identity and institution. The territorial rights claims can be understood within such context. Secondly the control over land and natural resources are very important for their future economic well-being and thirdly, governance of their traditional resource regime enable forest dependent community to design and implement policies that honour their culture, customs and also reflect their priorities. The local biodiversity which provides livelihood to the forest dependent communities are getting degenerated. The claims for Community Forest Rights (CFR) have provisions for bringing the territorial forest area under the jurisdiction of gram sabha (village council). Thus, by understanding this legal power, people started defining the biodiversity of the village through assessment of their forest area, but the major challenge has been translating them into conservation practice in the context of people's livelihood.

People have the knowledge and expertise of biodiversity and their uses, but not allowing them to practice their knowledge base led to deterioration of their norms and rules of forest management. Thus, it was necessary that the broken norms of management be put back in operation and follow a number of strategies for self-governance for community initiatives. The tribal communities felt they could benefit from community claims as this being an opportunity for them to access and control over their ancestral lands. Thus, they took up the initiative of conservation and protection to safe guard their home and their livelihood.

The communities' willingness to adapt to the prevalent conditions led to redefining and broadening their traditional knowledge. The traditional biodiversity and forestry management are transferred over generations by cultural transmission and these are their relationship with forests and environment. Traditional forest management is historical continuity which has been snatched away from them since colonial times. Community based forest management with its own set of rules which made participation mandatory and aimed to build community institutions as well as strengthen their capabilities to achieve the conservation and sustainable use of local biodiversity. The important aspect of the indigenous communities in Chhattisgarh has been their emphasis on plantation and regeneration of insitu tree species. Many of the traditional practices which existed in Chhattisgarh was modified and implemented like *beej* (seed) mela and *beej* bank, biodiversity register and value addition to their traditional craftsmanship, etc. became integral part of the community plans.

Panchayat Level Conservation Initiatives through Local Governance

Context

The indigenous communities in Chhattisgarh, which are the custodians of forest and resources, are the worst affected communities. The FRA has the potential, as a comprehensive system for area-based conservation measures at the local government level, to preserve the natural habitat and ensure the livelihood of the forest-dependent communities on sustainable basis. The NGO Navrachna, along with the local communities, has tried to implement the site-based conservation mechanism in five villages of the Kota block of the Bilaspur district. Here we discuss two case studies with a view to highlighting the initiatives taken by the community that are rarely integrated into the planning process or regional development strategies, which are lacking in India.

Threats and Problems Faced by the Communities

- The communities currently face a threat from the expansion of national parks and tiger reserves, forced relocation and loss of access to community forests.
- Rain-fed one-time rice cultivation (with danger of crop-raiding by elephants), decreasing NTFP and minor forest produce because of the presence of monoculture plantations, and/or no access to NTFP/minor forest produce have led to increasing livelihood crisis.
- This situation is further exacerbated by the loss of grazing ground and the lack of availability of natural fodder leading to a 70–90 per cent decrease in livestock and cattle.
- Women, who go into the forest to collect fuelwood and fodder, face harassment from both the forest guards and security forces.
- The forest departments, while not recognizing the FRA 2006, are channelling various government schemes, benefits and funds through Panchayats and Joint Forest Management Committees and not Gram Sabhas, leading to nepotism and creation of wedge between and within the communities.
- The complete lack of recognition of FRA 2006 and recording of CR over forests is severely hampering the communities' own initiatives to manage and govern their forests and the autonomy to define their needs and way of life.
- Communities' own initiatives to formulate their own rules and practices, to patrol forests, to stop the felling of natural forests and to restore their own forest lands are facing flak from the forest departments and government officials. The timber mafia is intimidating the communities and many community leaders and forest dwellers are slapped with multiple cases by the police.
- Currently, the communities' traditional relationship and cultural ties with the forests are at stake. The forests are no longer seen as a viable entity by the younger generation leading them to opt for other employment and livelihood options outside the realm of their traditional habitat, forests and territories. The very ethos of conservation is at stake.
- The traditional role of women is changing. With the invasion of patriarchal values, the customs and traditional practices during

festivals and marriage are changing. With men increasingly making the decisions, women are increasingly sucked into household responsibilities and child-rearing. Though women are still involved in agricultural activities and fuelwood collection, such activities only increase their workload and hours of work.
- While the political parties and leaders are doing the least to ameliorate the lives and conditions of the communities, their electoral practices, seeing the communities merely as vote banks, are driving a wedge within the communities.

Approach

The lack of knowledge and awareness of the importance of Community Forest Act, which, when translated, can become a conservation mechanism for local sustainable development, is an impeding factor. Navrachna's commitment is intended to fulfil the following major objective, that is, conserve biodiversity and increase livelihood opportunities for the indigenous communities through effective and equitable management of Protected Areas.

The measures proposed build on Navrachna's experience, gained from its initiatives. They entail a multilevel approach: Our emphasis has been on the following:

- Developing local panchayat capacities: The existing practices of Forest management and panchayats initiatives were studied and systematized and used as a basis for developing, adapting and applying appropriate tools for the mobilization of the local governments. Also, these panchayats received support in developing local biodiversity strategies and action plans for the protection of local forest areas.
- Embedding the panchayats' role in biodiversity conservation more firmly in legal and institutional frameworks by filing community forest rights claims. Appropriate policy recommendations were prepared through the participation of the Gram Sabha in the villages. Based on the analysis of existing management systems, institutional frameworks were developed.

- Continuously communicating by discussing with the people on (a) the challenges and benefits of local forest areas and other conservation mechanisms; (b) the pressure on the forest by different stakeholders and (c) the opportunity provided through community forest claims. The provisions of the FRA and the importance of the local governments' conservation action were communicated to the community forest management committee (CFMC). The lessons learned were disseminated at the Gram Sabha and village events and other key sector forums organized in the village.

In the two remarkable cases, the panchayat and its representatives were actively engaged in the management and protection of the forest, giving them an opportunity to become involved in the planning and implementing their forest protection measures. In Chuhiya, women were actively involved in planning and extending the dialogue on forest rights and conservation beyond confrontation with the hegemonic forest department at the block level to set an example of a forest protection system, while in Semariya, the youths were active in establishing regulations on forest protection with village conservation rules and new environmental rules at the panchayat.

Interim Recommendations

In principle, a transferable development right program can minimize the social cost of achieving a target for the area conserved and can reward those undertaking conservation. On a larger scale, a government could allocate development or conversion rights (denominated in hectares) to a particular habitat. Trading of these rights would tend to allow conversion of the plots most suitable for agriculture and retention under natural vegetation of the areas with the lowest opportunity cost. If the rights were freely and equally allocated among property holders (a fiscally inefficient but politically expedient procedure), those who maintained forests would profit from the NTFP sales. An efficient NTFP-based program is thus the conservation analogy of environmental permit programs that regulate pollution or forest access.

- The communities very strongly feel and are struggling for the immediate implementation of the FRA 2006 as passed by the Indian Parliament, in not only recognizing their rights but recording them and upholding the role and power of the Gram Sabha.
- In the sites, the communities have already taken the initiative to take over their forests. A formal recording of the rights and allowing the Gram Sabha to function will have a multiplier effect on the community conservation initiatives and facilitate the process of community control over and governance of the forests.
- The livelihood crisis that the communities are undergoing at present could be addressed largely with the recording of their tenurial rights over land and community forest resources. The communities also feel that the government should allow, support and facilitate the restoration of their forests according to their traditional wisdom and knowledge, requirements and local needs, benefitting both the communities and wildlife leading to the protection of both forests and biodiversity. A very powerful opposition exists against plantations, which ruin their livelihood, health, ecology and the economic value of the forests.
- Governments' and related agencies' support through funds and developmental schemes should be channelled through related and responsible committees formed under Gram Sabhas only.
- Women from the communities strongly feel that their traditional rights and security should be ensured while accessing the forests to collect fuelwood, NTFPs, or minor forest produce.
- Women have also voiced their opinion that the formation and strengthening of the Gram Sabhas will also strengthen their participation and role in the decision-making process dealing with the well-being of the community and conservation initiatives.

Youth Brigade in Semariya Pledges to Protect Forest

The Semariya Gram Sabha faced many difficulties in filing their CFR claims. This village, with more than 200 households, consisting predominantly of Gond tribes and a sizeable Schedule caste population, is a village on the roadside, which was a hub of timber theft. The village, with a significant forest adjacent to the Achanakmar buffer area, has been the convenient means to get wood logs for sawmills, and the people of the area. They bribe the forest department and get wood stolen out of the forest. Till now, the village council had not acted, and they had little knowledge of Community Forest Rights and thought that conservation and restoration of the forest is the duty of the forest department alone. After a prolonged process of making a claim, they filed the CFR application in April 2018. The panchayat sought information from the administration about the recorded history of land and forest, which the block administration did not provide under Section 12(4) of the FRA.

While conducting the ratification of the claim from the nearby villages, they also faced difficulties as this is the only village where there is a forest, and the adjacent village is dependent on this forest. Majhgawan, which is also a big village, refused to give its consent at first, but thanks to a meeting with the elders later agreed to give the consent. The intervention by the elders in Semariya and their coordination with the leaders of nearby villages led to the completion of the application and the staking of their claims on the management and protection of the forest.

However, making claims would in itself not fulfil the objective of the claim. The youth force of the village that has been active in the village wanted to ensure the equitable distribution of resources, a system, which in itself can protect biodiversity and the forest. It has been seen that the benefits from ecosystems are seldom equally distributed, with more well-endowed actors (especially wealthy urban actors in the global economy) being able to benefit better even without contributing to forest protection, while some people are not at all able to derive well-being from certain ecosystem services. The youth argued equity in the panchayat, which they wanted to see as an integral aspect of human well-being and development. Thus, they wanted to make an effort in this matter of conservation. Navrachna has been in constant dialogue with the youth group, and they felt that, in community-managed forests, there is generally a 'one-to-one' relationship between the forest as a resource catchment and the user community. Moreover, in this management form, there is a clear connection between the provisioning and distribution of forest ecosystem services and village-level social institutions, which are, in turn, embedded in social organizations and relations.

The effort made by the youth resulted in making more enemies rather than friends. The forest officials could not swallow this, as it was restraining them from getting their share through corrupt practices. They instigated the mafias. On a few occasions, this led to a case of conflict and police case. The youths were not intimidated, and they faced all the challenges strongly and showed their claims and even approached the district collector. The recent progress, in support for environmental and forest management interventions made by the Semariya Panchayat has paid considerable attention to the notion of legitimacy and the associated ideas of fairness and justice. The fairness of the actions by which they exercise their authority, the favourability of the outcomes that they dispense and the degree of outcome-control that they possess shows their commitment to and their dependency on the forest. The nearby forest-dwellers have slowly understood the identified connections between these different determinants of legitimacy and the power of community forest claims.

Chuhiya's Strong Women Force Battles the Hegemony of Forest Department

Chuhiya, a remote village in the Bilaspur district, is facing lots of problems due to being on the buffer area of the Achanakmar sanctuary. Prior to making the claims, the entry of the villagers into the forest was restricted. Men were beaten up, while women faced all sorts of harassment. The continuous mobilization and training by Navrachna have helped in translating the rights into powers devolved to the community, which enabled them to be empowered to conserve, manage and sell forest produce and get access inside the forest for strengthening their livelihoods. Navrachna aims to improve their livelihood opportunities through the development of their skills to generate long-term employment.

> As one of the Women FRC said 'the Forest department has been harassing us and did not allow us to enter us into the forest. We asked Navrachna to help us to find a way out of this problem. We came to know about the Forest Rights Act, as we had attended training sessions and meetings. We made the Community forest Rights claims and even went to meet the collector and the Tehsildar. We formed our sangathan, which gave us the strength and the power to resist the Forest department's hegemony. We even went to the nearby villages asked them to approve our claim forms and recognize our rights of the forest. This is our agricultural land, traditional forest. We get forest resources (*Mahul patta, Kariya kanda,* etc.) which are not available elsewhere. The forest department used to say, "*humare dharti ko mat kodo hamare suar khayega*" (do not plough our forest land to get tubers as they will be eaten by wild boars). The forest is everything for us. Our whole livelihood depends on this forest, we came earlier and later the Wildlife Sanctuary.
>
> The pressure on food supply from the commons is negatively affecting the customary diet and food culture, particularly making women vulnerable. The protection of natural resources such as forests, as a customary source of food, has a value on which you cannot put a figure. Yet for the traditional forest-dependent people, it is part of the daily physical and spiritual reality. They hold valuable the traditional knowledge of food and medicines. Now, after the claims, we bring bamboo. We have put a signboard that this is our forest, which was once pulled down by , forest department, and after a confrontation by the women's group, it has been put back' (*Personal Interview of Forest Right Committee Member, Chuhiya, Interviewer* D. Nandi).

Through the FRA 2006 and community forest claims, the forest-dependent tribal communities have legal access to the forest land that they have inhabited and empowered to exercise the management rights over forest produce such as NTFPs. This has been possible due to active women's organizations that are from the Baiga community and who have fought the feudal forest department to get their legitimate rights. The Baiga women in this village are very strong, and they took the decision to file claims after many meetings and threatening from the forest departments. The claims were made following the due process. The women had also written to all the levels of committees about the status of their claims without getting any responses from the authorities. Finally, they wrote a letter to the State level committee, which wrote back to the district administration to reply to the FRC. On 12 December 2017, the representatives of the village met the district collector, the President of the District Level Committee, and asked him to expedite the process. They also had a discussion on other issues of the village. This gave the confidence to the Women and Gram Sabha, in particular, to overcome their fear against the forest department and involve in the management and protection of forests. The CFMC was formed, with 16 members, with an equal number of women members. The committee planted 2,000 bamboo plants in the monsoon. There were termites, and the plants were eaten up. Excessive dryness due to terrain was another problem. The women found out a way of developing drip irrigation by putting plastic bottles over the plants. This is how around 800 saplings could be saved. Nurseries have been established under this project, and seedlings for plantations have come from these nurseries.

Struggle for Territorial Rights in Fulwaripara

Women from Fulwaripara, a village in the Behramuda Panchayat of the Bilaspur district of Chhattisgarh, have fought a long battle against the odds to retain their livelihood from the forest. A village displaced for the sake of a dam some 25 years back, and settled on the fringes of the Achanakmar Wildlife Sanctuary, Fulwaripara has seen all sorts of harassment and exploitation. The village has 70 households, consisting mostly of Baiga tribals. This village had been displaced, and their traditional lifestyle of forest-dependency destabilized by the ban on the practice of Bewar (Shifting Cultivation) from 1980 onwards. Later in the early 1990s, they were displaced from Madhav Rao Jalashay and settled in the limits of the Behramuda Panchayat, at the foothills of *Kukdur pahad*.

The wild edible food and resources collected from the commons such as forests and mountains continued to be the main or supplementary source of many a household's daily consumptions. The indigenous peoples and other traditional commons-dependent populations, including women and children, are increasingly facing challenges to access, consume and manage these wild edible food and resources. The supply of subsidized rice through food security policies were doled out to these communities, thereby undermining the locally grown millets, which have been consumed traditionally. The subsidized and market food where industries are involved rarely benefits the indigenous entrepreneurs but mainly creates risks of losing traditional rights and resources as regards indigenous populations, particularly women, the elderly and youths.

CONCLUSION

SDGs ought to be oriented towards a nature-based solution. The government should focus on such kind of interventions to uplift the lives and livelihood of the Indigenous community. Our study found out that there are many pathways through which nature and the functions that it carries out can help us achieve our development targets and guide nature-based solutions to achieve the SDGs.

Biodiversity is an important common property resource and offers potent options for the development of sustainable economies. In the forest and tribal areas, sustainability is only possible through efficient management of biodiversity. Biological diversity, or biodiversity, encompasses the variety of all life on earth. Biodiversity manifests itself at three levels: species diversity, which refers to the numbers and kinds of living organisms; genetic diversity, which refers to the genetic variation within a population of species; and ecosystem diversity which is the variety of habitats, biological communities and ecological processes that occur in the biosphere. The biodiversity we see today is the outcome of over 3.5 billion years of evolutionary history, shaped by natural processes and increasingly, by the influence of humans. Biodiversity forms the web of life of which we are an integral part and upon which we so entirely depend. Biological diversity is the natural biotic capital of the earth and affects us all. Humanity derives its supplies of food, medicines, energy and many industrial products from biological resources.

Biodiversity rich areas do ensure not only plentiful supplies of a very large number of products of special consumptive use-value but also fulfil many more functions, for example, maintenance of local hydrological cycle moisture circulations, nutrients flows, soil conservation and so on, which are vital to the sustainability of production systems (Singh 1991). To ensure gains on a sustained basis, biodiversity restoration should be central to the CPR management strategy.

The one way forward is by engaging conservation with the well-being agendas of indigenous people and help them maintain their livelihood by preserving their traditions, customs, and the hope of having a society with its own identity based on traditional knowledge of the people (Janasoy 2005).

REFERENCES

Asher, M. 2007. *Recognizing the Historical Injustices: Campaign for the Forest Rights Act 2006*. Pune: National Centre of Advocacy Studies.

Bailey, F. G. 1960. *Tribe, Caste and Nation: A Study of Political Activity and Political Change in Highland Orissa*. Manchester University Press, Manchester 13.

Choubey, J. 2014, 13 February. 'Chhattisgarh Villages Pledge to Develop Wildlife Sanctuary on Their Own'. Down To Earth. Available at: https://www.downtoearth.org.in/news/24-chhattisgarh-villages-pledge-to-develop-wildlife-sanctuary-on-their-own-43491 (accessed on 23 April 2020).

Cornell, S. (1988). The return of the native: American Indian Political Resurgence. Oxford University Press. New York

Jansasoy, J.S. and Perez, A.L. 2005. Life Plan. Proposal for the Cultural, Territorial and Environmental Survival of the Indigenous villages. Foundation Zio-Ai, Union of Wisdom. The World Bank Environment Department, Washington, D.C.

Lasgorceix, A. 2009. 'Displacement and Relocation of Protected Areas: A Synthesis and Analysis of Case Studies'. *Economic & Political Weekly* 44 (49): 37–47.

Mahapanchayat, B., and N. G. Morcha. 2010, 31 December. 'Land Rights Violation in Achanakmar Wildlife Sanctuary, Chhattisgarh'. *A Fact Finding Report*. Available at: http://www.equitabletourism.org/files/fileDocuments1001_uid18.pdf (accessed on 21 July 2016).

McNeely, J. A., and R. Norgard. 1992. 'Developed Country Policies and Biological Diversity in Developing Countries'. *Agriculture, Ecosystems & Environment* 42: 194–204. Available at: https://doi.org/10.1016/0167-8809(92)90027-9 (accessed on 23 April 2020).

MoLJ. 2007. *The Scheduled Tribes and Other Traditional Forest Dwellers (Recognition of Forest Rights) Act, 2006.* Gazette of India. Ministry of Law and Justice. New Delhi: Government of India.

Michon, G., de Foresta, H., Kusworo, A. and Levang, P. (1999). The Damar Agroforests of Krui, Indonesia: Justice for forest Farmers. In Malcolm Cairns (Ed.), *Voice from the Forest: Integrating Indigenous Knowledge into Sustainable Upland Farming*, 528-563. Resource for the Future (RFF) Press, New York.

Nandi, D. 2015. *Chhattisgarh Case Study*. CFR-LA, Citizen Report, 46–48.

Shivaramakrishnan, K. 1999. *Modern Forest: State making and Environmental Change in Colonial Eastern India*. New Delhi: Oxford University Press.

Springate-Baginski, O. Sarin, M., Ghosh, S., Dasgupta, P., Bose, I., Banerjee, A., Sarap, K., Misra, P., Behera, S., Reddy, M.G. and P.T. Rao. 2009. Redressing 'historical injustice' through the Indian Forest Rights Act 2006: A Historical Institutional analysis of contemporary forest rights reform. IPPG Working Paper: University of Manchester. Available at: https://pdfs.semanticscholar.org/94cb/f23f269d45e0947e3a6bf23ec1a6a37359cb.pdf accessed on (accessed on 17 January 2018).

Ramnathan, U. 2014. 'Law and The Constitution: Eviction of Forest Communities'. Briefing paper. Available at: http://www.ielrc.org/content/f0401html (accessed on 13 January 2018).

Rodriguez, I. 2007. 'Linking Wellbeing with Cultural Revitalisation for Greater Cognitive Justice in Conservation'. Lessons from Venezuela in Canaima National Park. Available at: https://www.ecologyandsociety.org/vol22/iss4/art24/ accessed on 20th January, 2018.

U.N. Sub-Commission on Prevention of Discrimination and Protection of Minorities, 1993. Discrimination Against Indigenous People, *Report of the Working Group on Indigenous Populations on its Eleventh Session* by the Special Rapporteur, Mrs. Erica-Irene A. Daes. U.N. Doc. E/CN.4/Sub.2/1993/29. Available at: https://www.refworld.org/pdfid/3b00f49e4.pdf (accessed on 27 January 2018).

Chapter 15

The Causes for the Despair of Farmers in France and India
A Literature-based Study

Geetha Ganapathy-Doré

The Commons movement believes that shared community resources (natural and human-made) must be protected and managed in such a way as to bring benefit for all peasants in India, as well as France, who are victims of the construction of barrages without regard to the environment in the name of the greater common good. This article proposes to identify the common causes for the sad predicament of French and Indian farmers through a literature-based study.

In the post-communist world of multipolar power relations, we have witnessed suicide as an extreme form of political protest or war by non-state groups. Like military might, economic clout is an aspect of hard power. The victims of overindustrialization have been, first and foremost, the farmers. Just as the craftsman lost his space of freedom in the industrial order as Richard Sennett has shown (Sennett 2008), the farmer is losing his or her power in the course of the Third and Fourth Industrial Revolutions.

Every day, a farmer takes his life in France according to the Mutualité sociale agricole (Terre-net 2019). Every day, some 33 farmers commit suicide in India if we rely on the statistics of over 330,000 farmer suicides having occurred in the past 22 years (Giri and Sinha 2018). On an average, some 12,000 farmers commit suicide in India every year (FP Staff 2017).

Farmer suicides occur not only in India and France but also in other European countries like Ireland and Italy, not to mention the United States and Australia. These acts of despair are the consequences, a definite article needs to be added before consequences of rural distress. The farm crisis of the 1980s in the United States (Weingarten 2018) foreshadowed the impending doom of farmers elsewhere. Market prices crashed. Loans were called in. Interest rates doubled. Farmers were forced to liquidate their operations and got evicted from their land. The suicide rate soared (www.saveashorefarmer.org). 'World's economic growth model is killing farmers,' says the agricultural expert Devinder Sharma (Giri and Sinha, 2018). The premises for my comparative study of France and India are threefold.

Both India and France are huge agricultural producers in their respective continents. According to the Eurostat Statistical Factsheet (2018), France has the highest percentage of the rural population in Europe (21.5%). The share of the agricultural sector in the Gross Domestic Product (GDP) is 14.9 per cent. India ranks number 2 in the world in terms of the total value of agricultural production (Ross 2019). Agriculture is the primary source of livelihood for about 58 per cent of India's population (www.ibef.org). Even as Indian economy has diversified and grown, agriculture's contribution to GDP has, however, steadily declined from 1951 to 2011, according to the FAO. Today, it stands at 18 per cent (www.fao.org).

The income of French and Indian farmers has not ceased falling year after year. According to the Mutualité sociale agricole, the average salary of a French farmer is €1,250 per month. In 2007, it was €2,375 (*Le Monde avec AFP* 2009). Indeed, one-third of them were made to do with less than €350 per month in 2017 (Houdayer 2017). Twenty per cent of agricultural concerns are unprofitable. The Mutualité sociale agricole has put in place a telephonic assistance called Agri'écoute to help peasants overcome loneliness and despair. In India, the farmers' average income is about ₹6,500 per month, according to the Dalwai committee report

(FE Bureau 2018). Economic Survey 2018 predicts that climate change is likely to lower Indian farmers' income by 25 per cent. Nevertheless, the government's target is to double the farmers' income by 2022.

The problems of the agrarian world are not only economic but social. There is a search for recognition and status. The feminization of agriculture is a trend both in India (due to rural depletion) and France (change in paternalistic attitudes, technical improvements which make manipulations easier, sustainable development are some of the factors that led to this shift). Indeed, women who have been either wives or daughters of peasants who have committed suicide were the first to bear witness to farmer distress, thanks to their autobiographical narratives. Notable among them are: Ludivine Le Monnier (*Le jour où on a vendu nos vaches*, Flammarion 2017), Camille Beaurain (*Tu m'as laissé en vie*, Le Cherche Midi 2019) and Mélanie Paquet (*Une fille d'agriculteurs, sans répères*, self-published 2019. In India 'at least 35 per cent of the agricultural work force is female and likely to grow. Indeed, unless we alleviate women's constraints, future farmer agitations may be led by women,' opines Bina Agarwal (Agarwal 2017).

In order to explore the agrarian crisis in India and France, this study relies on a comparative and interdisciplinary approach. It takes up for analysis two French narratives, on the one hand: *Paysans des Terres englouties*, a fiction biography of a peasant woman with true photographs of the period by Claire Van-Kinh published in 2016 and *La Louve*, a modern agricultural fable by Paul-Henry Bizon published in 2017, staging the confrontation between two economic models—a cooperative of environmentally conscious farmers and an amoral profit-seeking and consumerist enterprise. Bizon's story may have been inspired by the real fiasco of the project *Jeune Rue* combining ecology, gastronomy and design whose creator Cédric Naudon was in prison till February 2018. On the other hand, it examines three fictional narratives from India (two written in English and one translated into English), namely, Na d'Souza's novella *Dweepa* (published in 1970 and translated from Kannada into English in 2013), Kota Neelima's novel *Shoes of the Dead* (2013) and Sonora Jha's *Foreign* (2013), to give an overall picture of Indian peasants' suffering. Its conclusion emphasizes the return to nature after decades of agricultural productivism.

As Antoine Compagnon points out in his essay entitled 'A la recherche de la ruralité perdue', published in the *Philosophie Magazine* on the occasion of the Agricultural Fair in 2013, France is a land of culture, both agriculture and the culture of the intellect. Literary work and agricultural labour are not thus far from each other, for both the writer and the peasant who dig, stir, overturn, plough and harrow either the land or the language (Compagnon 2013, 32). The truth is that there are more visitors to the agricultural fair than to the book exhibition, which shows the attachment of the French to their 'terroir', or soil, their way of maintaining the bond with the countryside in the city. Compagnon notices the presence of agribusinesses that attract crowds with slogans like 'From the prairie to the plate' (Compagnon 2013, 34). Such publicity campaigns reverse the trend of agricultural fairs by taking the city to the countryside the year around.

In the late 1960s, when India was witnessing the green revolution, a premonitory book was written in France on *La Fin des paysans* (The End of the Peasants) by Mendras (1967), a sociologist who had conducted his inquiries not only in France but also in America. The replacement of the local Basque red corn by hybrid corn was presented to the French peasant as something harmless. However, it meant that they had to invest in the purchase of seeds, fertilizers, new tools and machines and thus get into debt (Clavreul 2008). Slowly the majority turned into a minority. They now face administrative and technical difficulties due to EU requirements. The majority is now a helpless witness to water and soil pollution and monocultures.

'What would be a world without the peasants?' was the question Henri Mendras raised. In the recently published essay called *Le Contrat naturel*, the French philosopher Michel Serres ([1987] 2018, 19) asked the same question: What if a peasants' party comes into being and announces a strike on food production?[1]

---

[1] It is a common knowledge that after the industrialization of agricultural activities, trade unions of the peasants are very active in France. José Bové of the Confédération paysanne, who is well-known as an anti-globalization activist, was a candidate of the Green party (Europe-Écologie-Les Verts) during the French presidential elections in 2007 and is currently an elected member of the European Parliament.

The greatest event of the 20th century is undoubtedly the disappearance of agriculture as the leading activity of human life, according to Michel Serres ([1987] 2018, 71). He does not refer to farmer suicides but calls them 'patricide' (Serres [1987] 2018, 19). It is the insensitive behaviour of the modern urban dwellers, which amounts to 'a collective suicide' (Serres [1987] 2018, 18). Michel Serres extols the peasants as the nourishing fathers of humanity. Their numbers have not ceased decreasing, while their misery is forever increasing owing to the exploitation of which they are victims. The loss of fertile land to concrete buildings is a sign of urban distribution, the correlate of global mobility. It is devouring everything on its way, according to Michel Serres. He wonders whether we should not rethink history as a multi-millenary conflict between the countryside and the city, rural and urban civilizations (Serres [1987] 2018).

This clash between rural and urban civilizations is a theme that Claire Depaix-Van Kinh had explored in her third novel *Gamin des villes, gamin des champs* the title of which harks back to the fable by La Fontaine, *Le rat de ville et le rat des champs* (The City Mouse and the Country Mouse). Her two previous novels, *Louise Paysanne en côte roannaise* and *Le Bastien des Sources*, are also narratives about the rural world. Her fourth novel *Paysans de Terres englouties* (Peasants of Submerged Lands) evokes the condition of the farmers at the mercy of nature and political power and the violence prevailing in their world in a realistic but much less brutal fashion than Emile Zola in his novel *La Terre*. In this 21st century narrative, the protagonist is a woman, Marthe Henriette. The novel is a fictionalized biography of a family friend of the author, and she intends it to be a tribute.

Abandoned by her teenage mother at birth in Lyons, Marthe Henriette has been brought up by peasant families who are paid by the state's social assistance. 'Working a lot and always much more' was her lot. She finds escape in marriage and becomes the wife of Antonin Dalmet, a fisherman from the village of Saint-Maurice-sur-Loire who possesses some arid land. Most of the males in the village are alcoholics. They commit petty offences like poaching or big crimes like rape.

The village itself is drowned by the construction of a barrage decided in 1974 and completed in 1982. The pretext was to muzzle the Loire river. Not even the existence of a gallo-roman village and its artefacts would deter the government. In truth, the objective was to cool the nuclear reactors downstream.

The author interviews and collects testimonies from peasants who were properly compensated, but nevertheless feel depressed and lonely because they had been uprooted and had lost their former way of life, memories and marks. Marthe traces her mother's family, but when she goes to her, she is already dead. Marthe's unfulfilled quest for her mother mirrors the modern urban dweller's quest for his roots. A quest that is always and already too late. Marthe's son's tragic death at a young age in an industrial accident and her own death in a car accident are the author's ironic winks to the modern sense of progress. Marthe is an embodiment of dignity, courage and resilience. We find the same traits of character in Na D'Souza's heroine, Nagaveni.

Paul Henri Bizon's *La Louve* (*The She-Wolf*) uses the codes of the classical French novel but gives it a contemporary twist. Two brothers from the butcher Vollot's family in Monfort-sur-Sèvre, Camille and Romain, grow apart after the suicide of their brother Antoine who went to Paris to study. While his brother Romain inherits the family business and puts to good use his knowledge gained from a business school, Camille, thanks to his benefactor Anne-Marie Perrault and wife Victoire's support, turns to permaculture and struggles to initiate a new market 'La Louve' where small farmers can sell their organic produce.

Paul-Henri Bizon uses the character of Anne-Marie Perrault to get across his message in favour of permaculture by mentioning the names of all the pioneers in the area. Trained as an engineer at the National Institute of Agronomy, Anne-Marie Perrault starts working in a petrochemical factory. At the end of the 1960s, when scientific research started showing the toxicity of the petrochemical products, she resigns from her job, and devotes herself to studying ethno-agriculture to explore the connection between living organisms. Her friend is Robert Hart, the Englishman who invented the concept of forest gardening (Bizon 2017, 46–49).

Camille's path, unfortunately, crosses that of Raoul Sarkis, a megalomanic swindler who had spent some 16 years in Poland, obsessed with money, booze, sex and the city. His larger than life project, a sort of marriage between Peggy Guggenheim and Alain Ducasse, turns out to be a disaster. The journalist Hakim Khalil exposes his fraud, and Camille's wife Victoire is able to confront Sarkis and save Camille's property. The rivalry between Romain and Camille in this novel may remind us of the Biblical story of Cain and Abel. Nevertheless, the structural pattern of the novel resembles that of a fairy tale. We have Camille, the hero, Victoire, the princess, and Raoul the villain. Antoine is the dispatcher, Hakim, the helper, and Anne-Marie, the donor. Paul Henri-Brizon's play with names makes us guess the name of some real and corrupt politicians behind the fictional mask. The author's purpose is to show how the agricultural world, caught between its own stagnation and the financial interests of mass merchandisers and supermarket, is unable to find a viable economic model in a world of bourgeois bohemians who think that they can have the best of both worlds.

The economist Silvia Pérez-Vittoria's *Manifeste pour un XXIe siècle paysan* published in 2015 is a cry against the elimination of peasants by the commodification of Nature that is occurring in France. It denounces urban agriculture as a modernist imposture. Indeed, a threat to the rural world implies a threat to the French culture as such. When confronted with rural distress, the response of French politicians is to propose to renegotiate the European Union's Common Agricultural Policy because French peasants, cattle breeders and fishermen cannot survive without EU subsidies.

From the suffering Mother India to the grieving of widows of Vidharba, India seems to have taken an inexorable path to loss and pain. For postcolonial critics who are familiar with the fiction of Bhabani Bhattacharya and Kamala Markandaya, farmer suicide narratives look like a 'literary recession', a plunge back into rural poverty and despair that the green revolution of the 1970s was supposed to have eradicated as the postcolonial nation took a decisive step towards food self-sufficiency. Indeed, R. K. Narayan's *Financial Expert* makes a comeback in Kota Neelima's *The Death of a Moneylender*. The combined reading of the three Indian narratives enables us to piece together a general picture of the transition of the Indian economy from Gandhi's vision of self-dependent villages through Nehru's dream of growth to the hyper-individualization of globalized modernity.

In *The Greater Common Good*, Arundhati Roy denounced dam building in the name of easier access to water, more power production and better flood control, because it dispossessed millions of people of their land and livelihood. *Dweepa* is a story of dispossession and displacement of peasant families from the Hosamanehalli village at the foot of the Sita-Parvatha hillock by government authorities in order to complete the Linganamakki Dam. It is told by a third-person omniscient narrator. As the author himself belonged to the public works department and was involved in the Sharavathi River valley hydro-electric project, it is clear that he is transfiguring his first-hand knowledge of a family's history into fictional material. The novel's seven chapters are named after seven stars, to indicate a different sense of time as well as seasonal change.

The farmer Ganapayya refuses to leave his land though he knows that it will be submerged by water, unlike other peasants who have accepted compensation, given up their land and taken up other professions elsewhere. His old father Duggajja supports his decision before he dies. In any case, as Ganapayya's file for compensation is said to be lost by a corrupt peon, he feels like a man hounded by a tiger in a forest. However, Ganapayya's wife Nagaveni suggests a provisional retreat to her native place. As both the men reject her idea, her family sends her old playmate Krishnayya to help the couple. A semblance of respite and happiness exists in the household before jealousy sneaks into the mind of Ganapayya like the water snake that finds its way into the kitchen. When her husband beats her up, Nagaveni becomes fully aware of her oppressed condition and her irrepressible desire for Krishnayya. Krishnayya yields when he sees the woman's depression but tries to get away out of a sense of guilt. He jumps into the rising water and is followed by Nagaveni. Although Ganapayya tries to avoid this watery grave, he falls prey to the tiger on the prowl that had earlier killed his cow.

That the heroine Nagaveni is the allegorical figure of earth makes no doubt. The bond between a man and his land is like the inalienable bond of desire that connects his body to his being in the world. The lesson from this postcolonial fable is that people who thwart earth's desire do so at their peril. It is because of deforestation that the man-eater impinges on the territory of Ganapayya.

Desire is embedded in the novel almost literally in the form of Sita-Rama's bed, for it is believed that the Sita-Rama-Lakshmana triangle took rest in a cave at the hillock during their exile from Ayodhya. The reckless and individualist consumption of desire between Nagaveni and Krishnayya, however, is intended to open the eyes of the reader as to the temptations of capitalism. The submerged island is a metaphor for our consumerist self that risks to be overwhelmed by the flood of greed.

This novel in which the geography of the Malenadu, its fauna, and flora, are faithfully etched in the narrative canvas is not merely a tale rooted in the soil but ventures into the zone of primeval desire in which a woman is attracted to a forbidden brother-like figure, while a suggested parallel is made between the cow wounded by the tiger and the woman undergoing physical intercourse in a situation of forced marriage. Gender violence and disregard for the environment are two sides of the same coin. Ganapayya is let down both by earth and his wife as if to punish him for his patriarchal sense of possession and property. Dweepa had been made into a national award-winning film in 2002 by Girish Kasaravalli.[2]

Kota Neelima's novel offers a different take on the issue of farmer suicide by portraying an epic struggle between an honest farmer and an ambitious politician in a dynastic democracy, both of whom taunt the boundaries of ethics, with an independent journalist, Nazar, playing the mediator. The journalist's character may have been inspired by P. Sainath, author of *Everybody Loves a Good Drought*, who won the Ramon Magsaysay award in 2007 for his 'passionate commitment as a journalist to restore the rural poor to India's national consciousness' (Magsaysay Citation). In the search for truth and social justice against

---

[2] Within the framework of this chapter, a comparison between the novella and the film would have been extraneous. There exist about a dozen films on farmer suicides in India. *Mitti: Back to the Roots* (2018) directed by Anshul Sinha is a well-documented and poignant movie. In France, Hubert Charuel's *Petit Paysan* (2017), Mélanie Auffret's *Roxanne* (2019) and Edouard Bergeon's *Au nom de la Terre* (2019) deal with peasants unease and suicide.

the tactics of 'diverting, subverting and converting' voters (Neelima 2013, 15), a woman researcher married to an industrialist plays the role of the facilitator. This narrative incidentally sensitizes us to fake news.

Sudhakar Bhadra kills himself, following the footsteps of his father, crushed by crop failure and the burden of debt. In order to take care of his sister-in-law and her two kids, Sudhakar's brother Gangiri resigns his job in the city as a teacher and comes back to the village of Mitiyala. By exercising some pressure on the district collector, he gets appointed as a member of the district committee, which has formerly been dismissing the claims of the farmers for government compensation with the complicity of the Lambordar and the moneylender among others. His determined defence of the victims invites not only hostility but death threats because each claim recognized is a sign of failure by the first-time MLA Keyur Kashinath, son of the respected secretary of the Democratic Party, Vaishnav Kashinath and a blot on the party's image. Obliged to beg on the doors of the very moneylender he denounces to treat his nephew for tuberculosis, the brave Gangiri commits suicide when his nephew dies. The fall of the hero, paradoxically, brings about a social change with the other actors having a pang of conscience.

Though this novel reads more like reportage than a fiction, it has the merit of clearly identifying the causes for and the number of farmer suicides, the solutions proposed by the government, and those recommended by academics, the obstacles, the actors and institutions involved in solving the crisis. The conspiracies of survival in the political, media and agricultural worlds are as merciless as any other, making the novel a modern-day treatise on 'the new game of money, power and fame' that seems to hold India in its grips.

Farmer suicide is a national tragedy. However, the crisis points are in several states, such as Andhra Pradesh, Karnataka, Gujarat, Maharashtra and Punjab. Like Narayan's Malgudi, Mitiyala is an emblematic fictional location in which 28 suicides occur within 40 days. Crop failure due to lack of rain, investment in cost-heavy fertilizers, pesticides and genetically modified seeds, land fragmentation, technological stagnation, exposure to volatile markets, the difficulties to get bank loans, the weight of debt, private money lenders who lend additional amounts to borrowers who are not creditworthy with the ulterior motive of confiscating their land and selling it for profit, corrupt local officials who connive with high-level politicians to put industrial development before sustainable development (Neelima 2013, 7) and the humiliation and despair of the farmers are the general causes. Into this nexus are woven the dilemmas of doctors and journalists who have to choose between the pursuit of their careers and their humanitarian inkling.

This narrative of farm distress is twisted by several actors who point to individual causes: aspirations for city life, laziness, depravity, alcoholism, depression, disinterest, disease, extravagant spending and pride. The government introduced a relief package in 2008. But the district committees put self-interest first and despise poor widows, indeed even ill-treat and torture them. In the novel, the adjective that qualifies the village headman is 'apatra' (rejector of petitions). The collector and the agricultural officer try to cope with the situation more or less efficiently. The police harbours a violent and hostile attitude towards protesting peasants.

The author mocks at academics who sit in plush offices and drive fancy cars, offering their spin on the issue to the media. Vaidehi recommends rather flimsy remedial measures: customizing agricultural services, cutting subsidies to dissuade people from engaging in agricultural activities, making urban youth interact with rural youth and setting up centres for spiritual counselling. The activist Gandri Bhadra (Kumar 2013) comes up with solid counter-proposals: forgiving debts, rescheduling loans, granting loans with zero interest, giving guaranteed farm input, incentives for repayment, and ending intimidating procedures of debt recovery. Indeed, some of these ideas could be found in the Pradhan Mantri Fasal Bima Yojana implemented in January 2016. The din and noise of debate coming out of the book is a testimony to the vitality of democracy in India despite its conspicuous shortcomings—hereditary power, corruption and criminality. The novel also bears witness to the moral susceptibility flickering in Indian society.

The purpose of this new variety of political fiction is to stage the fourth column of democracy. The author demonstrates an intimate knowledge of the grassroots, local and party hierarchies. Finally, it is the education that stands out as a safety valve. Educated Gangiri is able to move out of his low social status and stand up for his rights. Education is what gives him the lucidity not to cross the line between activism and a political career as MLA. Though Gangiri, who initially does not want to stand in the shoes of the dead, ends his life, he chooses to pass on his knowledge to his friend Vadrangi so that he, in turn, could take up the cause of the farmers in the district committee.

Sonora Jha's novel explores the same territory of farmer suicides in the real village of Pandharkawada in Maharashtra. In her novel, a single Indian mother and academic from Seattle takes a flight to rescue her 14-year-old son who has run away to meet his long-lost father, who is an activist and a Muslim. She, who is familiar with the depressingly unending rain and high rate of suicides in Seattle, comes to grips with the failing rain and equally high rate of farmer suicides in Pandharkawada. Indian in America and American in India, this exiled woman does not belong. She is forever a 'foreigner'.

Her heroine Katyayini seems to be a fictional double of the author, as this exiled woman and a former journalist is poised between the freedom and well-being that America represents and the dignity and strength of Maharashtrian farmers. What distinguishes her narrative from Kota Neelima's is, first, the paradoxical insider/outsider point of view, then the portrayal of the blogging youngster Kabir as a Krishna-like trickster who easily navigates the two worlds, and finally, the emphasis on the empowerment of the female farmer whose predicament is just touched upon in Neelima's *Shoes of the Dead*. It is also in Jha's account that we get to know that a farmer's suicide must fulfil 40 criteria to qualify for compensation. Indeed, Sonora Jha uses Gandhi's Dandi march as an archetype of protest marches in postcolonial India.

This novel resorts to the tested Hindi cinema formula for its plot: unfulfilled love between Katyayini and Ammar, the good farmer couple Bhajirao and Gayatribhai, the kidnapping of Kabir, Gayatribhai's rape, Meera's wedding in a mass marriage ceremony, Bhajirao's sacrifice of a kidney for his daughter's dowry and his life for his sick wife, the joining hands of Katya and Gayatribhai to write a book entitled *Bhajirao's Choice: Life and Death on India's Cotton Farms* which refers to the probable documentary version of the author's own fictional run of the incidents.

The novel itself is not very convincing from the purely literary point of view. Nevertheless, the story of cotton in India interwoven in the narrative is authentic. Cotton was thought to have been given to Gujarat by sage Kapasi 10,000 years ago. When the British came, they (Jha 2013, 83) exploited this 'white gold', and slowly, Mumbai became the centre of India's cotton economy. The dynamics changed in 1977 when the Indian government introduced Bit Cotton seeds imported from America. When the conditions were fine, the seed worked. However, the farmers were vulnerable, and one little thing could compromise the yield. After the liberalization of India's trade, Vidarbha's farmers had to compete with subsidized American farmers. The suicides began in 1997. The farmers hanged themselves, drowned in the river, and died by swallowing the very pesticide they used to protect their crops. Only the National Crime Record Bureau kept stock of these suicides as if they were crimes. By 2010, 20,000 farmers had died in India.

Jha's narrative avoids miserabilism and reads farmer suicides in the larger context of what drives human beings to commit suicide. While the novel's evocation of Indian mythology (Katyayini is the goddess who grants wishes for a bridegroom), the legendary love between Krishna and Rukmini via street theatre and its use of names of the wandering minstrels of India such as Kabir and Meera might seem rather easy strategies for rooting the narrative in India, its laying bare of the power struggle at play in gender and social relations in India is quite realistic. The author takes extreme care to make Bajirao's voice heard and not to make Gayatribhai sound like a subaltern to Katya. Although Jha does not assimilate the human to the Western liberal subject, the shocking end in which Gayatribhai hears that one of her sons-in-law has committed suicide gives a totally pessimistic twist. Gayatribhai's destiny of widow has caught up with her daughter, making injustice challenge the hard-won agency.

Nilotpal Kumar has argued that farmer suicides have to do with the farmers' sense of masculinity, status and honour (Kumar 2016). However, the disrupted life of the farmers in India and elsewhere is a symptom of malaise in the liberal economy. We tend to look at it as a sign. We interpret it as the symptom of the malaise felt by the farmers due to the precarity of their existence. Because we do not realize we are killing them, the farmers show that they are dying. The truth is that their absent bodies are signs of the presence of our indifference and lack of awareness that it is our own death that they are enacting. Farmer suicide is a symptom of the illness of modern civilization.

By dramatizing the confrontation between national sovereignty and individual responsibility in the context of rural distress, these narratives have started the process of societal resistance. Farmer suicides like the sale of body parts and the rape of women commodify the body. The whole of humanity is under threat when lives have become disposable, while bodies retain value. They spectralize the price of the cost of living that some of them cannot afford.

The NGO Citizens Resource and Action and Initiative had taken the matter of farmer suicides to the Indian Supreme Court. The justices of the Supreme Court have opined that 'the government is going in a wrong direction [...]. The remedy to the problem is not to pay money to farmers after the suicide, but [...] schemes to prevent this (www.firstpost.com).' The outcome of the litigation between Montsanto and Nuziveedu regarding the patentability of the genetically modified cotton seeds Bollgard and Bollgard II to be decided by the Delhi High Court, if positive, can restore the seed ownership to Indian farmers and this might protect them from exploitation and abuse by multinational companies.

Michel Serres asks us to rethink our relationship to the world because the human being is no longer merely a being. He or she has been transformed into a being equipotent to the world, thanks to the weight of the network of relations he has to build and the world objects he has to possess. In this process of commodification of the world and oversizing of human beings, we have lost the world. In order to restore balance, we have to put human beings at the periphery and the world at the centre. Such a change can happen only by recognizing the natural contract, by realizing that we are but a tremor of nothing in the universe's permanent quivering. Michel Serre's proposal responds across cultures and languages to Amitav Ghosh's (2016) lament in *The Great Derangement* about the lack of inventiveness of the human imagination and social sciences to foresee and find answers for the challenge of climate change. Pope Francis recommends the same remedy in his

Laudato Si' when he advises us to move away from modern anthropocentrism and its technocratic paradigm to care for our common home (Francis 2015).

REFERENCES

Agarwal, B. 2017. 'The Seeds of Discontent'. *Indian Express*, June 15. Available at: https://indianexpress.com/article/opinion/columns/the-seeds-of-discontent-madhya-pradesh-farmers-crisis-4704397/ (accessed on 23 April 2020).

Bizon, P. H. 2017. *La Louve* (trans. The She-Wolf). Paris: Gallimard.

Clavreul, L. 2008. 'La Fin des paysans' (trans. End of Peasants). *Le Monde*, August 1. Available at: https://www.lemonde.fr/idees/article/2008/08/01/la-fin-des-paysans-par-laetitia-clavreul_1079462_3232.html (accessed on 23 April 2020).

Compagnon, A. 2013. 'A la recherche de la ruralité perdue? (trans. In search of lost rurality?)' *Philosophie Magazine* 68: 31–35.

D'Souza, N. A. 2013. *Dweepa* (Island). Translated from Kannada into English by S. Punitha. New Delhi: Oxford University Press.

European Union. 2019. *Eurostat Statistical Factsheet*. Available at: https://ec.europa.eu/agriculture/sites/agriculture/files/statistics/factsheets/pdf/eu_en.pdf (accessed on 23 April 2020).

FAO. 2020. *India at a Glance*. Available at: http://www.fao.org/india/fao-in-india/india-at-a-glance/en/ (accessed on 23 April 2020).

FE Bureau. 2018. 'Economic Survey 2017–18: Agriculture—Climate Change Likely to Lower Farmers' Income by 25%'. *Financial Express*, 30 January. Available at:https://www.financialexpress.com/budget/economic-survey-2017-18-agriculture-climate-change-likely-to-lower-farmers-income-by-25/1035560/ (accessed on 23 April 2020).

FP Staff. 2017. 'Over 12,000 Farmer Suicides Reported per Year Since 2013: Centre to Supreme Court'. *Firstpost*, 3 May. Available at: https://www.firstpost.com/india/over-12000-farmer-suicides-reported-per-year-since-2013-centre-to-supreme-court-3421748.html (accessed on 23 April 2020).

Ghosh, A. 2016. *The Great Derangement*. Chicago, IL: University of Chicago Press.

Giri, A., and S. Sinha. 2018. 'Devinder Sharma on India's Agriculture Crisis'. *The Diplomat*, 20 June. Available at: https://thediplomat.com/2018/06/devinder-sharma-on-indias-agriculture-crisis/ (accessed on 23 April 2020).

Houdayer, G. 2017. 'Un tiers des agriculteurs français ont un revenu inférieur à 350 euros par mois' (trans. One third of France's farmers earn lesser than 350 euros per month). *France Bleu*, 10 October. Available at: https://www.francebleu.fr/infos/agriculture-peche/un-tiers-des-agriculteurs-francais-ont-un-revenu-inferieur-a-350-euros-par-mois-1507639289 (accessed on 23 April 2020).

India Brand Equity Foundation. 2018, October. *Agriculture in India: Information About Indian Agriculture & Its Importance*. Available at: https://www.ibef.org/industry/agriculture-india.aspx (accessed on 13 March 2020).

Jha, S. 2013. *Foreign.* Noida: Random House India.

Kasaravalli, G. 2002. *Dweepa.* Available at: https://www.youtube.com/watch?v=EY-qzjFtda8 (accessed on 23 April 2020).

Kumar, A. 2013. 'Kota Neelima's "Shoes of the Dead" Takes India to Bharat'. *The Hindu,* 7 August. Available at: https://www.thehindu.com/features/metroplus/the-inside-story/article4999568.ece (accessed on 23 April 2020).

Kumar, N. 2016. *Unraveling Farmer Suicides in India: Egoism and Masculinity in Peasant Life.* New Delhi: OUP India

Le Monde avec AFP. 2009. 'Les revenus des agriculteurs chutent de 34% en 2009'. *Le Monde,* 14 December. Available at: https://www.lemonde.fr/economie/article/2009/12/14/les-revenus-des-agriculteurs-chutent-de-34-en-2009_1280572_3234.html (accessed on 23 April 2020).

Mendras, H. 1967. *La fin des paysans* (trans. End of Peasants). Paris: SEIDES.

Neelima, K. 2013. *Shoes of the Dead.* New Delhi: Rupa.

Pérez, V. S. 2015. *Manifeste pour un XXIe siècle paysan* (trans. Manifesto for a Peasant 21st Century). Paris: Actes du Sud.

Pope Francis. 2015. *Laudato Si'* (trans. Praise be to you), the Vatican. *Word on Fire.* Available at: https://laudatosi.com/watch (accessed on 13 March 2020).

Ross, S. 2019, 15 February. *4 Countries That Produce the Most Food.* Available at: https://www.investopedia.com/articles/investing/100615/4-countries-produce-most-food.asp (accessed on 13 March 2020).

Roy, A. 1999. *The Greater Common Good.* Bombay: India Book Distributors.

Sainath, P. 1996. *Everybody Loves a Good Drought: Stories from India's Poorest Districts.* New Delhi: Penguin.

Saveashorefarmer.org. *Why Do Farmers Take Their Own Lives?* Available at: https://www.saveashorefarmer.org/why-do-farmers-take-their-own-lives.html (accessed on 13 March 2020).

Sennet, R. 2008. *The Craftsman.* Yale, CT: Yale University Press.

Serres, M. (1987) 2018. *Le Contrat naturel* (trans. The Natural Contract). Paris: Editions Le Pommier.

Terre-net. 2019, September. *Un agriculteur se suicide chaque jour selon la MSA* (trans. Each day a farmer commits suicide according to MSA). Available at: https://www.terre-net.fr/actualite-agricole/economie-social/article/un-agriculteur-se-suicide-chaque-jour-selon-la-msa-202-152192.html (accessed on 13 March 2020).

Van-Kinh, D. C. 2016. *Paysans des Terres englouties* (trans. Peasants of Submerged Lands). Self-published.

Weingarten, D. 2018. 'Why Are American Farmers Killing Themselves?' *The Guardian,* 11 December. Available at: https://www.theguardian.com/us-news/2017/dec/06/why-are-americas-farmers-killing-themselves-in-record-numbers (accessed on 23 April 2020).

Conclusion
Imagining Multiple Worlds in Fifty Years

S. Ashok

This concluding chapter is an exercise in imagination, coupled with possible explanations for that imagined vision, followed by macro-level descriptions of such imagined pictures.

There are actors, and there is the setting. The stage is only a stage we think, because of the time it takes for the stage to change. That is the essence of the stage. However, a stage can become the stage only in relation to the actors. The stage is usually constructed for a purpose, through a particular set of relationships with a given set of actors, constructed each time differently.

Look at this stage, for instance, the stage in which we are set—our immediate environment—was constructed by the hard labour of various actors for a particular purpose. It could be a reading room, a library, a room in a building, the metro we are travelling in on while reading or the toilet seat on which we are seated while reading this article. From a macro perspective, the period of change of the stage is more prolonged than that of the actors. Often, the stage is identified or misidentified, depending on the actors' sense of participation or even belonging, through several micro-interactions. Actors play different roles over time, but the stage itself is 'institutionalized' in a sense, differently from the actors.

For example, the readers might all go in different directions from here. However, the article itself and the work behind it are institutionalized differently. The institution of the stage happens through multiple actors, acting in various capacities across varying time periods—some longer than the others. Even though some actors themselves can become institutionalized, what we are trying to say is that certain individual actors may reproduce certain institutions beyond their physical existence at the stage itself. For instance, all readers will read, possibly internalize and critique and reproduce the possible knowledge from this article differently. However, it is the same material piece of knowledge that is reproduced differently by different readers.

From the point of view of the actors, the stage—these institutions—lasts just long enough to become only partially perceptible to the actor at a later point of time. The stage becomes a memory. From the macro perspective, however, some actors, some stages are more 'memorialized' than others. The act of remembering is structured, and the institutions are reproduced through the act of remembering. For instance, when the readers will finish reading this chapter, we will all remember different things about this same chapter. We could even feel differently about it. However, we may reproduce different experiences of the same stage, for example, the article under review.

IDEOLOGICAL CONSTRUCTION OF THE METHOD OF EXPLORATION

Let us take a larger stage, for instance, the institution of the nation. Memorialization and institutionalization are crucial, as Benedict Anderson argues, in the construction of an 'imagined community' (Anderson 1983). It is in this sense that individual actors may reproduce institutions. The stage, therefore, seems to have a relative fixity, with the actors' perceptions themselves. However, institutions or 'stages' themselves, are structured through material relations of production. Karl Marx in his 'Critique of Political Economy' points out,

> In the social production of their existence, men inevitably enter into definite relations of production, which are independent of their will, namely relations of production appropriate to a given stage in the development of their material forces of production. {…} It is not the consciousness of men that determined their existence, but their social existence that determines their consciousness. (Marx 1859, 4)

There is that connection between the stage and the actors. That is where each interacts with the other and affects each other very differently. In the long run, this article takes a reasonable standpoint, which stems from the fact that, as Heraclitus, the ancient philosopher of Ephesus in contrast to Parmenides, puts it, 'everything changes' or 'τὰ ὄντα ἰέναι τε πάντα καὶ μένειν οὐδέν' (Plato and Reeve 1998, xxix).

We live in a reality that is continually changing, which is in a constant state of flux. However, right now, this article aims only to imagine. Also, for constructing any imagined vision of the future, we will need to identify, for our purposes, what we think is the stage, and who, and what are the actors.

Since we are aiming to imagine our existence as a *species-being* (a collective, that determines our existence as a human being) across a significant time-span, one way to imagine is to think what could be the boundaries of a frame of reference—a stage—that we could, as human beings, consider as relatively fixed, in relation to us, as human beings, for an imagination to be made possible? One answer is to imagine a space-time boundary. The important thing about setting the boundaries of the space-time matrix is that we can begin to articulate the drama within its confines. It is like a canvas through which we can express our imaginings.

There could be an equally valid method of going about setting the boundaries from inside out, of going from the micro to the macro levels of analysis. The possibilities of imagination from the micro outwards seem to be infinite. One cannot seem to imagine how difficult that method could be, or if there would even be a need to set boundaries in that method. The objective categories for analysis, in that methodology of going from the micro to the macro levels, seem to be indeterminable for us, at this juncture. Where do we start from in that case? Idea or matter? Alternatively, is that an imposed Cartesian dichotomy? Alternatively, do we start from the fact of existence as a given and work our way outwards? However, then, inwards, we are infinity all the time, and sometimes we even have glimpses of knowledge of its existence. What description of existence can we possibly fix, against which we could measure change? The stoic philosophers might point us towards the *logoi* but unpacking *the particular logos* would require a lot more time than we have presently for this article. That would involve qualitative research that maps experiences using wholly different and more complicated methods of measurement.

USING THE METHOD TO DESCRIBE REALITY
Level of Analysis

Thus, for the present article, let us start with a macro perspective and use a space-time definition to set the boundaries of our imaginations. The time axis is presently taken as 50 years. The space we exist in, at a macro level, could expand to cover more than just the Earth by then. Looking outwards, human reach has already expanded to beyond the edge of the solar system. Space probes like the Voyager have already reached interstellar space (Roemelle 2014). Human habitation beyond the space of our planet seems possible, and in fact, maybe even likely in the next 50 years, especially given the necessities arising from what can happen to our climate, at home.

Setting up the canvas, thus, would involve marking out the axes of space and time. In 50 years, how would space fill out, materially? When looking at long term-patterns of social relations, it is always a difficult task to explain fundamental discontinuities across time. These phenomena get even more complicated as we try and understand what could be described as 'epochal changes'. As John Ruggie points out in 'Territoriality and Beyond: Problematizing Modernity in International Relations', for understanding epochal change, 'we lack even an adequate vocabulary, and what we cannot describe, we cannot explain' (Ruggie 1993, 144).

He argues,

> The global ecological implosion inherently invites epochal thinking. Analytically informed empirical studies of "ozone diplomacy" or attempts to save the Mediterranean inevitably focus on negotiation processes and the dynamics of regime construction, as opposed to exploring the possibility of fundamental institutional discontinuity in the system of states. They do so because, among other reasons, dominant modes of analytical discourse lack the requisite vocabulary. (Ruggie 1993, 143)

At the risk of over-determinism, we venture to suggest that in 50 years, the fundamental factor that would materially, and hence spatially determine the human condition the most crucially, will be our environment. According to an official expert group that presented the recommendation to the International Geological Congress in late 2017, humanity's impact on the Earth is now so profound that a new unit of geological time scale, a new epoch—the Anthropocene—needs to be declared (Carrington 2016). Scientists argue that mid-20th-century phenomena such as carbon dioxide emissions, rising sea levels, global mass extinction of species and deforestation, have ended a nearly 12,000-year-old Holocene epoch. Ever since the end of the 1940s, with the human species going nuclear, we are *directly causing* species to go extinct, warming the planet so much that Antarctica is melting, and, by 2050, there is going to be more plastic than fish in the ocean. The Anthropocene marks a new period, in which, according to Professor Chris Rapley, a climate scientist at the University College London, 'our collective activities dominate the planetary machinery' (Carrington 2016). The term 'Anthropocene' was coined only in 2000 by the Nobel Prize-winning scientist Paul Crutzen, who believed the name change for this geological time scale was overdue. *The Guardian*, a British daily newspaper, writes, quoting him, 'This name change stresses the enormity of humanity's responsibility as stewards of the Earth' (Carrington 2016).

The Grim 'State of Nature'

Human activity has pushed the extinction rate of animals and plants far above the long-term average. The Earth is on course to see 75 per cent of species become extinct in the next few centuries if current trends continue. Levels of climate-warming CO_2 in the atmosphere have been increasing at the fastest rate ever in the past 66 million years, with fossil-fuel burning, pushing levels from 280 parts per million (ppm) before the industrial revolution, to 400 ppm, and rising today. We have doubled the nitrogen and phosphorus in our soils in the past century with fertilizers. This is likely to be the most substantial impact on the nitrogen cycle in 2.5 billion years. We have left a permanent layer of airborne particulates in sediment and glacial ice, such as carbon from fossil fuel burning. As individuals in general, or as a species collectively, we have not been conscious enough of the impact of our actions, let alone our existence.

Modernity might have been the epoch, as John Ruggie, saw it when the 'I' became important (Ruggie 1993). We might be slowly shifting to an age, well within the confines of Anthropocene, where 'we' will have to become relevant, necessarily, at the global level, if not anything, but for the survival of the human race. Collectively and individually, our very survival and continued existence on this planet on a 50-year-horizon depend on how we respond to the changes we have brought about to our environment over the past 200 years or so.

The Grim 'State of Social Relations' and the 'Units of Analyses'

Crucially, these effects would be distributed in society in a highly unequal manner. The link between poverty and capability has long been established. At the macro level, there is no doubting that the worst victims of the unravelling of the environment would be the most socio-culturally and economically deprived sections of the world.

In this context, what should the unit of our analysis be? If the space-time boundary of the stage is set, who are our actors—missing and present? Should we be treating the nation-state as the unit of our analysis? David A. Lake (2007), in his article 'The State and International Relations', gives good reasons to stick to the nation-state as the unit of analysis in years to come. He argues that by studying varying state structures, giving space for more unit heterogeneity and by incorporating the concept of hierarchy in the international system, we can stick to analysing the system by treating the state as the unit. This, he argues, despite the ebbs and flows of differing domestic politics, and the increasing autonomy of transnational actors (Lake 2007). The requirement of an organized collective power to deal with the challenges emanating from the environment, which are bound to affect human existence as a whole, is almost self-evident. And in a span of 50 years, whether this problem can be dealt with by a norm-based order that critically depends on the individual will of the states or sub-national entities, without any explicit coercive content, or whether it should be dealt with by one single supranational entity or a group of supranational entities that have coercive powers over the states, would be critical considerations to find out how the structure of international relations might take shape going forward, and what our units of analyses will be.

Possible Future Scenarios

Conflicts would mark the coming age, one assumes, of a different nature. Competition among the units of the human organization may be replaced by the chance of cooperation among them because, for mere survival against a common problem, they might need to unite. Even though Kenneth Waltz might argue that the 'ultimate concern of states is not for power but security' (Waltz 1988, 616), in the context of a common challenge facing humanity as a whole, the so-called 'rational' response of the states would be to cooperate. This is one-way human societies can tackle the issue. The world has indeed shrunk, in one sense, in time and space, through the use of technology and the expansion and division of global processes of production and distribution in the age of global capital. Even though these might have been the very processes that have put humanity against nature, material conditions have been made available for creating new kinds of human organizations that do not depend, as Ruggie suggests, on the exclusive territoriality that the modern state hinges on (Ruggie 1993). In the present analysis, we may identify new categories for differentiation of societies. For instance, at the international level, we might have a classification of countries on a scale of capability to deal with climate change. Even though such classifications already exist in the international political lexicon, the legitimacy they acquire may help them become axes for various realignments of power. A global climate budget might become necessary, with different categories of the 'climate capable' groups debating claims for just distribution. Climate bureaucracies, with a heavy reliance on science and technology, can give birth to powerful new technocrats at the global level. Since 'market mechanisms' have an inherent problem of incorporating environmental costs and also since markets generally work on the premise of unlimited natural resources, global capital may come to be regulated by 'limits to growth' possibly arrived at through deliberative mechanisms at different levels of the system. However, having such cooperative, inclusive modes of the organization at the international level, that stand in solidarity against such macro challenges which confront humanity as a whole, looks like only one of the possibilities.

Another possibility, however, seems to be the more likely one at this juncture. Environmental negotiations at the international level, starting in the 1970s, have progressed and taken a definitive shape. Even though principles of common but differentiated responsibility, historical responsibility, climate equity, global climate budget and the like have strongly figured in these discussions among the States, what seems to have come through in recent discussions like the Paris Climate Agreement, for instance, is a dilution of these themes. A non-coercive capability-based individual state-centred norm-based framework has been worked out. To add to this, the scheme that has been worked out at the international level does not seem to have any explicitly coercive element of enforcement machinery behind it. Recent withdrawals of some of the most significant contributors to global warming, like the United States, from the Agreement itself, are a significant indication of its lack of effectiveness in terms of social justice. Prominent, influential political leaders are echoing ideas that completely refute the fact of climate change itself—with impunity (BBC News 2018). These political arguments also serve the purpose of invalidating the material experiences of those who suffer more from the effects of climate change.

Moreover, these voices emanate increasingly from historical powers: the most significant contributors to global warming. If this condition is to pan out, we might witness increased crystallization of the divide between the States—and consequently, people—into those who own the means necessary to withstand pressures of the environment and those who have been dispossessed of their means. Even though the world would not ever be divided into such neat categories, the forces of division will tend towards this direction—some states occupying the middle ground, and the powerful prospering at the expense of the powerless. Such a split could completely change the structure of international relations. In contrast to previous situations where the world was divided into mostly opposing camps, for instance, during the cold war, this time, the competition would not just be between and within camps, but crucially, the competition will function against a timeline when the Earth simply would not be able to carry the human burden. Data and experience already suggest that we are racing against time. Even the meagre 'limits' prescribed in the much-touted Paris Climate Agreement might not be enough (Srishti 2018), even if the 'Agreement' is implemented well, which is highly doubtful in itself.

In conclusion, if the second possibility is to take shape, as data and experience suggest it would, the race among those in competition to survive would be a race to determine who survives *outside* our planet, not on it. Sadly, what could materialize in this case would probably be the ultimate irony—the hitherto have-nots will have an earth uninhabitable for the human species all to themselves, and the hitherto haves will not have their home—to be sure, they might be the have-nots on an entirely new environment—a post-earth habitat, maybe? However, even if this turn of events takes place, it would be powerful, who would be irresponsibly leaving behind and imposing a trail of death and destruction on the part of humanity that has been kept powerless. Technological innovations in contemporary societies have aided the accumulation of wealth and power in a dominant few social entities—nations and corporations. Several commentators of human society have observed that these entities have tended to be historically irresponsible towards the dispossessed. As several such commentators have pointed out, dispossession has been part of the very formation of these social entities. If that trend is to continue and sustain, the very sustainability of human civilization might be under threat. A structural reconfiguration of the spatial existence of humankind is a genuine possibility. In 50 years then, the stages would have permanently changed, along with its actors.

REFERENCES

Anderson, B. 1983. *Imagined Communities*. London: Verso.

Carrington, D. 2016. 'The Anthropocene Epoch: Scientists Declare Dawn of Human-influenced Age'. *The Guardian,* 29 August. Available at: https://www.theguardian.com/environment/2016/aug/29/declare-anthropocene-epoch-experts-urge-geological-congress-human-impact-earth (accessed on 16 March 2020).

Lake, D. A. 2009. The State and International Relations. *UC San Diego*. doi: 10.1093/oxfordhb/9780199219322.003.0002.

Marx, K. 1859. *A Contribution to the Critique of Political Economy*. Translated by S.W. Ryazanskaya. Moscow: Progress Publishers. Available at: https://www.marxists.org/archive/marx/works/1859/critique-pol-economy/ (accessed on 16 March 2020).

Plato, and C. D. C. Reeve. 1998. *Cratylus*. Indianapolis, IA: Hackett Classics.

Roemelle, B. 2014. What Human-made Object Has Traveled Furthest From Earth?. *Huffpost,* 28 December. Available at: https://www.huffpost.com/entry/what-human-made-object-ha_b_6062490 (accessed on 16 March 2020).

Ruggie, J. G. 1993. Territoriality and Beyond: Problematizing Modernity in International Relations. *International Organization* 47 (1): 139–174. doi: 10.1017/S0020818300004732.

Srishti, C. 2018. 'UNBody Sets CO_2 Emission Cap to Limit Climate Change Catastrophe'. *Livemint*. Available at: https://www.livemint.com/Politics/GIuu6pnaESkN5cogG53e0H/Humancaused-CO2emissions-must-reach-zero-by-2050-IPCC.html (accessed on 16 March 2020).

BBC News. 2018. 'Trump on Climate Change Report: "I do not believe it"'. BBC News, 26 November. Available at: https://www.bbc.com/news/world-us-canada-46351940 (accessed on 16 March 2020).

Waltz, K. N. 1988. 'The Origins of War in Neorealist Theory'. *The Journal of Interdisciplinary History* 18 (4): 615–628.

About the Editors and Contributors

EDITORS

Mohanan Bhaskaran Pillai teaches at the Department of Politics and International Studies of Pondicherry University and coordinates the UGC Special Assistance Programme in the Department. He is a teacher and researcher of 39 years' standing. Currently, he is the Dean, School of Law, Pondicherry University, and Chairman of the Department of Politics and International studies of Pondicherry University on a second term. He has served previously as Director of the UNESCO Madanjeeth Singh Institute of South Asia Regional Cooperation and Chairman, Centre for South Asian Studies of Pondicherry University. He has also served as Principal of Pondicherry University's Community Colleges located at Lawspet, Puducherry, and Mahe, Puducherry. His areas of specialization include South Asian studies, research methodology and international political economy. He has been a visiting professor at Paris 13 University and lectured at the University of Warsaw, Poland.

Over the years, he has earned a reputation as an institution builder in recognition of his role in setting up Pondicherry University's Campus at Mahe, an outlying region of Puducherry, and serving as the founder Head of the Mahe Centre. He is the Founder Editor of the Institute for the Study of Developing Areas (ISDA) journal—*Studies in Development and Public Policy*—and the flagship journal of Pondicherry University—*The International Journal of South Asian Studies*.

He was a recipient of the Middle Career Award of the American Studies Research Centre at Hyderabad (currently renamed as

Indo-American Centre for International Studies) in 1988. He received travel grants from the International Studies Association to attend its annual conference held at San Francisco in March 2018. He has been nominated as Chair of the Panel on Disaster Diplomacy, and Discussant in the Panel on Historical Issues in India's Foreign Policy at the annual conference of the International Studies Association in March 2020 at Honolulu, Hawaii, USA. Apart from the above accolades, he has been honoured for his paper on 'Indian Strategic Culture: The Debates in Perspectives' being accepted for presentation at the conference in the panel on Indian Philosophy as a site for theorizing IR.

He has authored and edited more than 10 books and published research papers in national and international journals of repute. His publications include *The Politics of Regionalism in South Asia*, *India's Foreign Policy: Continuity and Change*, and *India's National Security: Concerns and Strategies*. He has received multiple citations for his research papers. His hobbies are reading fiction and painting.

Geetha Ganapathy-Dore is an alumna of Annamalai, Madras, Paris 7 - Denis Diderot, and Paris Nanterre Universities. She is currently a research-accredited Associate Professor of English at the Law, Political and Social Sciences Faculty of the University of Sorbonne Paris Nord. She is in charge of the second-year master's degree in trade policies with emerging nations. She is the author of *The Postcolonial Indian Novel in English* (2011). She has co-edited 10 volumes of research dealing with postcolonial literature (including migrant and refugee writings), culture and cinema, on the one hand, EU law, and human and environmental rights, on the other. Her research papers have appeared in many international journals. She has also translated Tamil short stories and poems into French. She sits on the editorial board of *Atlantis, Journal of the Spanish Association for Anglo-American Studies*, and heads the Society of Activities and Research on the Indian World. She is a co-project investigator for the SPARC project entitled 'Engendering Development Goals, Action Plans and Strategies: Dialogues between India and Europe' and lectured at the Centre for European Studies, Pondicherry University, in the summer of 2019.

CONTRIBUTORS

S. Ashok is currently pursuing his PhD in political science from Pondicherry University, after having completed his master's degree in political science from Jawaharlal Nehru University (JNU), New Delhi.

He is actively involved in various social and political movements in solidarity with multiple subaltern sections of the society. He is deeply interested in social justice and civil rights movements and the socio-economic plight of the marginalized. Apart from his activism, he is interested in reading, writing, photography and music.

Bindu Balagopal is Associate Professor of Economics at Government Victoria College, Palakkad, Kerala, India. She has 25 years of experience in teaching economics at the PG-level and has guided several postgraduate research projects. Her research work in the economics of the music industry is pioneering. She has several research papers and conference presentations to her credit. She is also a poet, and her poems have been published in leading periodicals.

Julien Cazala is a full professor of international law at Université Sorbonne Paris Nord. Prior to this, he was a senior lecturer at Orleans University and worked from 2011 to 2016 for the French Ministry of Foreign Affairs in Istanbul (Turkey). He has been a consultant for the United Nations High Commissioner for Refugees (UNHCR) and the International Criminal Tribunal for Former Yugoslavia (ICTY). He is a well-known specialist in international economic law and is the author of extensive writings in many fields of international law. He has given lectures in many French and foreign universities (Belgium, Canada, Romania, Cambodia, Turkey, Netherlands). He is a member of the Board of the Francophone Network of International Law (RFDI). He is an expert for the *Agence universitaire de la francophonie*, the National Research Agency (France), National Fund for Research (Luxembourg), and the Social sciences and Humanities Research Council (Canada).

Most of his writings can be downloaded from https://univ-paris13.academia.edu/juliencazala

S. Chemmalar is Faculty in the School of Law, Pondicherry University. Prior to this, she had worked as Assistant Professor at the SRM Institute of Science and Technology, Chennai, for two years and as Guest Faculty at Dr Ambedkar Government Law College, Puducherry, for one year. Her research mainly focuses on the use of nuclear weapons and the doctrine of self-defence in international law. She is also interested in contemporary issues relating to the use of nuclear weapons for self-defence. She is currently pursuing her doctrinal research in the School of Law, SRM Institute of Science and Technology.

She has published research articles in numerous peer-reviewed journals and presented her work at various professional conferences. She earned both her bachelor's and master's degrees in law (BA, LLB and LLM) from Dr Ambedkar Government Law College, Puducherry, which is affiliated to Pondicherry University and she is also an MBA in human resource management from Pondicherry University.

Catherine Colard-Fabregoule is a Research Accredited Associate Professor of Public Law at the Université Sorbonne Paris Nord, where she teaches public international law. She studied public international law at the University Paris of 1 (Panthéon-Sorbonne) where she obtained her doctorate in 1999. Her recent research focuses on international environmental law, climate change and human rights. She has co-edited *Changements climatiques et défis du droit* (Climate Change and Challenges for Law) (2010), *Changements environnementaux globaux et droits de l'homme* (Global Environmental Changes and Human Rights) (2012) and *Sécurité et environnement* (Security and Environment) (2016). She organized, with the cooperation of the French Embassy in Warsaw and the Warsaw School of Economics, a symposium entitled 'Companies on Climate Change'. She participated in the European project 'Human Rights and Climate Change: EU Policy Options' (2011–2012) and was a member of the ANR CIRCULEX on the circulation of norms and actors in the international governance of the environment (2012–2015). Another field of her research activity is the law of the sea. She wrote the marine environment columns for *l'Annuaire du droit de la mer* (Yearbook of the Law of the Sea)

(INDEMER, Monaco—1997–2013). She participated in the 'The Governance of Seas and Oceans' research project under the aegis of the French Institute for the Exploration of the Sea and the Center for Strategic Studies of the Navy during 2016–2017.

Suja P. Devipriya holds a doctorate in environmental technology from the Cochin University of Science and Technology (CUSAT), Kerala, India. She was awarded the International Indo-US Raman Fellowship by UGC in the year 2013. She received her post-doctoral from Bowling Green State University, Ohio, USA. She has worked as an Assistant Professor in Pondicherry University and is currently posted as Associate Professor in CUSAT, Kerala. She has also been a CSIR-Senior Research Fellow (Chemical Technology) and CSIR-Research Associate (Earth Sciences). She has over 10 years of teaching experience. Her fields of interest are environmental photocatalysis, environmental nanotechnology, water quality analysis and treatment, solid waste management and industrial ecology. She has published multiple research works in her fields of interest in esteemed journals. Her publications have received multiple citations.

Kaushik Dowarah is currently a PhD scholar in the Department of Ecology and Environmental Sciences, Pondicherry University. He obtained a master's degree in environmental sciences from JNU, New Delhi, in 2016. He has worked as a field officer with the Assam State Disaster Management Authority (ASDMA). He is currently working on microplastic pollution in present-day Puducherry. He is keen on raising environmental awareness among local communities, especially in the perspective of pollution by plastics. He has published his work on the status of microplastic pollution on the beaches of Puducherry in the *Marine Pollution Bulletin*. His research on microplastic ingestion by various commercial marine organisms such as mussels and clams is under process.

Didier Guével is Professor of Private Law and Criminal Sciences at the University of Sorbonne Paris Nord, holder of a State Doctorate in Law, and a member of the IRDA Research Centre in Paris 13 (laboratoire

EA 3970; https://www.google.fr/search?q=irda+paris+13&oq=irda &aqs=chrome.4.69i57j0l5.3155j1j8&sourceid=chrome&ie=UTF-8).

He defended a thesis in the field of general theory of law, relating to the dispersion of the jurisdictional function. Author of many legal works in both commercial law and property law (including bills of exchange, business law and the law of inheritance and gifts) and a hundred academic research papers under a single signature, Professor Guével specializes in areas intersecting the borders of civil and commercial laws. He frequently teaches abroad (notably Greece, Morocco, Russia and Ukraine). He is Honorary Dean of the Faculty of Law, Political and Social Sciences of Paris 13 University and Honorary Professor of the Faculty of Mendoza (Argentina). He recently presented various papers abroad (including Canada, Chile, Korea, Japan, Mexico and Peru) on the rights of ecology, robotics, liability and contracts.

P. Chacko Jose, an academician, writer and research guide, is currently Associate Professor and Head, Department of Economics, Sacred Heart College, Chalakudy, Kerala, India. He has a teaching career spanning over 25 years in UG and PG courses. He has also served as Reader at the UGC—Academic Staff College, University of Calicut. He is a research guide of the University of Calicut and a visiting faculty for the MBA programme of IGNOU and the School of Management Studies, Calicut University. He has to his credit journal articles, editorship of books and paper presentations in national and international conferences.

Binu Joseph is currently pursuing his PhD in the Department of Politics and International Studies, Pondicherry University. He holds an MA in political science from St Thomas College Pala (affiliated to Mahatma Gandhi University Kottayam, Kerala).

His research interests lie in the area of India–Nepal relations, more specifically in India's new development partnership with its neighbouring nations. He is keenly interested in observing and analysing India's foreign policy changes towards its neighbouring nations. He has presented several research papers on India's cultural diplomacy, India and Nepal open-border problems and other related areas. He is also

interested in teaching and other academic activities. He is an observer of public issues and an analyst of public policies.

Sisira K. G. is currently pursuing her PhD in politics and international studies at Pondicherry University, after obtaining her master's degree in politics and international relations there. She hails from Kerala and has done her graduation in political science from Maharaja's College in Kochi, Kerala, India. She has completed an internship programme in local administration with the Kerala Institute of Local Administration in Thrissur, Kerala, India. Her research interest is in environmental commons, particularly climate change and its governance.

Anju Lis Kurian has completed her MPhil and PhD in politics and international relations and is currently pursuing post-doctoral research on the topic 'Climate Change and Environmental Governance: A Study on Livelihood Issues in the Western Ghats Region of Kerala' at the School of International Relations and Politics, M. G. University, Kerala, India.

She has more than 30 research publications such as journal articles, book chapters and a book to her credit. She has presented more than 25 conference papers at various national and international conferences across India. She was awarded the National Young Political Scientist Award, 2015, and Research Excellence Award in 2019. She is the editor of *mRNA*, a multidisciplinary journal and is a reviewer for *International Journal of Management & Social Studies*. She is professionally affiliated to Indian Women's Studies Association, Indian Political Science Association and the Institute of Scholars. She is the co-author of the book entitled, *Regional Integration and Energy security: The European Union Experience* (2014).

Jean-Jacques Menuret obtained his PhD from the University of Paris 2 – Panthéon Assas with a thesis on 'Litigation at the Competition Council' which was awarded the Varenne Foundation Prize.

He is currently Associate Professor of Law at the Faculty of Law, Université Sorbonne Paris Nord. He presides the public law section and is in charge of the master's degree in rights and fundamental freedoms (second year) and the master's degree in public law (first year). His research focuses on administrative law and litigation, the law of fundamental freedoms, procedural law and economic law.

He is the editor/co-editor of *Les formes renouvelées de la démocratie* (Renewed Forms of Democracy) (2019), *Le droit de la régulation audiovisuelle à l'épreuve du numérique* (Law of Audiovisual Regulation with Digital Technology as a Litmus Test) (2016) and *La collégialité, valeurs et significations en droit public* (Collegiality, Values and Meanings in Public Law) (2012) and the author of the following selected articles: 'L'utopie du statut général des AAI' (The Utopia of the General Status of Independent Administrative Authorities) (2018), 'AAI et démocratie participative' (Independent Administrative Authorities and Participatory Democracy) (2018), 'La place du Conseil supérieur de l'audiovisuel au sein des AAI' (The Place of the Higher Audiovisual Council at the heart of Independent Administrative Authorities) (2016), 'L'autorité de la concurrence' (Competition Authority) (2015), 'Les relations entre les tribunaux administratifs et les enseignants-chercheurs des facultés de droit' (Relations between administrative tribunals and the academics of faculties of law) (2014) and 'Bientôt des AAI territoriales' (Territorial Independent Administrative Authorities coming very soon?) (2013), 'Quelle collégialité pour les AAI?' (What collegiality for Independent Administrative Authorities?) (2012).

Govind N. completed his five-year integrated master's degree in political science at the Department of Politics and International Studies, Pondicherry University, in the year 2018. During this period, he had attended several national and international paper presentations/conferences/seminar/workshops and secured an internship the at Bureau of Police Research and Development (Ministry of Home Affairs), Government of India, and RCE Trivandrum (affiliated to United Nations University). He holds a certification in ethical hacking and has apt knowledge in graphic and web designing, and this had fetched him opportunities for developing a full-fledged website for the students' forum during his postgraduate studies. He was an active member of various student forums and served a term in Pondicherry University's Student Council as an elected member.

He is currently a UGC Special Assistance Programme Project Fellow in the Department of Politics and International Studies coordinated by Professor Mohanan Bhaskaran Pillai. He has worked on several areas such as virtual intrusion on female populi and Double Taxation Avoidance Agreement (DTAA). His current interests focus on cyber politics and Marxian thought and liberation. His preferred approach is multidisciplinary.

Devjit Nandi is a research scholar in agricultural economics at the Institute of Agriculture, Visva-Bharati (Central University), Sriniketan. He has worked on various tribal and forest issues and done a lot of policy research in the areas of forest restoration and management. He has successfully completed many projects related to tribal livelihoods and forest diversity with national and international donors.

Debashis Sarkar is Professor and Head, Department of Agricultural Economics, Institute of Agriculture, Visva-Bharati, Sriniketan. He also served as Director, Agro-Economic Research Centre (Sponsored by the Ministry of Agriculture and Farmers' Welfare, Government of India), Visva-Bharati for two years (2011–2013). He was awarded a doctoral fellowship in agricultural economics and national scholarships by the Government of India at both UG and PG levels. He is an active researcher and has been teaching for the past 28 years. He has completed many research projects sponsored by UGC, National Institute of Agricultural Economics and Policy Research (ICAR-NIAP), Directorate of Jute Development, Government of India, Directorate of Crop Production, Government of India, and Directorate of Plant Protection, Quarantine & Storage (PPQ&S), Government of India. He has published 10 books (4 edited) and many articles in reputed national and international peer-reviewed journals.

Arsha V. Sathyan is a research scholar whose research interests focus primarily on the areas of rights, citizenship, civil society, social movements, local governance and indigenous political mobilization.

She pursued her BA (Hons) in political science at Hindu College, University of Delhi, and MA in politics and international relations at Pondicherry University. She completed her MPhil in development practice at Ambedkar University. She has also worked as a research consultant for the Ford Foundation in a project entitled 'Unlocking the Value of Non-timber Forest Products' at the Centre for Development Practice. The project focused on the lac markets and the processing units of Balarampur, Purulia District of West Bengal. She holds expertise in ethnographic researches on the study of rural India.

She has presented academic papers at various national and international conferences with numerous publications in the field of international relations as well as rural development.

Arsha V. Sathyan is currently working as Assistant Professor at the Department of Political Science, P. M. Sayeed Calicut University Centre, Androth.

Namita Sharma received her master's degree in politics and international relations from Pondicherry University and has been engaged with associations like the Assam State Commission for Women as an intern. She has actively participated and presented papers at national and international conferences during her postgraduation. During her UG, she had also volunteered for the global campaign of Kailash Sathyarthi Children's Foundation organized by the Nobel Laureate Kailash Sathyarthi held in the Rashtrapati Bhawan, New Delhi. Her UG was in political science and history from Indraprastha College for Women, University of Delhi. Her interest areas include India's foreign policy, international migration, diplomacy, minority issues and international politics.

Currently, she is engaged as a junior researcher at the Centre for Policy Analysis, New Delhi. With immense interest in the developments in international affairs, she wishes to continue her higher studies and contribute towards academic research in global sociopolitical issues.

Anusha Sooriyan completed her master's degree in politics and international relations at Pondicherry University. She has been associated with a couple of NGOs and policy think tanks, based in India, as part of her interest and internship requirements. She has worked in local and international projects (city transport integration). She has a published paper to her credit: 'The Unofficial Ambassadors: A Comparative Study of Indian and Chinese Diaspora in Southeast Asia' (August 27 2018, Chennai Centre for China Studies website). Her interest drives her to pursue a career in international relations. She holds a distinction in her undergraduate degree in journalism. It has fetched her opportunities to work with a few media organizations and publish news articles. Her experiences in working for the college community radio, producing news videos, designing magazines and her skills in photography have brought her many accolades.

K. R. Sreelekha holds an MPhil degree in international studies from JNU, New Delhi. She has worked as a project fellow at the UGC Centre for Southern Asia Studies, Pondicherry University, and as an Assistant Fellow at the Institute of Social Sciences (ISS), Regional Centre, Puducherry. Her area of specialization is Southern Asia studies, and her area of academic focus covers India's foreign policy, Afghanistan–Pakistan region, strategic studies and international political economy.

She has published works on India's foreign policy, Pakistan's military regimes, etc., and is currently working on her PhD thesis 'Pakistan's Afghan Policy—1999–2008: Security and Strategic Concerns'. Since 2018, she has been working as a Guest Faculty at the Department of Politics and International Studies, Pondicherry University.

C. Vinodan is Associate Professor and Director, School of International Relations and Politics and Honorary Director, Institute for Contemporary Chinese Studies, Mahatma Gandhi University, Kottayam, Kerala, India. His current areas of teaching and research are: international relations; security studies; foreign policies of India, USA and China; South Asian studies; Chinese studies; rise of Asia and the Indo-Pacific; BRI; energy, environment and human security.

He was awarded a visiting scholar fellowship (2003) by Claremont Graduate University, California, USA. He was a visiting professor at Jinan University, Guangzhou, China, from 22 November to 5 December, 2019. He had attended numerous courses in international relations in India and abroad. These include the 2019 ISA Asia-Pacific

Conference at Nanyang Technological University, Singapore; 2017 ISA International Conference at University of Hong Kong, Hong Kong; 2016 Sino-Indian Cross-Cultural Dialogues held by the Institute of Advanced International Studies, Sun Yat-sen University, Guangzhou, China; the US Department of States Fulbright American Studies Institute (FASI) course on Foreign Policy at the University of Delaware, Philadelphia in 2000; the Regional Center for Strategic Studies (Colombo) Summer Workshop on Defense, Technology and Cooperative Security in South Asia at Katmandu, Nepal in 2000, etc. He is currently a member of the editorial board of the *Journal of Human Security* (Canada), the *Indian Journal of Politics and International Relations* and the *South Asian Journal of Diplomacy*. He has published more than 50 research papers and 9 books.

Index

Achanakmar Tiger Reserve, 223
Achanakmar Wildlife Sanctuary, 225, 239
Action Plan for the Protection and Management of the Marine and Coastal Environment of the South Asian Seas Region, 179
Adivasis, 221
AERB, 199
Agricultural Fair (2013), France, 246
agriculture
    as primary source of livelihood in India and France, 244
    disappearance in the 20th century, 247
allocative
    efficiency, 4
    productivity, 4
Anderson, Benedict, 260
Antarctica, 62
Anthropocene, 263
ARCH-Vahini, 214
atmosphere, 62, 66, 69, 78
Atmosphere Summit (2015), Paris, 79
Atomic Energy Act of 1962, 201
Atomic Energy Commission, 193
Atomic Energy Regulatory Board (AERB), 195
atomic minerals, 201, 203
Atomic Minerals Directorate for Exploration and Research, 197

Baiga primitive community, 224, 225, 238
Bakelite synthetic plastic, 141

Baviskar, Amita, 214
Beaurain, Camille, 245
biodiversity, 20, 223, 240–241
    loss, 223
    marine, 177
    misfortune, 3
    panchayats role in conservation, 233
bird flu, 33
Bizon, Paul-Henry, 245, 248
blue economy, 189
Borloo, Jean-Louis, 96

Cartesian dichotomy, 261
Cement Sustainability Initiative (CSI), 76
Central India, tribal provinces ruled by tribal kings and feudal lords, 221
Central Pollution Control Board, 185
Chicago Climate Exchange (CCX), 76
Chorzow Factory case, 91
Chuhiya women, battle against forest department hegemony, 237–239
chunking method, 133
civil society organizations (CSOs), 211
clean energy, 96, 192
climate budget, global, 265
climate bureaucracies, 265
climate capable groups, 265
climate change See also global commons, concept of, 62

climate change, agencies role in governance
　local government role in, 75
　national and sub-national governments, 74–75
　private actors, 76
climate change
　USA, mitigation measures adopted by, 74–75
　adaptation and mitigation at local level, 74, 76–79
　affects global commons, 66
　and rise in sea level, 86
　challenge of mitigation, 63, 70
　effectiveness of polycentric strategy, 79–80
　forms of governance, 73
　governance, 62, 63–64, 70
　impact of, 61
　predictions and assessments on, 61
　preparedness, 77
　regime, 62
　states contribution to, 91
climate refugees, concept of, 91–92
　international perspective, 86
　issue of, 85
　problem of, 84
Coase theorem, 7–8
Coase, Douglass, 10
Coase, Elinor, 9
Coase, Ronald, 4, 7
Coastal Regulation Zones 1991, 202
common but differentiated responsibilities, notion of, 91
common concern, doctrine of, 64, 90
common heritage of humanity, 13
common heritage of mankind, 13, 15–16, 18, 20, 90
　and area resources, 19
common pool resources (CPRs), 3, 4, 7, 10
common property, 8
common resource, 9, 12, 14, 17, 19

commons movement, objectives of, 243
commons
　basic premise of, 12
　definition of, 12
Community Forest Management Committee (CFMC), 239
community resource rights (CRR), 227
community-based organizations (CBOs), 211
Compagnon, Antoine, 246
compression method, 133
Crutzen, Paul, 263
cyber
　attacks, 130, 134
　threats, 130, 134
cyberspace (or digital ecosystem), 135–136
　as a new global common, 135
　definition of, 127
　governance of, 129
　international summits on governance of, 129–130
　national-level governance mechanisms, 130–132
　origin of, 127
　physical dimensions of, 128
　social dimensions of, 128
　technical techniques for management of, 133
　UN initiatives, 133–135

deep geological repositories, 200
Deep Sea Ventures corporation, 15
Department of Atomic Energy, India, 193
Department of Defence (DoD), United States, 127
Development of Regional Action Plan on Marine Litter in the South Asian Region, 179

Directorate General for Maritime Affairs and Fisheries of the European Union, 105
displacement of people, reasons for, 86
domineering externality, 52
Draft Articles on the Responsibility of States for International Wrongful Acts, 91

ecological
  debasement, 4
  issues, 3
El-Hinnawi, Essam, 84
electricity demand in world, 98
encroachers, 222
encyption method, 133
energy scenario in India, 193
environment
  mainstream economics treatment to, 4
environmental democracy in France
  citizens information and participation, before and after decision-making process, 110–116
  control of procedures by public authorities, 116–119
  environmental lawsuit, limitations of, 119–121
  importance of, 110
  motivated by 1789 revolution, 108
environmental refugees, definition of, 85
environmental responsibilities, global, 90
Environmental Survey Laboratories (ESLs), 196
environmental
  degradation, 3, 4
  goods, 4
European Birds Directive, 99
European Commission and the Bureau of Maritime Affairs, 100
European Union (EU), 103, 189
  efforts to add fisheries, 104
  internal programmes on climate change, 74
European Union's Common Agricultural Policy, 249
exclusive economic zones (EEZ), 105

farmers in India and France
  agrarian crisis, 245–246
  and feminization of agriculture, 245
  average income of, 245
  distress among farmers, causes of, 253
  Green Revolution in India, 246
  reasons for suicides, 253
  suicide rates of, 244
Forest Rights Act (FRA) 2006, 217
Forest Rights Act 2006, 223
Forest Rights Committees (FRC), 224
forest-dependent people, 227
FRA 2006, 235, 238
  advantages of, 226
  aims and objectives of, 226
  contribution to conservation, 228
  provision for community rights, 227
  rights of PVTGs and nomadic tribes, 227
France Revolution of 1789, 108
Fukushima disaster, 193
Fulwaripara women, territorial rights struggle by, 239–240

genetic-biological method, 28
Ghosh, Amitav, 256
Ghosh, Dipak, 198
global commons, concept of, 14, 16, 19, 20
global commons, concept of See also climate change, 62
global commons, concept of

284 | Global Commons

challenges faced by, 65–66
covers large part of planet, 62
definition of, 124
effectiveness of, 65–66
features of, 63
governance of, 63–64
international law recognition to, 63
need global regulation, 20
open access to, 63
origin of, 124
principles of, 124
speciality of, 124–126
treaties signed at global level to protect, 125–126
global ecological implosion, 262
global resources, degeneration of, 123
global warming, 64
impact on marine areas, 96
globalization, 63, 222
Gond community, 225
Gram Sabha, 233, 234
grassroots support organization (GSO), 211
green house gas (GHGs) emissions, 66
greenhouse gas (GHGs) emissions, 69, 70, 73, 75, 77
grim
state of nature, 264
state of social relations, 264–265

Hardin, Garrett, 5, 7, 8, 10
high seas, 62
human-made radiations, 197–198
hybrid climate change governance, 73

ideological construction of method of exploration, 260–262
imagined community, 260
Indian Ocean garbage
Action Plan of India, 184–187
coastal population, impact on, 177
consensus and responsibility in South Asian region, 182–184

generated from South Asian coastal states, 174–175
impact on marine life in South Asian waters, 177
international laws on maritime boundaries protection, 177–179
national laws, scope of, 180–182
pollutants, sources of, 175–176
programmes and laws in South Asian region, 179–180
Indian Ocean Rim Association (IORA), 180 189
Indian Rare Earth Limited, 202
Indian-based Neutrino Observatory, 200
indigenous communities initiatives, in exercise their rights
conservation mechanism for local sustainable development, 233–234
panchayat level conservation initiatives through local governance, 231–232
threats and problems faced by communities, 232–233
transferable development right program, 234–235
individual forest rights, 224
Indo-US Nuclear Deal of 2005, 193, 194
objectives of, 192
institutionalization, 260
Integrated Coastal Zone Management (ICZM), 104
Intergovernmental Oceanographic Commission, 105
Intergovernmental Panel on Climate Change (IPCC), 86
Special Report on Global Warming of 1.5°C, 85
Internal Displacement Monitoring Centre, 92

International Convention for the
  Prevention of Pollution from
  Ships (MARPOL Convention
  73/78) 1973, 179, 181, 182,
  186
International Convention Relating
  to Intervention on the High
  Seas in Cases of Oil Pollution
  Casualties, 178
International Council for the
  Exploration of the Sea, 101
International Court of Justice (ICJ),
  41
International Criminal Court, 13
International Geological Congress
  (2017), 263
international heritage, 13
International Maritime Organization
  (IMO), 178
International Oceanographic
  Commission, 101
  Guide for the Assessment of
    Maritime Spatial Plans, 105
International Seabed Authority, 17–18
International Telecommunication
  Union (ITU), 128

Jha, farmers in India and France, 254
Jojo, Sunilkumar, 197
Jus cogens, notion of, 91–92
Jégouzo, Yves, 39

Kasaravalli, Girish, 251
Kennecott corporation, 15
Kerala Minerals and Metals Limited,
  202
Kumari, Neha, 197
Kyoto Protocol (KP), 63, 64

Lake, David A., 264
land debasement, 3
legal regime, 13
literary recession, 249

Lloyd, William Forster, 5

Maastricht Agreements of 1992, 38
Mahatma Gandhi National Rural
  Employment Guarantee Act
  (MGNREGA) 2005, 209–210
Marine Occupation Plan (2007), 101
marine
  currents, 96
  debris, 173, 174, 177
  environment, 18, 95, 100, 101,
    178, 180, 184
  litter, 173, 174, 188
  pollutants, 172
maritime spatial planning
  administrative framework, 97–100
  definition of, 99, 100
  features of, 100–101
  strategies adopted by European
    countries, 101–106
market mechanisms, 265
Marx, Karl, 260
Mazdoor Kisan Shakti Sangathan
  (MKSS), 217
membership support organizations
  (MSOs), 211
memorialization, 260
Mendras, Henri, 246
micro-beads, 143
microplastics, factors contributing
  abundance and distribution of
  atmospheric fallout, 145
  biofouling, 144
  domestic sewage and industrial
    sewage, 143
  fishing and recreational activities,
    144
  hydrographic factors, 144–145
  long-range transporatation, 146
  maritime activities, 144
microplastics
  contamination effect on human
    beings, 164–165

crustaceans, 163
definition of, 142
in algae, 164
in biota, 152–160
in crabs, 161–162
in fishes, 160–161
in marine environment, 149–152
in marine worms, 164
in mussels, 163
in oysters, 162
in sediments and freshwater bodies, 146–149
physical and chemical damages to animals, 160
size denomination of, 142
Ministry of Tribal Affairs, 227
mitigation effectiveness, 64
MKSS, 218
modernity, 249, 262, 264
Monnier, Ludivine Le, 245
monoculture, 224
Moore, Charles, 173

Nansen Conference on Climate Change and Displacement 2011, 86
principles of, 88–89
Nansen Initiative 2012, 90
Narayan, R. K., 249
Narmada Bachao Andolan, 214
National Campaign for People's Right to Information (NCPRI), 217
National Commission for Public Debate (NCPD or CNDP), France, 111–114
National Human Rights Commission, 197–198
National Maritime Foundation, 187
National Rural Employment Guarantee Act (NREGA) 2005, 217
natural resources, 124
Neelima, Girish, 251
Neelima, Kota, 245, 249

neopopulism, 30
New Economic Policy of India (1991), 191
NGO Citizens Resource and Action and Initiative, 256
NGOs in India
activity in rural areas, 214–215
Dudhera community demand for unemployment allowance, 215–216
types of, 211
NGOs
agendas of, 217
culmination of private interests and individual desires, 211
function of, 213
vision of professionalization of community, 213
non-governmental organizations (NGOs)
definition of, 211
Non-Governmental Organizations (NGOs)
role of, 213
non-refoulement, 88, 92
non-timber forest products (NTFPs), 227
North Atlantic Treaty Organization (NATO), 127
North, Douglass, 9
NTFPs, 232, 234, 238
Nuclear Power Corporation of India Limited (NPCIL), 193
nuclear power industry in India
expansion post-2005, 193
politico-economic aspirations, 194
strategic security ambitions, 194
nuclear power reactors in India
and indirect chain of hazards, 196
and UCIL engagement in feeding reactors, 196–197
emission of carbon dioxide, 200
environmental impact of, 195–196
nuclear waste generation, 200

thorium mining see thorium, 201
water, air and soil contamination,
 198–200
Nuclear Suppliers Group (NSG), 193

oil spills in India, 176
onion routing (Tor), 133
Oraon community, 225
Organisation for Economic
 Co-operation and Development
 (OECD), 124
Ostrom, Elinor, 8, 10, 70, 71, 76
Ostrom, Vincent, 70
outer space, 62
over-determinism, risk of, 263
overindustrialization victims, 243
Ozone Protocol Convention, 91

Pacific Ocean, largest garbage found
 in the 1990s, 173
Paquet, Mélanie, 245
Paris Climate Agreement of 2015, 63,
 65–66, 195, 266, 267
 objective of, 87
particularly vulnerable tribal groups
 (PVTGs), 226
patricide, 247
planet earth, 63
planet-wide temperature boost, 3
plastics
 biodegradable, 142
 domination in everyday lives of
  human beings, 141
 features of, 141
 microplastics See, 142
 microplastics see microplastics, 142
 waste, rise in generation, 142
polycentric governance approach for
 climate change
 challenges and loopholes in, 79–81
 meaning of, 70–72
 origin of, 70
 stakeholders participation in,
  importance of, 74

 to explore institutional arrangement and rules, 72–74
PRADAN NGO, 210, 211, 215
precaution
 and prevention, difference between
  see prevention and precaution,
  difference between, 24
 meaning of, 24
 origin of, 24
precautionary principle, 23
 definition of, 26–27
 progress in the implementation of,
  44–52
 progression in the reception of the
  concept, 29–44
precautionism, 30
prevention and precaution, difference
 between, 24–26
proficient appropriation of assets, 4
property rights, 4, 8
protected areas, 224
protected areas, restrictions on local
 people and relocation from
 forest, 223
prudence, 24
PVTGs, 227
Pérez-Vittoria, Silvia, 249

Rajasthan Atomic Power Station
 (RAPS-5), 193
Rapley, Chris, 263
rare-earth mining, 202
Refugee Convention 1951, 85, 86,
 87–88
Regional Oil and Chemical Marine
 Pollution Contingency Plan for
 South Asia (2000), 186
renewable energy, 96, 96
Report on Trends in Global CO2
 Emissions (2016), 195
resource conservation, 224
Right to Education Act 2009, 218
Right to Food campaign, 217
Right to Information Act 2005, 217

Right to Work campaign, 217
Rio Declaration on Environment and
    Development (1992), 36, 90,
    108
Roy, Anupama, 214
Roy, Arundhati, 250
Ruggie, John, 262, 264, 265

Sadeleer, Nicolas, 44
Safeguarding and Preservation of
    Moving Images adopted by
    UNESCO 1980, 14
Sainath, P., 251
Samaj Pragati Sahyog, 218
SDGs, 240
    ecological concerns, 223–224
seabed minerals, 15
self-governance, 8
selfish-interest, 15
Semariya Gram Sabha youth, pledge
    to protect forest areas and rights,
    235–237
Serres, Michel, 247, 256
Sharma, Devinder, 244
shifting cultivation (or bewar) practice
    in Central India, 222
Single European Act of 1986, 38
Sinha, R. K., 193
Smith, Adam, 6
social movements, 214
Sonowal, C. J., 197
South Asia Cooperative Environment
    Programme (SACEP), 173
South Asian Association for Regional
    Cooperation (SAARC), 179
South Asian Seas Action Plan (SASP),
    173
South Asian Seas Environment
    Programme (SASEP), 179
state responsibility, 91
Suresh, V., 201
sustainable commons, 8–10
Sustainable Development Goals
    (SDGs)

components of, 223
Swachh Sagar Abhiyan, 187

technological innovations, 267
territorial rights, 227
The Guardian, 263
thorium, 196
thorium mining
    as viable alternative, 201
    environmental cost of, 201–203
Tiebout, Charles, 70
Traditional Knowledge Digital Library
    (TKDL), 51
tragedy of the commons, concept of,
    3, 10, 17
    case study, 6–7
    depicts assets exploitation by
        individuals, 6
    highligt difficulites for
        non-exclusion to CPR, 4
    solution to, 5
Treaty of Rome (1957), 38
Treaty on the Functioning of the
    European Union (TFEU), 37

UN Convention on Biological
    Diversity (1992), 20
UN World Tourism Organization
    (UNWTO), 177
UNESCO Intergovernmental
    Oceanographic Commission,
    105
United Nations Conference on
    Oceans (2017), New York,
    105
United Nations Convention on the
    Law of the Sea (UNCLOS)
    1982, 13, 16, 18, 19, 178
United Nations Environment
    Programme (UNEP), 84, 178
United Nations Framework
    Convention on Climate Change
    (UNFCCC), 63, 66, 70, 86–87

United Progressive Alliance (UPA)
    government, 217
United States Nuclear Regulatory
    Commission, 199
UN's Sustainable Development Goals
    2030, 105
uranium, 196
Uranium Corporation of India Ltd
    (UCIL), 196–197
Use Less Plastic slogan, 166

Van-Kinh, Claire, 245
Verhoeven, Joe, 13
Vidharba, 249
virtual private networks (VPNs), 133
voluntary climate change governance,
    73

Waltz, Kenneth, 265
Warren, Robert, 70
water shortage, 3
wave
    energy, 96, 97, 104
    production, 98
Wildlife Protection Act, 222
Williamson, Douglass, 9
wind energy, 96, 98
World Business Council for
    Sustainable Development
    (WBCSD), 76
World Conservation Charter of 1982,
    36
World Energy Council, 97
World Wide Fund for Nature,
    175